THE HOLE IN THE SOUL

THE HOLE IN THE SOUL

FROM CHAOS TO CLARITY

A MEMOIR BY
SUZIE BROWNE

The Hole in the Soul

First published October 2025

ISBN 978-1-7643505-0-1 Paperback
ISBN 978-1-7643505-1-8 Epub

Copyright © 2025 Suzie Browne

 A catalogue record for this book is available from the National Library of Australia

All rights reserved. No part of this publication may be reproduced, stored in a retrieval system or transmitted in any form or by any means, electronic, mechanical, photocopying, recording or otherwise, without prior written permission of the copyright owner.

DISCLAIMER

The material in this book is intended to be of general informational use and is not intended to constitute legal, medical, financial or professional advice. All specific legal, medical, financial or other decisions should be made in consultation with a qualified professional.

The authors and the publisher disclaim all responsibility for any liability, loss or risk, personal or otherwise, which is incurred as a consequence, directly or indirectly, from the use or application of any of the contents of this book.

For the purposes of consumer law in Australia, including the Australian Consumer Law, the reader is advised that this book comes with no warranties, either express or implied, that the information contained herein is accurate or complete. The reader should seek independent professional advice to confirm the relevance and applicability of the book's contents as may be required.

This book is a memoir. It reflects the author's present recollections of experiences over time. Some names and characteristics have been changed and some dialogue has been recreated.

For Greer – my heart

*I disappeared from your life when you were very young.
You were the one who saved me.
As I grew distant from you, you found a sense
of familiarity within yourself.
Maybe by telling my story, you can tell yours and so be free.*

Courage is telling the story of who you are with your whole heart.

Brené Brown

*This memoir is dedicated to the late Jennifer Hutchinson
who was my inspiration and guiding light.
God Blesss you, Jen.*

From the author

My life has been a rich tapestry of experiences – coloured by addiction and ultimately transformed through recovery.

I have worn many hats: cook, dishwasher, caterer, barista, retail assistant, restaurateur, secretary, account executive, barmaid, child care worker, mature age student, actress, volunteer worker, rehab assistant, nanny, cleaner, trolley-dolly, housekeeper and accountant.

And no matter the circumstances, I have given it my all.

Throughout my journey, people often told me I should write a book – so I did. My hope is that this raw and unfiltered memoir brings readers a sense of relief, healing and perhaps a few answers of their own.

From my heart to yours,

Suzie Browne
MELBOURNE 2025

Table of Contents

Is That You, God?	1
I Wanna Be Famous	7
305 Bluff Road	10
Hepburn Springs	14
What Now?	19
My Family	24
The Leading Role	34
Torquay	37
The (Unofficial) Original Puberty Blues	44
Cherry Popped	51
East and West Coasts	58
Progressive Disease	65
If Nothing Changes, Nothing Changes	73
What Is This Thing Called Sex?	77
UK, Here We Come Aye	80
Europe	83
London, Again	95
Return to Oz	101
Tex	112
I'll Be Home on a Monday	116
Brighton Hilton	120
Where's the Cheese?	124
You're in My Heart, You're in My Soul	129

Advertising – Take Three	134
New Beginnings	139
The Next 20 Years	143
Brownies Café	150
Machello's	156
How Could This Possibly Happen?	160
I Don't Want a Nice Little Simple Life	165
Getting Serious	176
Get a Real Job	185
The Brown Conspiracy	190
Free At Last	194
Central America Here We Come	199
From Playa Jaco to Australia	216
Home Is Where the Heart Is	221
It's So Not Fair	230
Living in Heaven	234
Back to School	247
Return to Melbourne	258
I saw the Light	264
I Want to Feel Again	273
We Are the Fortunate Ones…	281
Toning Body Mind and Spirit	289
The Simple Life	297

Is That You, God?
Or is that the devil?

Mum and Dad are hosting another fabulous party. Once again, my sister and I press our faces against the frosted glass doors, breathing in the heady mix of Tabu perfume, whisky, and cigarette smoke. as we watched them jive to the music - the old 78's spinning on the gramophone, filling the room with tunes from the Glenn Miller Band and Burt Bacharach. The women's skirts swished as they twirled, and the men strutted about in their ball-crushingly high-waisted trousers.

Full of wonderment, whispering to my sis, 'I can't wait to grow up so that I, too, can drink and smoke and dance. Look at how much fun they're having.'

My first drink happened around this time; at ten years of age. Offering to clean up after a shindig, the oldies nursing their sore heads and none the wiser, I sculled the dregs from the half-full glasses, puzzled at how much booze was wasted.

I loved the instant buzz; loved it way too much. A warm, fuzzy glow enveloped my whole being. In a twilight zone, I looked up at the heavens and asked, 'Is that you God?' I had found my best friend, a friend who served me well for five decades. That friend saved my life until it almost killed me.

~

I was born in Melbourne on 14 May 1954 and have a sister who is two years older than me. I am a Taurean – stubborn, loyal, passionate, creative and a hopeless romantic. Most people who know me would strongly disagree, but I am also introverted, shy, self-conscious and insecure. I have early memories of feeling lonely, disconnected from others, uncomfortable in my own skin. I envied everyone and wanted their lives, any life but my own. Saying 'I love you' was absent in my home. I have no doubt I was loved, but I ached to hear those three words. So began my lifelong quest for validation and acceptance.

I was an inquisitive child, fascinated with other people's lives. On family car trips, my face pressed to the window, I would wonder, longed to know, about the things I saw. 'Hey, Dad, who do you reckon lives in the room of that old pub with the venetian blinds? How did his life lead him there do you think?' 'What sort of people live in those commission flats and why?'

I ached to know whether these people were happy or sad. I wondered what my life would be like if I lived in that hotel room or those commission flats. I wanted to get into people's minds, to look through their eyes, feel their feelings and know their stories. Still today, I want to know all about the nail technician and the hairdresser. Where are they from? How many children do they have? Are they happy?

I was also a determined child. When I was four, we lived in a tiny apartment on Church Square, St Kilda. Dad, my sister and I were walking sis to her first day at St Kilda Primary School. A gust of wind blew my tartan skirt up around my ears, revealing my bare bum. Earlier that morning, I had insisted on dressing myself. 'I do myseff. I dress myseff!'

I reasoned that if my sister could dress herself so could I. The difference being, she remembered her undies.

'What am I wearing today?' State school mornings began with me yelling to Mum.

The reply was always the same, 'Wear what you wore yesterday.'

I dreaded hearing those five disgusting words. I would become distraught, 'Waaah, waaah, waaah. I am not wearing what I wore yesterday. I want to wear something different.'

Mum, recognising my penchant for perfectionism and tired of the disturbing morning ritual, sewed pinafores in a different tartan for each day of the week, which I wore with white puffed sleeved shirts and black patent leather shoes. I looked fabulous.

I had no fear. When I was five, I stood on top of our swing set and called out, 'Watch me, Dad. I can fly,' while launching myself off the swing, arms spread, my head landing on a six-inch nail as I hit the ground.

At kindergarten, I didn't just hang from the monkey bars like the other kids; I stood on top of the unit, throwing myself off. 'Hey, watch me, guys,' I called, while attempting to grab on to the bars on my way down. Twice unsuccessful – two broken arms.

~

My sister and I have nothing in common in the looks department – she's a blonde and I'm a brunette. When I was born, Dad said I looked like Joe Louis, the boxer. Mum told me he would joke with his mates, saying, *'I'm pretty sure the hospital gave us the wrong kid. I reckon there's an Aboriginal family running around with our blue-eyed, blonde-haired child.'*

When I was old enough to understand, hearing this simply cemented my belief that I had, in fact, been dropped from a spaceship, that I was an alien in a human suit. But raised with the 'disease to please,' I laughed on cue.

Sis and our neighbour decided that I, the younger sister, would be their source of entertainment.

'Suzie, do you want to play a game with us?'

'Oh yes,' I would beam.

They put a table under the clothesline. 'Stand on this'.

Once I was up there, they pegged my skirt to the line, wound the handle as high as it would go, spun the clothesline, removed the table and, giggling, ran away. After what seemed like an eternity, I became panicked. The sun was going down, the wind coming up, my mouth dry, my tummy rumbling. I thought about un-pegging myself but the drop would have broken my little legs. I wondered how long they would leave me there. I wondered if this was my lot. *Am I to never be taken seriously? Ridiculed? The butt of others' jokes? Forever trying to please others at my own expense?*

Turns out they forgot about me. My furious father eventually rescued me. I felt sad and confused and incredulous that my sister didn't seem to notice the torment she caused me.

Another time, 'Hey, Suzie, would you like to sit in my sister's hairdresser's chair?'

'Yes, please.'

'While you're there, do you want us to trim your hair?'

'Oh, yes please.'

There was no mirror, so I was unaware they were cutting a straight line around my head, above my ears. Again, traumatised, I made sure I was out of sight before I sobbed.

At seven, I was a member of the Sandringham Calisthenics Club. Mum came with me to the Scout Hall every Saturday for practice. One morning, she dropped me off and left. Apparently, I had lost the note given to me informing us there was no class that day. I panicked when I realised no one was there. I ran to the street, yelling, 'Mum! Mum! Come back, Muuum!'

I saw the back of her car turning the corner. My paranoid seven-year-old mind convinced me that I had been abandoned. I decided that Mum must've known class was cancelled and that's why she hadn't come in; she wanted to be rid of me because she didn't like me. A desperate sadness came over me. I ran home through pouring rain, tears streaming, my feet aching in my ballet shoes. No one was home and the doors were locked. I sat on the doorstep, shivering.

Some things we never forget.

I didn't have a name for it then, but I now know it as anxiety – a condition that would haunt me throughout my life, as would a visceral sense of feeling unsafe.

From a young age I would wake in the middle of the night, fear tightly wrapped around my rib cage, like it was sucking the air out of me. 'Go away,' I would scream inside. Will this feeling ever leave me I wondered?

Adding to my insecurities was the debilitating condition of an extremely weak bladder. Mum said that even as a baby, I would take off my nappy and wee on the carpet. As I got older, when I laughed, I wet myself. In later years, at dancing class, my urine splashed on the highly polished floorboards, ricocheting onto those around me. The music stopped, and the room cleared. The silence was deafening. I can still see my stern-faced teacher heading towards me with a mop.

At school, I weed on the oval, the tennis court and the hockey field. My sister became tired of hearing, 'Hey, your sister wet her pants again today.' At church, I weed on the pew, wetting every bottom. I weed on the Rotor amusement ride at Luna Park, my urine flying around the circular unit, not missing a soul.

I used to think my bladder had a mind of its own, conspiring against me at the very worst moments. Almost every school day ended the same way, damp tights, a hastily tied school sweater around my waist and a silent prayer that no one would notice the spreading stain. At school, my friends and I found a cupboard under the stairs where we would go at lunchtime to hold seances. Our seats were large piles of old yellowing newspapers. At one of these séances, placing our fingertips on an upside-down jam-jar, we invited the spirits in. Suddenly the jam jar shuddered under our hands and, inch-by-inch traced the letters J-U-D-I-T-H, which was the name of my friend Carole's mum who had recently passed. We knew it was she as none of us were privy to her name. I got such a fright, before I could clamp my muscles tight, warm wee poured down my legs, soaking the stacked newspapers under me. My friends scrambled out into the hallway, squealing half from fright, half from the thrill of believing we had summoned Carole's mum. I stayed behind, heart hammering, the smell of ink and urine rose around me. I couldn't move.

Mum had started tucking a spare pair of undies in my schoolbag. This day I quickly changed, 'what to do with the wet pair?' I found a rusty grate so I pushed the undies inside it. When I returned to class I noticed a bunch of giggling students crowded around the outer wall and there, protruding like a white flag of surrender was the elastic waistband of my sodden underwear visible through the vent that opened onto the passage. Shame lingered long after the hallway cleared. It wasn't just the wetness, it was believing something was wrong at my core. If I could speak to that ashamed me now, I'd tell her that my worth is not measured by the dryness of my undies. But back then, it debilitated me.

Many times, my friends would hop up to leave. 'Come on, let's go, Suzie.'

I would freeze, flippantly stating, 'you guys go ahead. I'll catch up'. *Please God, dry my pants.*

And here's the thing, I would become hysterical at anything and everything. I laughed loud and hard. I laughed at inappropriate times; I laughed when no one else did; I laughed when it wasn't funny; I laughed when it was funny, continuing to laugh when everyone else had stopped, repeating the punch line over and over, in order to keep on laughing, I laughed with embarrassment. Inside, I ached with shame.

I Wanna Be Famous

> Talent is God given. Be humble. Fame is man-given. Be grateful. Conceit is self-given. Be careful.
>
> **John Wooden**

From an early age I aspired to be a famous singer. I sang enthusiastically into a hairbrush in front of the mirror, gesticulating to the imaginary audience. I adored country music; the sad songs resonated with me, those darker-hued, deep-voiced ballads, tales of lonely highways, unrequited love, empty promises. My most cherished possession was a portable pink record player for listening to my vinyls. I loved Patsy Cline and her heartbreaking voice. I'd sing *Crazy (I'm crazy for feeling so lonely)*, and like Patsy, I had a natural country twang. Singing was so therapeutic; singing was like sucking serotonin through a straw.

Mum would bust me a lot, her head poking through the door. 'Sue, you are supposed to be studying, not singing'.

I replied, 'Mum, who needs school? I am destined for the stage. One day I will be a star'. Stardom was the answer, the solution.

I'm not sure what happened to me when I heard these tragic country love songs, causing tears to flow. I wondered if this was because of my developing unaddressed psychological issues or simply the tragedy of the song. A sensitive child, I cried a lot. Other's pain would cause a deep sympathetic response in me; my empathy seemed innate, as true to me as the colour of my eyes.

My empathy manifested in many ways, as I would exhaust myself trying to please, worrying about others' comfortability. Did they have what they needed? I felt as if it was my place to service others at all times.

One of my earliest performances, at age ten, was at Firbank Junior School when I sang Nancy Sinatra's *These Boots Are Made for Walkin'*, dressed in a white mini dress, vinyl lace up boots and a long blonde wig. Sashaying down the stairs, I pointed at a handsome boy, a playful look on my face, and sang, 'One of these days these boots are gonna walk all over you.' I loved the effect I had on him as he blushed. A sense of power, a small potent current ran through me. I surprised myself. *I am so good at this.* At that young age I became aware of the feminine expression, and how it could shape the world around us. I wondered if in fact I had a split personality. Where was the introverted, shy girl now?

My gut told me that I was destined for big things, that I would make a difference to the planet. I thought I was gifted, special, a creative genius. I envisioned my name up in lights, my face plastered on billboards, or maybe the lead singer of an all-girl band, 'Suzie and the Sapphires' or 'Suzie and the Slab'.

In 1960, I attended my first school – Sandringham State. I begged my teacher to allow me to join the school band.

'What can you play?' he asked.

'Nothing,' I admitted, 'but I'm an excellent singer.'

'There is no singing in this band,' he frowned, as he thrust a recorder in my face. 'Here, make like you can play this.'

Because I was small, they put me in the front row. I wore a red and white gingham frock that had puffed sleeves and a wide red velvet sash and black patent leather Queen Anne shoes, my shiny hair in a short bob. I fake-played my way through *Swing Low, Sweet Chariot*, rolling the recorder around in circles to give my playing theatrics. I'm pretty sure everyone knew I wasn't playing but my family clapped. 'Bravo, bravo,' I heard my dad yell. I was elated.

It was at this school that I became aware of the opposite sex but not in a good way. 'Hey, sis, I have a boyfriend. His name is Russell Thompson; he has greasy hair and looks like Elvis Presley but with acne.'

I had my first kiss with Russell. His breath smelled of pie and sauce. I wondered if all boys smelled. I also experienced my first heartbreak with Russell when he dropped me for Melanie

Thorogood. I wanted to die when I saw them walking hand in hand across the oval. I figured he had chosen her over me because she was blonde and had legs up to her neck. That was a new sort of pain; one I wished I didn't have to feel, ever again.

After state school, I attended Firbank Junior School in Sandringham.

I was the leader of one of two gangs, full of bravado, but riddled with fear. As a child, I wore the mask of a leader. At school I formed a posse, influencing others to think like me. It all seemed so simple. For a time, I was popular – the one others followed, the one who set the tone. On the surface it looked like confidence, but beneath it all I was scared of life. I bullied not out of strength but out of an early need to control, to shape the world around me so it felt safer. I didn't know how to process my feelings so I gave my energy away. I spilled it out in dominance, in bossiness, in care-taking, in fussing over others' choices as if their lives were mine to manage. This 'power-tripping' became part of my fabric throughout most of my life and was no doubt part of the 'isms' of alcoholism born to me. As a child I didn't know that what I called leadership was really an attempt to escape myself.

I was smart but I didn't understand the curriculum and the useless information fed to us, like in Grade 5, learning about the Battle of Hastings 1066. For Christ's sake, we had to bash our fists on the desk, repeating over and over, 'The Battle of Hastings 1066'. What are we suppose to do with that? Why didn't they teach us about the evils of alcohol and drugs, and how to practice safe sex? None of that, just the Battle of fucking Hastings 1066. Hence I had trouble taking school seriously. Granted I have never forgotten that piece of information. Maybe if we had slammed our fists repeating DON'T DRINK AND DON'T TAKE DRUGS, I may not have ended up here!

My school reports stated, 'Sue is a born leader, but unfortunately she leads in the wrong direction.'

305 Bluff Road

Mi casa es su casa

Our family home for seventeen years was at 305 Bluff Road, Sandringham. One of my first memories in our new house was Mum being heavily pregnant. I was six and my sister was eight, and we were so excited for a little sister, whose name was to be Sally. We bought a new washing machine and a Westinghouse drying cabinet with rods for the nappies. I remember being fascinated by Mum's humongous belly. I so wanted to touch it but that wasn't the done thing. We went off to school with the promise of coming home to a new baby.

I came running into the house after school, so excited, when I saw my dad bent over, his head in his hands, his body racked with sobs. I knew there was no baby. The room was so quiet and still. I wanted to hug Dad, but he didn't look at sis or me. The three of us cried, separately.

We picked Mum up from hospital; she was pale and quiet. She didn't want to talk about it. Apparently, we were to process this devastating news on our own. I didn't know how. Sis didn't know how. I believe this set a precedent. *Don't let your emotions get in the way of life.*

What are we going to do with the Westinghouse dryer with the rods for the nappies? I mused.

I cried in my room. I prayed, 'Dear God, can you tell me if she looked like me? How would she have turned out? I am so sad that I didn't know her. I am sad that I can't talk about her with my family, ever.'

Now a spirit, one who never breathed air and never saw light, this baby was so invisible, so evanescent, that our language doesn't even have a word for her. I wonder if the seed of my addiction began during early traumas such as these. Much later we were told that due to the horrendous birth, the doctor had asked Dad who he should save, the baby or mum. Guess that was a no-brainer.

~

Ours was a popular house where all were welcome. There were after-school play dates during the week and sleepovers with school friends most weekends. Our friends loved Dad. He always made them laugh.

Dad made the absolute best mashed potato, and to check it was perfectly whipped, he would hold the pot upside down over our heads. One night, performing his trick on a school friend, the potato wasn't set properly and it landed on her head.

Sis and I shared a room. This was okay until we fought; when I would then gaffer tape a line down the centre of the room. 'So, sis, there is the line, and you are not allowed to cross it.'

She would become incredulous. 'Then how am I supposed to leave the room? The door is on your side!'

Dad decided to build another bedroom. I grew to love Saturday afternoons, hanging in the new room with Dad, just the two of us, with him on a ladder, painting, whistling, the radio blaring with footy and races, ciggie smoke wafting, the smell of fresh paint so pleasing. 'How about a sandwich, darl?' he would call from the ladder. He loved my sandwiches. He never asked mum to make him a sandwich, as she would have forgotten the cheese, the ham, the butter or the bread.

By her own admission, Mum was a terrible cook. Nightly, she served either chops or sausages with lumpy mash and rock-hard grey peas. When she wasn't looking, Dad put his sausages on the TV Week under the table for our dog, a corgi named Genevieve. Even the dog became sick of sausages.

Hence, dinners were deserving of distraction. My naughty behaviour saw me banished to the kitchen where I would slowly slide open the servery window, poking my head through and quoting Dad's hero, Alfred E. Neuman, 'Goodbye cruel world.' They struggled to keep straight faces. I struggled to hide my joy.

By the time I turned ten, I was fed up with what Mum laughingly called her 'cooking'. I decided I needed to learn to cook. I was surprised how naturally it came to me. On weekends, I offered my family menus in bed. Dad called it 'Sue's Diner'. Nothing was said when I served them a teapot of boiling water with both tea and coffee in it.

~

When I was ten, Dad came home with our first black and white television set. We would excitedly run home from school to watch *Kommotion*, a popular Top 40 pop show. We imitated the singers, miming the latest pop hits including Tina Turner's *It Takes Two* and Sonny and Cher's *I Got You Babe,* perfecting dance crazes like the Swim and the Sprinkler, adoring Ding Dong go-go dancing in her wire birdcage, her huge boobs bouncing, her cleavage resembling a baby's bottom. I practised over and over, becoming frustrated when I couldn't master the moves. I noticed my desire for perfection becoming alarming, adding to my ever-present anxiety. *If I can't do it perfectly, then why do it at all?*

Dad had a half-brother, Mardy. They had the same father but different mothers. Because Mardy's parents lived in the country, they sent him to boarding school which he despised, and therefore came to live with us for the duration of his school years. I loved having my uncle living with us. We called him 'bro' and he called us 'sis'. Mardy was older than me and younger than sis. I flirted with his gorgeous schoolmates, looking so handsome in their Wesley College uniforms. Alas, I was seen only as Mardy's little sister.

My bro was such an enthusiastic fella. He longed to be a drummer and was forever tapping tables, furniture and walls with knives and forks. He put together a band that rehearsed in our garage on Sunday afternoons. They were loud and out of tune. I didn't care how bad they sounded, as it was a place to hang with my favourite people, unsupervised. These were impressionable times.

I felt an internal buzzing, causing excitement and anticipation, a sense of freedom, and yet I was so aware of myself, analysing my very essence, feeling fractured, never whole.

We experimented with drinks like Cinzano and lemonade, cherry brandy and Pernod, all stolen from Mum and Dad's well-stocked liquor cabinet. I noticed I drank more than my friends, but I dismissed these thoughts as irrelevant.

On one of these rehearsal days, I experienced my first period and, having had no information from Mum, turned to my sister. Humiliated, I asked 'Hey, sis, I've got blood coming out of my hoo-ha. What do I do?'

Inside, sis presented me with a cotton pad the size of a surfboard. 'OK, so you have to hook this on to this and put this between your legs.'

I couldn't believe this was happening. I wailed, 'How long do I have to put up with this?'

She grinned and said, 'only for another forty years. Now, pull yourself together and come back to the party.'

I sat on the floor and sobbed. I wondered what us girls did to deserve this. Now, I praise the Lord that I wasn't aware this was the beginning of a lifetime of being held hostage by my hormones.

I replaced my highly anticipated floral summer frock with a windcheater of Dad's that came to my knees and, as a deterrent, practised my newly acquired kissing technique—more on that later—on my new boyfriend. Everything was going just swell until he put his arms around my back and pulled me into him. 'What's that?' he questioned. It seemed the ginormous pad had ridden up to the middle of my back.

My bro's band didn't come to much, nor did my boyfriend and I. Not long after we broke up, one of his friends told me that he had decided he was gay. I wondered if it was the elephant pad incident that turned him or the dancing class incident when I covered his shoes in urine. Either way, that relationship was doomed.

Hepburn Springs

The enchanting mineral waters of Hepburn Springs are considered among the best in the world.

Dr McKenzie Meldrum from Washington

Dad and Mardy's father, Grandy, was an interesting chap. Sophisticated, well educated and handsome, he had shades of Eric Pearce, the English-born broadcaster. Grandy's full name was Richard Walter Harding-Browne, the same name as his father before him. Grandy served in the Second World War. Grandy's parents came from County Cork, Ireland, and were Protestant Irish free settlers. Our surname used to be double barrelled, Harding-Browne, but, apparently, they had to drop the hyphen when my great-great-grandfather was hung for rape. I'm guessing a double-barrelled name wasn't appropriate for descendants of a rapist.

Dad, Mardy and Grandy shared many things including Wesley College, selling insurance for Australian Mutual Provident Society (AMP) and an insane obsession with the St Kilda Football Club. Grandy was fifty-five when he had Mardy. His first wife, Dad's mum, died when Dad was very young. Grandy's second wife, Aunty Merle, Mardy's mum, was twenty years younger than Grandy. Her actual name was Norma Merle, and she was a ripper. I called her Norma Jeane because the resemblance was uncanny.

Grandy, too, was an alcoholic. Due no doubt to a nasty stomach ulcer, he drank brandy with milk and smoked a packet a day of Craven A non-filters.

Grandy and Merle moved from Melbourne to Hepburn Springs in 1959, after Grandy was threatened several times by the Victoria Police to stop his illegal bookmaking. He and my dad had an office in Chapel Street, St Kilda, where they carried out their business. The first time they were raided, upon instruction from Grandy, Dad jumped out the window. The second time, Grandy was arrested, fined and threatened with prison. Disgusted, they packed up and moved to Hepburn Springs, where they purchased the Hepburn Mineral Springs Hotel. We spent many years there, with Dad having to run the pub for a time as Grandy became quite ill.

Some of my most precious memories are of that idyllic, intoxicating part of the world. I can still recall the aromas of the gum trees, rose bushes and wood smoke, which billowed from the chimneys, the frost on the lawns, the crisp air biting our faces, and the joyous birdsong which was a constant.

Up there, we ran in a pack. In addition to Mardy, sis and I, there were the children of the regular guests. There would be a daily journey to the springs to sample the mineral waters, while the mums soaked in the old brick tubs that were bubbling with hot mineral water. A large octagonal-shaped rotunda with a dome roof, a stage and fabulous acoustics provided the perfect setting for us to sing and dance unashamedly. We threw coins into the wishing well, gazing at our reflections in the water. How simple and uncomplicated our lives were then.

The Hepburn Mineral Springs Hotel was, and still is, an iconic old pub. There was a large lounge with an open fireplace, a dance floor and jukebox. We were heavily into The Beatles, our favourites including *Love Me Do* and *Hold Me Tight*. Every night, Aunty Merle supplied us with a pile of slugs, the same size as a ten-cent piece, to use in the jukebox. At six o'clock every evening, she would line up hours of dinner music such as Herb Alpert and Perry Como. In secret, we would swap her slow numbers for The Beatles. While the dinner guests were anticipating *This Guy's in Love with You*, they got *Roll Over Beethoven*.

There was a staircase from Aunty Merle's accommodation on the upper level to the foyer on the ground floor. At 5.45 p.m. on the knocker, she would saunter down those stairs, dressed in a pencil-thin skirt, sheer stockings, stilettos and a rabbit-fur cardigan covered in pearls and wearing matching pearl earrings. Her hair would be fresh out of rollers, teased and sprayed, her lips red and glossy and she would have a ciggie in one hand and a sherry in the other. She looked like a movie star, she looked like Marilyn Monroe, and I adored her. Her family came from Spotswood; they were refreshing, earthy, honest, hardworking, hard drinking middle-class folk. I remember their shrieks of laughter.

Mardy and I were well-rehearsed jivers, The Beatles *Hold me Tight* being our favourite. He would twirl me and roll me across his back, with me wrapping my legs around his waist, my full skirt swishing. After dinner, commandeering the dance floor and wearing Beatles wigs and suits, with tennis racquets for guitars and Mardy on pots and pans for drums, we performed enthusiastically, imitating our favourite band.

It was around this time, when I was eleven years of age, I noticed alcohol was ubiquitous. The hotel had footy clubs booked in on weekends – they were a bunch of larrikins. I would sneak out of bed in my pyjamas, hiding in the cupboard under the stairs where I had a bird's eye view of the goings on. Peering through the dense layer of smoke, I took it all in – the boisterous merriment, the drunken discourse. They drank with gay abandon. I wanted to chuckle like them, talk incessantly without a conscience. It seemed as if this was a normal part of life, what all adults did, and I couldn't wait to be normal, to feel normal, to feel whole, with a sense of connection.

~

While on the subject of Mardy, over the years we have attended three of his weddings. He first married a girl I went to school with, they were eighteen. I warned him. That marriage finished before the wedding photos were printed, and as planned, with his money she built herself an extension on her house. Bitch.

His current wife, Barb, who he is still with today, having had two daughters and now a grandchild, superseded the second wife, Janet. Barb was chosen as they met at The St. Kilda Football Club and she, like him was an avid follower of his beloved Saints, therefore the third marriage was a match made in heaven.

At their engagement party, with sixty people in attendance, dad was asked to make the speech. Having had a couple, he talked about how they met and he used the previous wife's name, Janet, he then talked about how happy he was that Mardy had finally met his perfect match and he used the previous wife's name, Janet.

Finally, he made the toast, and asked that we all raise our glasses to the newly engaged couple, Mardy and Janet! The crowd were aghast. Barb burst into tears, screaming at dad, 'for fuck's sake Dick, should I have had my name tattooed on my forehead?" I was finding it hard to not lose it completely. I grabbed dad, 'Jeez dad, you should have quit while you were ahead, three times!' He too was feeling terrible. He said, 'from now on I will start with her name… Barb and Mardy, Barb and Mardy.'

Mardy, who was also upset but stifling a grin, told his brother that, under no circumstance was he to speak at the wedding. Of course, the wedding was held at the St Kilda Football Club in Moorabbin. It went smoothly, and no one called Barb, Janet. When everyone had left the venue, Dad, grabbed Sis and I by the hands, dragging us onto the dance floor where we jumped up and down, screaming MARDY AND JANET, MARDY AND JANET, MARDY AND JANET… It felt so damn good.

~

I had a feeling Firbank Senior School was to be taken more seriously. Again, I was popular and a leader, and again, alas, I led them astray.

In domestic science class, I beckoned to my friends. 'Hey, Debbie, say you're going to the toilet, meet me on the roof, bring the olive oil.' And 'Penelope, excuse yourself from class, meet me on the roof and bring the dried oregano.'

The roof was corrugated iron and a magnet for the sun. The olive oil was for tanning our legs. It was crucial they were golden brown for the after school catch up with the Brighton Grammar boys, when we hitched up our skirts, though not so high that the test answers on our thighs were visible. The oregano was for mixing with tobacco for the joints. This was no doubt a placebo effect but it sure got us cackling.

We were the trendsetters. We sat at the back of the school bus practising the drawback, our socks pulled down, hats and gloves off, lips blotted out with skin-coloured lipstick and eyelashes thickly layered with a week's worth of mascara The nerdy girls sat at the front of the bus, hats and gloves on.

Mum and Dad spent a lot of time in the head mistress's office. Dad asked her if it was possible to have an adjoining room, '… to save going back and forth.'

Barely recognisable as Firbank girls, my friends and I were continually caught smoking in the toilet block with the Brighton Grammar boys. We were suspended, sent home for a week with enough homework for a month. We spent the week at the beach, smoking and drinking Cinzano and lemonade.

In hindsight, I made some good, solid friends at that school – artists and academics who went on to achieve great things. However, these friendships ended when my drinking career began, when I needed to find my tribe.

We found it hard to take school seriously; we were hell bent on having a good time, in and out of the classroom. In year seven, a health worker talked to us about STDs, sex and the like. On the subject of crabs, she said, 'And by the way, you can't get crabs from toilet seats.'

My friend yelled out, 'So strop trying.'

Our algebra teacher was German. She finished every single sentence with, '… so we know where we stand.' This particular day, we were learning how to design a house. She held up the floor plan and said, 'So, we shade in the floor, so we know where we stand'.

We would shriek!

Our headmistress bore an uncanny resemblane to Lurch from The Addams Family – a towering six feet tall, with a ghostly powdered face and vivd red lips. I often wondered if she was, in fact, a he. Partially deaf, she became our unwitting source of amusement as we silently mouthed words to her, delighting in her confusion.

I was super alert, always on the lookout for the joke. Where was it? Where could I create it? Where was the pun, the play on words? I was desperate to make others laugh. I missed a lot, but laughing was more important than learning.

What Now?

You are braver than you believe, stronger than you seem, and smarter than you think.

A.A. Milne

When school finished, my friends were sorted. They were either going to university or teachers' college. That all sounded way too difficult. *No, thanks.* I had more important things to do. I had an addiction to nurture, an addiction that required my full attention.

At the same time, there was no encouragement from home to pursue anything of substance. I went to work just five minutes up the road as an accountant, in a local supermarket. This was ironic, as throughout my schooling I had failed maths. I would copy the answers in the back of the book, referencing the wrong exercise, be caught out and told to leave the classroom. In case of passers-by, I would pretend I was getting something from my locker. Feelings of shame evolving.

So there I was, checking off invoices from nine in the morning until five at night, causing my eyes to glaze over. When I couldn't balance, I would throw the invoices in the bin and then empty the bin into the dumpster. My boss, confused, would ask 'Where is the invoice for (so-and-so)? I'm sure it was in that pile. Where is that pile?'

I had half an hour for lunch whereby I would walk home sobbing. *Don't tell me this is now my life?*

Not daring to express my feelings or show emotion as regards concern for my ominous future, my folks were clueless. Eventually Mum sent me to Business College in the city to learn typing and shorthand – Pitman's Shorthand – which I have never forgotten.

I met a like-minded girl there. She and I wagged a lot, using our fake IDs, spending time at one of the many city hotels. I somehow managed to come top of my class, typing ninety-two words per minute.

With the benefit of hindsight, and still regrettable to this day, I would have made a wonderful teacher.

As an aside, my weekly paycheck from the supermarket was $14.50. My dad framed my first payslip; he was so proud of me. I still have it.

REBEL REBEL

I had a healthy disrespect for the law and figures of authority in general – a bit of an outlaw, if you will. There were several law-breaking incidents over the years.

The first one that comes to mind was when I was thirteen and staying with mum's sister in Frenchs Forest, north of Sydney. My girlfriends and I lied to my aunty and uncle, saying we were going to the movies. Instead, we jumped on a train to Maroubra, two hours away, to catch up with some surfie mates of ours. Unbeknown to us, these boys were drug dealers, and we found ourselves in the middle of the 'Maroubra Mafia'. We were all arrested and instructed by police that we weren't to leave the precinct until family collected us. I was allowed one phone call. 'So Hollywood,' I commented.

I rang, hoping Aunty Niecy, would answer the phone, but alas, it was Uncle Les, who was a strict disciplinarian.

'Hi, Uncle Les, it's me. I hope you're having a lovely day.'

'Hello. How was the movie?' Les asked.

'Well, you see, a funny thing happened. We didn't actually go to the movies. We are in the Maroubra Police Station. Do you think you could come and pick us up?'

Les banned me from visiting for two years.

Another encounter happened one night at the drive-in with a mate of mine. He had a bad back and asked me to drive. I had made it home when a police car arrived. Shining the torch in my face, imitating a wind-down-your-window action, the officer asked, 'Care to explain why you have an unconscious man's head in your lap and, more to the point, why you were driving without your lights on?'

Damn. I knew I had forgotten something. He then asked for my licence. 'I don't have one yet, officer, but I will soon as I'm currently having driving lessons and my instructor says I'm doing really well,' I proudly announced.

'Where are your parents?' the officer enquired.

'Inside, sir.'

Seemingly ignoring the unconscious man, the police officer frogmarched me into the master bedroom. Dad sat up, turned on his bedside light and squinting at the policeman asked, 'What's she done now?'

I was fined and banned from getting my licence until I was nineteen. Of course, that didn't stop me driving. I'm not sure why but that incident got a mention in the local paper.

Throughout my life, it seemed every time I broke the law the media got hold of it.

On a separate occasion, in 1975, a girlfriend and I boarded a train to Geelong to watch a football match between the Bloods and The Geelong Cats. The Bloods were our football team, made up of ex-Haileybury and Brighton Grammar boys. Us female supporters were called the 'blood clots'.

My friend and I drank a cheap cask of red wine on the train trip to Geelong. We were in the public dunnies, she throwing up, me comforting her, when the door was suddenly kicked open by two burly looking policewomen. 'We know what you're up to!' one of them said. 'Get out of there now.'

I turned to them and slurred, 'Just because you fucking dykes are in uniform doesn't mean you can speak to us like that.'

Next thing I know, I am being handcuffed and thrown into the back of a police van where I loudly sang, 'I'm goin' home in the back of a divvy van ...' They dragged me out of the van and threw me into the Geelong lock-up. The young policemen were clearly amused. One officer asked, 'so, love, what was the charge? Abusive language or drunk and disorderly?'

'Both,' I grinned.

Pointing to a concrete box, the officer stated, 'So, what you have to do now is remove your jewellery and hop into that cell.' This took me some time as I was not only blitzed and uncoordinated, but I was going through a 'more is better' costume jewellery stage, and that morning I had put the whole lot on. As punishment, I was to miss our return train.

The cell smelled like stale urine. I had recently read Papillon, so I decided to copy his *modus operandi* and pace, counting my steps. In the meantime, my mate, a solicitor, rang some friends of his who lived nearby and asked them to come and get me. My friend explained that he would train it home and drive back to pick me up. Perfect.

A short time later, I was in a house full of total strangers and, to add insult to injury, my cask wine hangover was reaching monumental proportions. The house was adorned with Queen Anne furniture and aromatic fresh flowers in Georg Jensen vases. The velvet drapes felt like the robes at a four-star hotel. The lovely lady smiled sympathetically and, in a voice like Queen Elizabeth's, asked, 'So, Suzie, is there anything you don't eat? I have a lovely roast lamb in the oven. I hope that's suitable?'

'Oh yes, that sounds lovely,' I whispered so as not to disturb my throbbing head any more than I had to.

Why weren't they asking me why I was in jail? I was desperate for a drink, but I could not possibly ask for one. What would they think? We sat at the dining room table, lovely lady, her husband and their two adult children. 'Suzie, would you care for a chilled Chardonnay?'

Are the Kennedys gun shy? Do wild bears shit in the woods?

'Yes, thank you,' I whispered.

The dinner conversation was a little strained, and still no mention of my jail time. I was ravenous and the meal was delicious. The wife had even made her own mint sauce. I tried to make small talk but my mind was spinning. *I wonder whether lovely lady is going to refill my glass with that liquid gold or,* I shuddered, *are these the 'one-glass-of-wine-over-dinner-then-cork-the-bottle-for-later' peeps?* Shit. To this day I find these types fascinating.

My friend eventually arrived at ten that night and drove me home, for which he expected sex in return for his good deed. 'Are you fucking kidding me?' I screamed, my head about to explode.

No wonder I had a healthy distrust of the opposite sex.

I was charged with drunk and disorderly behaviour and abusive language and had a court date set. And, as usual, the next day there was a rather large article in the local paper about the misdemeanour.

Twenty years later, I joined the local tennis club down the coast. By coincidence, the woman who bailed me out that night was a member of my team. We became great mates, and she has never asked?

There was also a misdemeanour that occurred on June 2, 1976 whereby I was jailed in the Spanish capital, Madrid. More on this later.

My Family

*In my family, weirdness isn't an option –
it's a requirement*

Before I go any further, let me tell you about my family. I'll start with my dad.

An extraordinary, charismatic man, my father had the handsomeness of Carey Grant, including the smooth, black, slicked-back hair, and a wonderful sense of humour. He worked for forty-five years as an AMP insurance salesman. Refusing to join the technological age, Dad's filing system comprised entirely of shoeboxes. 'I don't know how to use those fucking computers, and I'm not about to learn,' he declared.

Dad was a paradox. He was entertaining, a lover of life, yet he had a dark side. A daily drinker – I have no doubt he was an alcoholic – however labelling wasn't hip back then. Labels were sticky. At times Dad suffered from depression and experienced monumental highs and even greater lows. I admired him. I was in awe of him. I ached for his approval.

A party man, the more Dad drank, the funnier he became. He was a devoted follower of the Rat Pack and knew every word of Dean Martin and Frank Sinatra's comedy skits. Channelling the man himself, Dad would pull his hair onto his forehead like Frank's and recite:

Frank – 'So, Dean, I need to speak to you about your drinking.'
Dean – 'Why, Frank? Did I miss a round?'
Frank – 'So, Dean, do you ever fall over?'
Dean – 'That's the only time I get any rest. What do you think these are? Cuff links? They're kerb feelers.'

We would yell 'more Dad more' and there was always more. Dad loved an audience. There were a lot of 'Dick' jokes, as per his nickname – his actual name was Richard Neville Harding Browne. We religiously watched Rowan and Martin's *Laugh-in*, which would sign off with Rowan saying, 'Say goodnight, Dick,' and Martin replying, 'Who's Dick?'. This became a family nightly 'ritual', as in unison we would all yell 'who's Dick?'.

The dick jokes flowed thick and fast in the caravan park when it was camp erecting time. The place would be buzzing.

Over the din we would hear shouts of, 'Have you got any string on ya, Dick?'

Dad would reply, 'What do you think it is, a fuckin yo-yo?' and, 'Have you got a glass, Dick?'

'No, it's real for Christ's sake!'

Once he had successfully put our caravan and annex together, he would shout out, 'Hear ye hear ye, my loyal subjects, I hereby declare that King Dick has just completed his (for example) fifty-fifth erection'.

On the camp fridge dad stuck a newspaper clipping, the setting being a nudist beach. While walking along the beach, one couple passes another couple. One wife says, 'wasn't that dick brown? Her husband replies, 'yes dear they get that way in summer'.

~

Dad had a superb baritone voice and, as well as singing at Wesley Lodge evenings, he did a mean rendition of *New York, New York* and *My Way*, sounding uncannily like Frank Sinatra. He also crooned Herb Albert's 'this guy's in love with you', and Bull Moose Jackson and the Flashcats' line, which he would yell out when anyone jumped on a table, a regular occurrence, 'Get off the Table Mabel, the money's for the Beer'. He did a wonderful rendition of Winston Churchill when he arrives home late and drunk, and his wife says, 'you're drunk', and Winston (dad) replies, 'yea and you're ugly, but at least I'll be sober in the morning'. And he did an excellent W.C. Fields impersonation (in a slow tipsy American drawl), ' You drove me to drink Bugsy (his nickname for mum), and I thank you for the ride'. He took on the essence of the character brilliantly.

I have a video of Dad and I, with stubbies as microphones, singing Nancy and Frank Sinatra's version of *Somethin' Stupid*, gazing into each other's eyes, '… and then I go and spoil it all by saying somethin' stupid like I love you.' I didn't care that he was sozzled, I loved that he sang those words to me.

My godmother, Helen Black, informed me that Dad loved and adored me, even though I was a constant source of concern for him. He recognised the disease of addiction in me, my reliance on alcohol worrying him.

She also told me that Dad had to borrow money to send my sister and I to a prestigious school because his horse gambling had taken its toll. He would reprimand me, his tongue firmly planted in his cheek, 'Jeez, Sooz. I paid thousands of dollars for your education and you swear like a trooper! Where's my return on investment?'

~

My parents had a good relationship. I remember a lot of giggling from mum as they flirted with each other. However, Dad's drinking caused problems over the years, including times of infidelity.

I witnessed one of these events when Mum was overseas. I was seventeen at the time and full of anger, which was exacerbated by the realization that my boyfriend was cheating on me. I came home unexpectedly and, as I stormed down the hallway, I heard noises coming from Dad's room. I threw open the door and there was Dad in bed with another woman. I will never forget the look of horror on Dad's face. In that moment, I didn't recognise him as my father. He was a stranger. For a minute I couldn't look away. I wanted to scratch the image of that dreadful scene from my retinas but I was transfixed. I thought I was going to vomit. I slammed the door and ran to my car, shaking and sobbing. I drove to the beach, where I sat staring at the waves crashing on the shore, as I drank vodka from the bottle, shedding a million tears.

My life changed forever in that moment. Nothing made sense. *Why did people take vows?* I wondered. *Doesn't a marriage union mean anything?* The world seemed unsafe. I felt fearful and uncertain.

The next day at work, I received flowers from Dad with a card that read, 'One day you will understand'. Fifty years later, I still don't understand. What happened that night gave me a sense that infidelity was an acceptable past time. If it was okay for my father and my boyfriend, it was okay for me.

~

A bit of history here regarding the Black and Browne families who shared parallel lives, which included a lifetime of camping together, our camp aptly named 'The Brindles', (black and brown). The two Black girls were a couple of years younger than sis and I and the four of us shared a four-bunk tent.

One Christmas Eve, Blacky and Dad were instructed to put our wrapped presents in our stockings which were hanging off the end of our four bunk beds. We were woken by giggling as pie-eyed dad fell on top of pie-eyed Blacky. Sis sat up in bed and said, 'So I guess there is no Santa?'

We lived opposite each other in Bluff Road Sandringham and attended the same school. Mum and Helen Black were best buddies, as were Blacky and Dad. Both empathetic women, mum and Helen worked at Bailey House in Brighton for forty years, caring for children with down syndrome, most of which was in a voluntary capacity. They also shared their first car.

Dad and Blacky competed in twelve Sydney to Hobart Yacht Races. When out on the wild seas these two morphed into wild adolescents. They would step off the boat, their faces weather beaten and tanned, smelling of body odour, stale beer and boat fuel, dad with mutton chops taking up most of his face, Blacky with his white hair died black which they did when he was passed out. Nicknamed Fred Flintstone (Brownie) and Barney Rubble (Blacky), the resemblance was uncanny. They also answered to Black-Dog and Brown-Dog. Refusing to grow up, they were an outstanding comedy duo.

But most prominent was Blacky and Brownie's footy rivalry, which began in 1944.

Dad barracked for St Kilda while Blacky went for Collingwood.

They were fanatics. The 1966 grand final was pending – Collingwood vs. St Kilda at the MCG. Dad held a meeting with sis, Mardy and I. 'OK, guys, we need a plan,' he said. Blacky lived across the road from us at 374 Bluff Road. He was a plumber, and while he was at work, we painted a block of his roof tiles red, white and black. The next day, Dad came home from work to find our letterbox painted black and white. 'This is war,' growled Dad. The following day, we tied red ribbons around their black and white cat's neck, the cat's name being Collingwood. Twenty-four hours later, covering our enormous chimney, that took up the better part of our house, was a huge black and white banner of a magpie. We were incredulous.

'Now this is fuckin' war,' Dad declared. 'Yeah, this is fuckin war,' we echoed, fist pumping the air. Off to Spotlight we went, buying metres and metres of red, black and white material. On the sewing machine, Mum produced a huge flag to which we attached a wooden pole, and when Blacky was at work the next day, we secured it to his fence.

The Herald Sun got hold of this story, as one of their reporters was driving down Bluff Road and noticed a ginormous magpie on one side of the road and a very large St Kilda flag on the other side. They interviewed Dad. The next day, on the front page of the Herald Sun, there was a fantastic photo of Dad holding the flag and standing in front of the magpie, with the headline *Friendly Rivalry* and the story of Blacky and Brownie's lifelong friendship, rivalry and passion for their teams. It was sensational or, as Dad put it, 'Saint-sational'.

It was 1966 and the big day had arrived. Collingwood versus St Kilda in the Grand Final. Stats: Collingwood had won twelve premierships, St. Kilda none. Dad, Mardy and Grandy attended and their excitement was palpable. When St Kilda, the underdogs, beat Collingwood by a point, the three of them became psycho, screaming, crying, their faces purple, high fiving, chanting 'Saint K-i-l-d-a, Saint K-i-l-d-a', followed by three thunderous claps, over and over, when suddenly Dad and Mardy noticed Grandy had disappeared and that's because he was on the ground having had an excitement-induced–heart-attack. As the ambulance carried him out on a stretcher, in his Wesley College King Charles voice, tears in his eyes, he was heard singing, 'carna mighty saints'!

And that my friends, was the one and only grand final St Kilda has ever won. For fifty-nine years now we've been waiting for another. And our motto, understandably, is 'strength through loyalty'.

~

Mum was a partier in her youth and pre-children days, but she slowed right down once she had us. She would say, 'you can't have two drunks in the family. How will we ever get home?'

I remember being carried from strange beds, wrapped in prickly blankets, and laid down in the back of the cold EH Holden. Dad would be singing in the passenger seat and good old reliable Mum driving, the faint odour of cigarettes and beer in the air as streetlights flashed past, upside-down power poles whizzed by and us kids, half asleep, shivered.

I have a feeling Mum aspired to be a loving, nurturing, caring woman although I also have the feeling she was not the maternal type. At twenty-two years of age, she certainly wasn't prepared for my sister's arrival. She was hoping for a couple of years honeymoon before kids, but it was not to be. My gut told me I was in her way most of the time and, in later years, she confirmed this was the case. Once, when I was four, she smacked me on the bottom for being rude. I was mortified. Too humiliated to cry, I grabbed her red lipstick, facing my bum to the mirror, and drew what I thought was the perfect shape of a hand on my little bottom. I bared all to her, wailing, 'See what you've done to me?'

Mum was an attractive, well-educated, classy woman. She was also accommodating, meeting our every need. She made our clothes, including our 'first date' frocks. Mine was a pencil-thin skirt with matching blazer in a stretchy purple mohair cotton, which I wore with a lacy lilac camisole. For my sister's prom, Mum made a long white muslin empire-line frock with a self-pattern of tiny blue flowers and a royal blue velvet ribbon under the bust, which my sis wore with white sling backs. That day, sis spent hours at the hairdressers, arriving home with a bouffant. Crying, she ran to the shower, washing it out. Dad said, 'Well, that's good money down the drain.'

Mum was a health nut. Our cupboards boasting wholemeal pasta, Ryevita biscuits, brown rice, and rye bread, and absolutely no sugar. We couldn't wait to go to our friends' houses on weekends where we stuffed our faces with sweet bikkies, and held midnight feasts where we would make butterballs rolled in white sugar.

Sis and I walked to and from state school and, on our way home, we would buy a bag of mixed lollies at the corner store, excitedly chewing on our clinkers and false teeth as we walked. Sometimes Mum surprised us by picking us up. We would see her car approaching, and one of us would shout, 'Quick! Mum's coming. Ditch the sweets,' and over the nearest fence they would go. As soon as we could, we would go back to retrieve them. And they were always where we left them.

Before getting married, Mum trained as an interior decorator. At home, she wallpapered every room in a different pattern, which included pasting the ceiling of the sewing room in stripes. Dad would joke, 'Hey, girls. Don't stand still too long. She'll paste you to the wall!'

During Christmas 1975, while Mum and her best friend, Gladys, were overseas, we were preparing for an upcoming party. Brownie and Blacky were in the roof cavity installing Pink Batts. Suddenly, we heard a commotion coming from the sewing room. We ran in to find Dad spread-eagled, half on and half off the bed, and Blacky's head appearing through the hole in the ceiling. 'Hey, while you're down there, Brownie, why don't you take the top off one?'

Mum rang from Europe, 'Hello darling. How are the Christmas party arrangements going?'

My voice cracking, 'The party arrangements are going swimmingly but Dad just fell through the roof of the sewing room'.

In a panicked voice, I hear Mum say, 'Oh no. He didn't ruin the stripes, did he?'

Dad was a hit that night, dressed as Santa, pointing out the hole in the roof to all and sundry, beaming, 'ho ho ho! Merry Christmas! I've had enough of fuckin' chimneys, now I come through roofs.'

~

I must make mention of my Nanna, Mum's mum, who was a fabulous woman. She, too, was an alcoholic. My mum swears I got her missing gene.

During our secondary school days, at lunchtime, we smoked ciggies with her at her house. 'Don't tell your mother,' she would say. In the cupboards would be half-full long neck bottles of beer. 'Nanna, why have you got all these bottles around the house?' I would ask.

'Oh, they're not mine darling; they're Reggie's'. Reggie was Nanna's dead brother. Her husband, Lionel, died when Mum was twenty-three years old. Nanna and Lionel were inseparable. On her own, Nanna was lost and lonely. She found the drink comforting.

At age fifty, after she first hit rock bottom, Nanna asked Mum to take her to an AA meeting, after which she announced, 'I'm not an alcoholic. I don't belong there,' and she continued to drink. After her second rock bottom, at age fifty-five, they went to another meeting. 'I am definitely an alcoholic,' Nanna declared, and she never drank again, nor did she go back to AA. On reflection, she had the symptoms of a 'dry drunk'.

Thursday nights were at Nanna's house for roast lamb. She would be tiddling and smoking in the kitchen so the lamb would be overcooked and the veggies murdered. We imitated her, wearing an apron, posing with a fag and necking a big bottle of beer. 'You belly children,' she would smirk.

My bro, sis and I sat on one side of the dinner table and would reliably get the giggles. One night, I was hysterical, rocking my seat, as I knocked my bro's chair over which knocked my sister's chair over. We all landed in a pile on the floor, our plates of food on our heads, and of course me wetting my pants. 'Oh, you belly children,' from Nanna, mum and dad looking like they were going to burst.

Nanna encouraged our performing, teaching us songs such as *Barefoot Days* '... We'd go down to the shady brook ... with a bent pin for a hook, we'd fish all day, fish all night, but the gosh darn fish refused to bite.' We would imitate a bent pin for a hook with our fingers, as we pulled up the imaginary fishing line, slapping our hips, and frowning.

Other favourite songs we performed were *The Little Shirt My Mother Made for Me* and *Let's Get Together* from *The Parent Trap*. Nanna clapped enthusiastically, big bottle of beer and ciggie at hand, her knitting on her lap. We performed whenever the chance arose.

One of these times was the talent quest at the Caloundra caravan park while on a family holiday. My sis and I performed *Barefoot Days*, playing toy ukuleles and dressed in matching homemade blue and white houndstooth playsuits, our hair in short bobs. We won. There were shouts of 'Encore! Encore!' We followed with *The Little Shirt My Mother Made for Me*. We won a box of Cadbury chocolates. We were chuffed.

The caravan park had a pool, and my sis and I swam all day long, until her blonde hair went green from the chlorine. We pined for luscious Queensland bananas but, sadly, the trees were bare. One morning, we noticed a big bunch hanging from the same tree we had checked only the day before. 'Wow,' I said to sis. 'How did those bananas grow so fast?' Dad feigned surprise.

This was a memorable time. I was eight years old and sis was ten. We travelled in Dad's old blue Holden sedan, towing a caravan. Bored, my sis and I fought in the back seat and chanted, 'Are we there yet?' We stuck chewing gum behind each other's ears which meant Mum had to cut big chunks of our hair off. Dad kept us amused by playing a 'James Bond' game, pretending there was a bomb at the border of the next town and if we didn't get there in time, then we would all die.

It was so exciting. We would count down the minutes to the next town shouting, 'Will we get there in time? Are we going to make it?' Once at the border of the next town, dad would pull over and sis, dad and I would jump up and down, excitedly running around in circles, throwing our arms in the air. 'We're saved, we're saved, Hallelujah, we made it.' Dad was such a funny dude.

It rained heavily for most of the trip so, with the help of our creative mum, we wrote a song:

> Rain, rain, go away
> Don't you spoil our holiday
> Rain, rain; go away
> Come again another day.
> We left Sydney Harbour on a rainy Boxing Day
> We travelled in our caravan till we were far away
> And then it started raining, it rained and rained and rained
> And that is why we started to sing this long refrain.
> Oh, rain, rain, go away …

Looking back, I never understood the family thing. I loved them but they didn't satisfy me, rather I felt suffocated by them. I knew this holiday was potentially quality time, but I didn't know how to bond. They were just there, shouldn't that be enough? I took them for granted. I felt disconnected from them, like I was the odd one out. They didn't fulfil my needs. I wanted more. I always wanted more. More is better.

The Leading Role

Be so good they can't ignore you.

Steve Martin

Nanna housed a border whose name was Michael and who was the director of a theatre company called The Adelphi Players. Clearly, he detected the Sarah Bernhardt in me and cast me in the lead role of Flora in *The Innocents*, a production based on the 1961 film starring Deborah Kerr. I was eleven years old. I had hundreds of lines to memorise for my part in this psychological thriller about ghosts possessing children. Late at night, following rehearsal, I was driven home to a dark, cold and silent house and would jump into bed, pulling the blankets over my head. I found the plot disturbing, but I was hooked.

On opening night, with my friends and family in attendance, I received fifteen bouquets, delivered to me on stage during the curtain call. It was such an exhilarating feeling. One of stardom, validation, adoration and success. *One day these bouquets will be academy awards,* I promised myself.

I loved the works of Shakespeare and instead of sleeping, with the help of a torch, I would read the large volumes under the sheets. I spent hours researching the lives of famous stars – Elizabeth Taylor, Vivien Leigh, Marilyn Monroe. I read *Valley of the Dolls* over and over. I became enmeshed in a Hollywood fantasy bubble, so envious of these stars and their glitzy, glamorous lives while, at the same time, so restless in my own.

In addition to theatre, I also had a short-lived television career. I appeared on the TV series *Bellbird* as Jeanie Hall, a child whose mother had died in the bushfires. They moulded putty wounds over my body and filled them with chocolate topping for blood, as the colour red wasn't visible on black and white television. I also had a small part on *Division 4* where I played the child of a crook. On both occasions, if you'd blinked, you would have missed me.

I continued acting for a couple of years, joining The Toorak Players and The Brighton Theatre Company. I performed in productions of The Pirates of Penzance, My Fair Lady and Oliver Twist, when I played the lead, 'please sir, I want some more …' I had found my niche and, with it, a new-found sense of confidence. Taking on another character and persona, removing myself from my head, was the answer.

Sadly, as soon as I discovered boys and booze, my acting abruptly ended. I found partying and flirting to be a full-time job. No longer was I taking on a character's role in a play, I was now playing the role the alcohol handed me.

Curious as to my 'disease of more', including feelings of emptiness and numerous unanswered questions, I read self-help books at the age of thirteen, searching for answers. *There has to be something more.*

~

Nanna's husband, Lionel, my maternal grandfather, was Jewish, and Nanna had two Jewish sisters-in-law whose names were Myrtle and Selena Levy – or Aunty Ena to my sis and me. When we were young, sis and I had sleepovers at Aunty Ena's unit in Elwood. She wore acrylic floral dresses and had a pinafore tied around her waist. I was so fond of her; there was something about the inner serenity of the Jewish people.

I can clearly remember the frosted glass dining room doors etched with flamingos, shag pile carpet and artificial flowers, which adorned the windowsills of Aunty Ena's home. There were knick-knacks everywhere. I spent hours playing with the neatly stacked cards, erasers, perfectly sharpened pencils and containers of elastic bands in Aunty Ena's roller-door desk. I still have a vintage art-deco china Buddha of hers that is over one hundred years old.

The unit smelled of fish as, whenever sis and I visited, Aunty Ena would reliably prepare our favourite juicy white flathead fillets with crispy batter. I sat patiently watching and waiting for the fish to go cold. I am unsure why but it tasted better that way. We so looked forward to 'Aunty Ena's cold fried fish'.

We would sleep on a hard sofa that folded out into a bed. The sheets and pillowcases were white and crisp, like the ones in a motel. Without fail, during the night, I would wet the sofa. Poor sis always woke up a tad damp. Dear Aunty Ena never complained as she took on the arduous task of washing the sheets in her manual washer, pulling them through the wringer. She got wise in time and put a plastic mattress cover over the sofa.

When we were older, at Aunty Ena's request, on the third Thursday of every month, my sis, her husband, my boyfriend, Lewis, and I went to her house for dinner, the smell of fish as we entered no longer appealing. She would put our good wine in her cupboard, pouring us a glass of warm Spumante. She fed us cold fried fish with lumpy mash and grey beans. For dessert, it was predictably blancmange. We avoided eye contact as we ate.

Ever resourceful, I would hide one of our uncorked good wines in the shower recess. I wondered if anyone questioned my many trips to the toilet.

At the end of their lives, Ena and Nanna were housed in the same aged care facility in Brighton. Nanna would call me, saying, 'Sue, Ena and I need these belly hairs removed. Can you get in here?' In I would go with the Nair, removing the thick black hairs growing out of their upper lips and chins. I remember that place smelling like a sushi dumpster on a hot day.

Aunty Myrtle wore a weird wig. It looked like it was on backwards. Maybe it was.

When Aunty Ena died, sis and I, with our well-rehearsed funeral faces, kept it together in the viewing room. That was until we saw the familiar black hairs sprouting from her chin. Sis said, 'well you obviously haven't visited for a while!' We lost control. Mum was horrified. Mazel tov.

Torquay

If there's heaven for me, I'm sure it has a beach attached to it.
Jimmy Buffett.

Our Torquay camping experience began when sis and I were babies and continued for the better part of our lives. My earliest memories as a toddler are of raucous people with a drink in one hand and a cigarette in the other. Mum and her cronies resembled movie stars, as they lay on their canvas beach lounges in their stylish floral two-piece bathers. They were smothered in coconut oil, with the only form of sun protection being the triangles of newspaper over their noses that were held in place by massive Jackie Onassis style sunglasses. Us kids loved to watch that coconut oil turn a solid white once the sun went down. They baked their way into their seventies. Once I overheard a couple of surfers down the beach a way, 'Hey, check out those ladies. They look like a bunch of old Big M Girls.'

I have followed suit regarding the sunbaking. When the sun's out, I'm in it. I call it 'tan-orexia'. All my problems disperse when I am baking. At the start of every winter, my mood would plummet to the depths, which confused me until my doctor diagnosed me with seasonal affective disorder. That made sense, another addiction.

When we were toddlers, pubs closed at 6 o'clock. I'm not sure why but the mums began getting ready at 5 o'clock, dressing in their white pedal pushers, plastic loopy ear-rings, their lips shimmering. In order to get what needed to be done in that short time, they would sit us on our potties and tie us to the tent pole to make sure our business was complete. Some may call that child abuse however, back then, considering their limited time frame, it was acceptable. When at the pub, while the mums drank and smoked, the blokes had been there all day by the by, us kids were allowed ten pence, (one bob), each, which bought us a raspberry lemonade and sixpence worth of hot chips from the fish and chip shop, which we would jump up and down on until the chips were smashed. Not sure why but they tasted better that way.

Pre-children, the oldies would drive to Torquay on Friday after work in the old 34 Plymouth Deluxe, with the running boards along the sides of the car, traditionally stopping at The Grovedale Hotel for a couple.

These drinking sessions regularly continued longer than planned and while the blokes would have a skin full, the ladies drank half lemonade, half beer so it was their job to drive to the camp, while the blokes travelled on the running boards singing loudly.

This ritual continued post-children and on one of these occasions, deep into the drinking session mum said to dad, 'oh shit, it's Sue's birthday!' They handed me a packet of chips and sang happy first birthday.

Our family maintained the same campsite for seventy-two years. So many wonderful memories were made there. We'd wake up at six a.m. to the sound of birdsong, waves crashing and the paperboy bellowing, 'Heraaaald, Suuun and The Aaaaage'. Sixpence in hand, we would run for the paper, which was used only for Dad's sports guide and Mum's crossword. We had a Coolgardie Safe as a fridge, in which Dad placed a large block of ice that was delivered to our site along with our milk in glass bottles with foil lids, an inch of cream at the neck.

My first nasty experience with alcohol occurred in the camp one New Year's Eve. I was twelve years of age. My camp bestie and I were home alone and got stuck into a bottle of Dad's brandy. I remember staggering on the beach and then nothing. When I awoke, I noticed I had vomited green bile all over the sheets and myself. I will never forget the look of concern on Mum's face. She knew. I threw up for the next forty-eight hours. I thought I was going to die. I wonder why this wasn't a deterrent, but, back then, I had no idea that the power lay with the brandy, not me.

Pre-teen years in the camp were so much fun. We had no choice but to entertain ourselves, as parental supervision was non-existent. We made aluminium sheets into slides, tearing down the steep slopes of the sand dunes. We converted big beer cans into stilts, threading string through the perforated holes and stomping around on top of the bricks adjoining the toilet block, chopping the heads off bull ants. The locals knew this brick space as 'the hot box'. In our teenage years, that hot box became a sacred place of worship, as that's where the hot surfers hung out. If you were accepted into that space, you knew you'd made it. Us girls were allowed to sit there but were not allowed to speak.

We frequented the local pinball venue, the front beach trampolines and Frenchy's jukebox and gelato café, dancing to tunes like *Young Girl* by Gary Puckett & The Union Gap and *Love Grows (Where My Rosemary Goes)* by Edison Lighthouse. My interest in boys was growing as my self-confidence flailed.

It was around this time that I noticed an electrical buzzing going on inside me, a state of heightened alertness and sensitivity. I was constantly worrying even though I had nothing to worry about.

Adding to my anxiety were the antics of a dude who camped near us. His parents were friends of my parents. He was older than us and looked like Robert Redford. He was a ladies' man, and his caravan doubled as a brothel. My camp bestie and I would watch through the curtains at the goings on, a different girl every time. One day he caught us out and chased us, grabbing me and aggressively throwing me on the ground. He sat on my back and, with the sulphur end of a matchstick, proceeded to engrave the initials J.R. just above my bum crack. J.R. stood for John Robinson, who was my Clayton's boyfriend – the boyfriend you have when you're not having a boyfriend. He was looking on laughing. I was crying with humiliation and pain, so scared I couldn't move.

Mum noticed my back and the obvious 'J.R.' engraved into it and went berserk. 'How dare he! I'm going to see his parents about this,' she said, as she gave them a piece of her mind. 'If I see your son near my daughter again, I will be calling the police.'

Another time, my girlfriend and I were running back from the Torquay cinema in the dark after seeing Alfred Hitchcock's *The Birds*. We were already understandably freaked out when we felt sharp 'claws' on the back of our legs. I had a feeling it was he and I was right. We screamed and ran faster. He stayed on our heels, scratching us with bushes and making maniacal high-pitched bird screeches. Oh, how he traumatised me, and how I feared him; yet, conversely, I enjoyed the attention. Truth be known, I had a huge crush on this good-looking, sexy man. Life was so puzzling.

A wonderful camp tradition was the Australia Day celebration, which involved an 18-gallon keg of beer, pavlovas, lamingtons and party pies with Aussie flag toothpicks. The men wore wife-beater singlets and board shorts, while the women wore wigs and Aussie flags as sarongs. Performing is mandatory. At one of these celebrations, a group of us imitated The Andrews Sisters, singing *Boogie Woogie Bugle Boy* and *Don't Sit Under the Apple Tree*. We wore belted polka dot dresses, black stilettos, bright red lipstick and Roaring Twenties hairstyles with hairnets. We made a microphone using a broomstick wrapped in coat hangers and shoo-whooed our way to raucous applause. That act was so well received; we took it around the camping area and then to the Torquay Surf Club where we rocked the crowd.

Our children also performed throughout their lives, starting as toddlers and the oldies entertained us way into their eighties, donning tutus and wigs.

We had a camping committee whose job it was to set the rules, keep law and order wherever possible and give out the camp awards on Australia Day. This time, my sis had just had her boobs enlarged, so she was awarded a size 40H sequinned leather and lace bra, painstakingly made by some of the women. There were awards for the most morning swims, lowest golf handicap, last man standing and so on, and involved a lot of yahooing and cheering from the sozzled crowd. Year after year, as previously mentioned, Dad was appointed King of the Camp and was presented with a beautiful gold painted crown with King Dick printed on it and a large decorated gold sceptre. I have some beaut photos of him with this large phallic object between his legs, the crown on his head, wearing a cheeky grin and addressing his loyal subjects. 'I guess you're wondering why I've called you all here,' he would say. He played the part well, and as far as making us belly laugh, he never failed.

One Aussie day, Dad and his buddy, Bruce, decided to crack the barrel early, making sure there was a perfect flow of beer. This was taking place while the hot sun was beating down on King Dick's bald head. Dad peaked too early and was rotten as a chop. I was horrified as I watched him fall backwards, hitting his head on a tree. Everyone rushed to him, and I grabbed a pillow to put under his very red sweaty head, noticing blood. I yelled, 'we need a nurse! Is there a nurse in the house?'

I hear my sister next to me say, 'I am a nurse. Get out of my way.'

'Quickly, we need a tourniquet. We need to stop the bleeding,' she shouted.

Someone ran over with the sequinned bra and we wrapped it around his head. The blokes then carried him to bed, which was no mean feat as he was a jolly chap with a large beer belly. He woke up at eleven p.m. with the bra stuck to the coagulated blood on his head, furious that he had missed the party.

In 1994, much to the disappointment of us all, the government decided to end the Australia Day long weekend. Horrified, King Dick decided to have a 'burial of the long weekend'. We made a coffin out of black balsa wood. Dressed in black outfits and top hats, straight faced and to the tune of Mendelssohn's *Funeral March*, with King Dick leading us, we slowly carried the coffin down the stairs to the beach. It was a very hot day and the beach was packed. All activity stopped, cameras clicking furiously, as we disappeared into the ocean holding the coffin above our heads, dad yelling, 'March on, loyal subjects.' I glanced across at Uncle Ronnie. A short chap, who had water creeping up to his nose, his cigarettes, glasses and hat floating above his head. Determined not to let go of the coffin, he marched on.

At Easter time, we held a traditional 'clubbies vs. tenties' competition, in which the surf club crew competed against the campers. On one of these occasions, we watched as a surfboat came down the filthy dirty creek carrying a dozen blokes dressed in armour splattered with tomato sauce, depicting blood. They swayed back and forward, holding big bottles of beer in one hand and spears in the other, yelling, 'plunder, torture, pillage!'

The mums, not to be outdone, sported bird costumes and were inside homemade bamboo cages, singing '… *I'm Only a Bird in a Gilded Cage*'.

One of my old aunties would get messy when she drank too much. Someone would yell, 'Norma's switch has gone off,' as she would be fine one minute and falling sideways the next. During one of these incidents, my mum whispered to me, 'Can you take Aunty Norma to her caravan? She's had enough.' I successfully undressed Aunty and put her to bed, locking the caravan door behind me. Next thing, there she was back at the party in her underwear, drink in one hand, ciggie in the other, twirling around in circles, having climbed out of her caravan window.

A popular game at the time was charades. This night it was Aunty Norma's turn to act. She was jumping up and down, pointing to her forehead on which she had stuck a Fosters beer label. So much hilarity.

Lifetime friendships were made from that camp. When someone dies, we have their wake at the Torquay Surf Life Saving Club and then their ashes are taken out in a surfboat and scattered at sea. We joke that there is a sandbank out there built entirely from 'Varicose Vein Valley' residents, our name for the camp.

Four generations later, the camp lives on through my daughter, her family, my nieces and their families who still holiday there. Mum pulled the pin and gave her site to the family when she was eighty-five.

~

Mum travelled overseas with Aunty Gladys every year. Dad, on the other hand, had no desire to travel, unless of course he was on a yacht. That all changed when Mum suggested Dad accompany her and Aunty Gladys on a trip to Ireland where he hails from. Dad researched before he left, discovering where his grandfather used to drink – a little pub in County Cork.

The story goes something like this. Dad walked into a bar … an original old Irish pub which was dark, had leadlight windows, sticky carpet and beer taps the full length of the bar.

As far as Dad could see, which wasn't very far, he was the only person there. He sat on a stool at the bar and introduced himself to the barman, explaining the reason for his visit. Thrilled with his story, the barman responded, 'Ah, to be sure, to be sure. 'Tis a grand story. We need to celebrate Dick's visit, so I'm shouting the bar!' Dad was amused as he was the only one there.

Then suddenly, from somewhere in the distance, he heard a small voice saying, 'Oil 'ave one,' and out of the darkness came a leprechaun look-alike who hoisted himself up on a stool next to Dad. The three of them got stuck into the Guinness while Dad regaled them with his family history.

It didn't matter how many times Dad told that story – and he told it a hell of a lot – it was well received. One Christmas, I bought two extra large white T-shirts, one for Dad and one for Dad's buddy Bruce. On the front I had printed the words 'OIL 'AVE ONE' in big green letters, the colours of the Irish. They were the most well received gifts, and Dad and Bruce wore them everywhere. They even slept in them.

This became the camp catch phrase and it is still used today. Whenever anyone has a bottle in their hand, the call echoes out in the ether, 'Oil 'ave one.'

On this trip, dad bought sis and I diamond and sapphire earrings, which he smuggled through customs in an Alpine cigarette packet in his shirt pocket. He was so proud of himself.

The (Unofficial) Original Puberty Blues

... *'bitchin barrel babe', 'yea whatever, where's me pie and sauce?'*

It's complicated.

In my early teens, considering myself in tune with the essence of the ocean and those who rode the waves, delusional and full of hope, my camp bestie and I began frequenting the share houses in town where our heroes lived. The (unofficial) original Puberty Blues was about to be re-written and my well-established low self-esteem set in cement.

There was a bunch of us surfie chicks, clucking our way to the beach with our hot, skinny bodies. We were skinny because we didn't eat, especially around the boys, as that would be way too awkward. However, I wasn't anywhere near as skinny as some of my friends. They were so thin I wondered where they kept their internal organs.

As I mentioned previously, I was kind of 'going round' with John Robinson, a narcissistic, chauvinistic, self-absorbed prick. He was six feet two, had masses of curly black hair, and was smoking hot and totally unattainable. I hung around him like a bad smell. When my eyes met his big, intense brown ones, butterflies slam danced in my tummy. When he asked, 'Where's me Chiko Roll and Coke?' off I would go, trudging over hot sand dunes in 30-degree heat, using the money I had pinched from Mum's wallet. *Jump, girl. How high, lover boy?*

We had our instructions from our boys. 'Hey, chicky babes. Make sure you're checking us out working the waves.'

We would watch them change from their clothes into their wetsuits, always leaving their budgie smugglers on. We were required to fold their clothes and warm their towels by sitting on them. We were to take an interest in surfing but not so much that we surfed. As instructed, upon their return we gushed, 'hey, dude, bitchin' left, unreal cut back, radical re-entry, epic green room ride, babe, filthy right. Cowabunga, dude.'

'Yeah, whatever. Where's me pie?'

We lay on our backs because our bellies looked flatter that way, not that we had bellies and not that they noticed, however there were those chicks who were vertically flaunting their perfect figures. We knew they put out. We, on the other hand, were frigid virgins pretending we put out.

Unlike the other girls, I hadn't yet developed breasts, so my mum would make my bikini tops with padding in them and a frill sewn on the outside. I think I got away with it.

~

Besides the seaside, my time with John played out in the beer garden of our popular seaside pub. Due to the heroin clashing with the beer, he often threw up or nodded off or both. It didn't matter what he did or how much he took advantage of me, I was besotted. I wondered if it was because he was unattainable or because he was a notorious figure in the town and the desire of many, or because he was so damn hot, but I had never felt love like it.

He became my heroin, an intoxicating presence that offered temporary highs but left me grappling with the lows. I was caught between the desire to save him and the need to save me. There is a thin line between love and self-preservation.

This triggers a memory. Fast forward to 1977 when I was flush with some money from the successful outcome of a court case instigated by my dad (more on that later). I bought an old Volkswagen, spending the balance on John and whichever girl he was 'tuning'. Mum was custodian of these funds. John would nudge me, 'Hey, Sue, we're out of cash. You need to grab another red back from ya mum,' Yes sir! Back to the camp I would go. Mum would begrudgingly hand yet another twenty-dollar bill over, tsk-tsking me, saying, 'surely you can do better than that, Sue? God only knows what you see in him.' How do I explain my obsession with this boy, this addict I thought I could fix, and make fall in love with me. I was already finding solace in undesirables, substance abusers, creating unhealthy boundaries from the get-go.

Truth be known mum had a soft spot for John. He could be so charming

One day, he stole my mother's car to drive to the women's prison to visit his other girlfriend. Guess he owed her that much as he had been the cause of her incarceration, convincing her to fill her vagina with heroin while travelling from Bali to Australia. This day, he nodded off at the wheel and smashed up Mum's car. And still I loved him.

~

I had my first acid trip with these Torquay boys at the local church fellowship dance. LSD played havoc with my psyche, and I convinced myself I was a massive lumpy green gherkin with no legs. I locked myself in the toilet, paranoid, my mates hanging over the top of the cubicle, begging, 'You have got to come out of there. You've been there all night. You are not a gherkin. Promise, we can see your legs …'

As we were coming down, we lay on the grass, carrying out a burial for a cigarette butt. My body felt like cotton wool. The sun was rising and all was serene, the sky a yellowish grey before the rain came and drenched us. A sense of euphoria enveloped me. I loved this feeling so much.

There was another phase we went through. We found that mixing cough mixture with Serepax caused a pleasant high involving dizziness, shaky legs, laboured breathing, buzzing body and uncontrollable merriment. You may well ask why; I still ask why. The answer is simple. It was all in the name of the eternal pursuit of mind-numbness.

> **Diary excerpt January 1971:** *I have come to the rather worrying conclusion that reality is just not for me. Dad once said, 'Sue, you were behind the door when God gave out moderation.' Was I determined to prove him right? Was this a self-fulfilling prophecy? I*

love the sensory amplification the acid produces and yet, paradoxically, I hate it. I love anything that allows me to escape, but being out of control of my senses frightens me. And yet, I must do this. To be accepted, I must do this.

Friday nights were the cream. We would wait patiently outside Hampton High School for our boys, inevitably hearing their names called for detention. Of course we stuck it out, it was worth it just to see John sauntering my way, with a fag in hand, Marlboro packet in the top pocket of his untucked shirt and that smile, the one that caused me to go weak at the knees. These nights were spent at the local disco, Stonehenge, where us chicks flaunted our semi-naked bods, wearing sequinned boob tubes and micro miniskirts, which looked more like belts. We would then throw trackies over our dance outfits, removing the glitter from our faces, and morphing from disco ducks into surfie chicks, while jumping into the combi van and heading to the coast. Traditionally, our mate Hilly would yell, 'Wish it was Friday,' and we, in unison, would scream, '*Fuck it is; fuck it is!*' We were living the dream.

These times would depend on whether my folks believed my lies about going to my girlfriend's house for the weekend. Strangely, they were generally trusting. That was until one Sunday when my camp bestie's brother saw us hitchhiking home from the seaside, and instead of picking us up, he dobbed us in. We were lucky to survive that ride. The hoons who picked us up were drunk; doing wheelies in paddocks and refusing to take us home, with us white knuckling in the back seat. When I arrived home it was dark and Mum and Dad were standing in the kitchen, looking pale and anxious. I caused them so much concern. I was grounded on a regular basis, this incident included, and I climbed out of my bedroom window on a regular basis.

This was all lived out to the soundtrack of some memorable albums including *Bob Dylan's Greatest Hits* and *Positively 4th Street*, as well as music from bands including Crosby Stills Nash & Young, Eagles, The Beatles (*Let It Be*), The Doors, Tamam Shud,

The Moody Blues, Blind Faith (*Can't Find My Way Home*) and Jimi Hendrix (*All Along the Watchtower*). And the song I sang to John, Build Me Up Buttercup by the Foundations … .'why do you build me up, buttercup baby just to let me down, and mess me around, and then worst of all, you never call baby when you say you will, but I love you still … .'

These were unforgettable times. Opposite the Torquay Pub was an old rambling house, a place of euphoric spiritual essence, home to followers of Krishna before it became hip to embrace his teachings. Here lived the much older, long-haired, caftan-wearing gurus, an aroma of Nag Champa incense and marijuana wafting. They were worshippers of Meher Baba, an Indian spiritual master, known as the 'Avatar'. I faked interest but this 'hippy-trippy' stuff was way too profound for me. I was more concerned with how I looked, whether I should iron my naturally Afro hair or just let it go, if I was acceptable, whether I fit in and if I was pleasing others.

However, it appeared these devoted surfers had a secret. They were spiritually connected to the ocean and nature in a sensory way. While I found it all a bit intense, being in their presence excited me and filled me with a sense of gratitude. They knew how to decomplicate their lives.

These people taught me that spirituality might just be that link between the façade of me and my true self, with a little precious help from the ocean. I so wanted to be like them. I wanted to be free of the anxiety that came with an uncomfortableness, a dissatisfaction, a desire for something unattainable, a feeling of separation between them and myself, like I had a hole in my soul which needed filling. My needs were never satisfied.

Back then marijuana was the go. No one drank much, except me, so I started hiding my drinking, my addiction already causing me shame.

One of the tribe, a brilliant musician, had a beautiful dark green restored Rover with a shiny wooden dashboard. It was his pride and joy. He had rules: no drinking or eating in his car. One day, he drove my girlfriends and I from Melbourne to Torquay. I had a hangover and needed a drink. I begged him, 'Please, Brew, can you stop at the bottl-o? I need a UDL. Pleeeeeease.'

Finally, he relented, pulling into the Werribee Bottle-O. When I got out, he drove off, leaving me there. I had to hitch back. When I saw him next, I asked why he left me there. He said, 'I didn't want you spilling your UDL.'

The women folk were so accommodating, welcoming me into their fold. I followed them around, wearing what they wore which were long hippy skirts and floppy hats. We held ceremonies in Taylor Park, sitting in a circle among the tea trees, singing along to their soulful guitar playing, me pretending to share their joints, pretending because that stuff made me so paranoid, exacerbating my perpetual imposter syndrome.

During my time with John, we witnessed a profoundly historical event when, on July 20, 1969 my friends and I, having been given the day off school, made our way to 34 Raynes Park Road, Hampton, which was John's family home, where we watched the men landing on the moon. While sitting next to John, his hand on my knee, witnessing this monumental occurrence, I remember feeling a great force of energy ripple through my entire being. I knew then that this was where I wanted to be forever. Not long after that John's eighteen-year-old brother committed suicide by hanging. John found him. A month later John's dad died of bowel cancer.

It was also at this time that John ditched me because I wouldn't put out. He wrote me a 'Dear Sue' letter, explaining that he couldn't be with a city chick as he was now a surfie dude and moving to the coast to live with Hilly. I read this letter during music class at school while listening to the soundtrack from *Romeo and Juliet*. I thought my heart had been broken by my first boyfriend at state school but that was nothing compared to this. I remember the room blurring around me, the music seemed to disappear into the walls, which were closing in on me, and I was struggling to breathe, my tears dripping onto the letter. I was shattered. I thought I would never recover.

Over the years I watched John deteriorate into horrific addiction until he died at a young age in a men's shelter, a broken soul. For a time he moved to Queensland with his mother, his last remaining family member, where his heroin addiction all but destroyed him. At that time, he was in the bedroom stoned while his Valium – addicted mother burnt to death on a bar heater. A fireman had to shake John into consciousness. In 1974 Phil (more on him later) and I were visiting his parents in Broadbeach, Queensland. Whilst crossing Cavill Avenue one day, we spotted John who tried desperately to avoid us as he owed Phil $3000 from a drug deal. 'Where's my money,' asked Phil. 'Up my arm,' replied John. And still I loved him.

To this day, I feel privileged to have been part of such a free-spirited group of warriors. Even though my imposter syndrome raged most of the time. I have no doubt that as young enthusiastic girls, our prettiness acted as currency, as did our will to please, not to mention the fact that we idolised and adored these legends, placing them on pedestals, laughing at everything they said, fetching whatever they wanted and generally boosting their already massive egos. Why wouldn't they want us around? It helped that we knew our place amongst these figures of worship. We knew when to speak and when to be silent, when to fade into the background, not drawing attention to ourselves or getting in their way, and we knew when to be present. Acceptance didn't come easily and none of it was on our terms. As I'm writing this, only one of that tribe is still living.

And at this point, I can't help but wonder, after all the years of questioning, confusion, anxiety, analysing and doubting our worth, was it simply all about us, as spiritual beings, having a human experience and doing our best to survive, while trying to make sense of it all?

As Paul McCartney put it: And in the end the love you take is equal to the love you make.

Cherry Popped

Why do they call it losing your virginity, anyway? It's not like I don't know where I left it.

Rachel Vincent

Having finally lost my virginity, I decided to use my new-found sex skills with the aim of securing my place in this very clicky surf town. My friends and I had come to the realisation that we had the power over men. It's called 'the power of the pussy'. Der. Why don't we use it? Sex became the stage, and we became the actors.

There was a plethora of willing participants. At our young age, we managed to transform ourselves into strong desirable women who effortlessly obtained what we wanted from men. Men were so easy.

I was sixteen when I lost my virginity to my camp bestie's cousin who eventually decided he wanted me as his girlfriend and I didn't question it. Why would I?

And so ensued a hell of a lot of pashing, causing gravel rash, which I decided was unacceptable for starters. But I was curious and excited at the idea of eventually achieving this orgasm thing I had heard so much about.

We were at his house the day he decided there would be penetration. He took me into the bedroom and talked me through the process. While he was negotiating my as yet unpenetrated vagina, I was climbing up the bedroom wall. 'Get away from me. Stop that. What do you think you're doing?'

Ouch. Blood. Pain.

His mother unexpectedly arrived home in the middle of this. 'Quick,' he said. 'Mum's home, get dressed and go say hello to her.'

I was aghast. *Oh my God. Is that it? Is that what I must do for the rest of my life? Kill me now. Where were the doves? The detonations of glitter? God damn it. I thought it would be like it was in James Bond movies, me straddling my fella, wearing a sexy black lace bra, arched back, parched lips, sucked in stomach, thrashing my arms in the air, swishing my long flowing locks, dim lighting, frantically fornicating, pretending I knew what I was doing, faking orgasm.*

It appeared us girls were forever being punished as, for the duration of our lives, we will have blood coming out of our vaginas and penises going into them.

When I finally orgasmed, I couldn't understand what all the fuss was about. *Whaaaaaaaat?! I don't need a bloke for that.*

I really wanted to be good in bed, but, then again, who wants to be bad in bed? To me, the whole thing was a waste of drinking time.

And let's face facts. Teenage boys would hump anything – the furniture, lampposts, you name it. I reckon if doors had holes, women would be obsolete. Their dicks are like divining rods.

I made a conscious decision then and there that if this sex thing is what is required of me, I would make sure I was completely inebriated, therefore numbing myself to the ordeal.

~

My Melbourne boyfriend spent a lot of time cray fishing on Thursday Island. We wrote letters to each other. He sent me Harry Nilsson's single, *Without You (Can't live if living is without you)*. It's true; you will always have feelings for the one who 'breaks' your virginity. What I didn't know then was that we would break each other's hearts.

With him came what I would like to believe was my tribe, although I didn't think for one minute that I was on a par with these private school kids. Affluent, good looking and snappily dressed, they were so much more sophisticated than the people I was used to. Truth be known, I was resentful and envious of them, my imposter syndrome rearing its ugly head again. My boyfriend's mum couldn't believe how shy I was, but that soon changed when I found booze. I put my heart and soul into keeping up with these seasoned drinkers and dope smokers from the city. It wasn't long before I outran them all.

These new friends enjoyed my company. I was fun, crazy, loose and accommodating. Over the years, I benefited greatly from this lot and their perks. Who needs holiday houses, ski lodges, snazzy cars, speedboats, yachts or swimming pools when you are a member of this set? I wondered if they noticed, or cared, that I had no way of reciprocating on a material level.

However, I still felt spiritually connected to the ocean and couldn't drag myself away from it entirely.

I had two lives effectively; one in Melbourne and one in Torquay, and I became magnificently adaptable. My fashion changed with the geography. My Melbourne life saw me in op shop clothes such as vintage lacy shirts, black velvet boleros, berets, long skirts, chokers and much 'Spakfilla', our term for make-up.

My Melbourne life in the early eighties was all about cabarets. These nights required extra adornment, including layers of foundation, false eyelashes and big hair – teased, sprayed and with the addition of a switch which was pinned to the top of my head to create the illusion of more hair. Depending on the seriousness of the night, sometimes two switches were called for. Once, I dyed my sister's switch dark brown which didn't go over too well. We wore silk dresses with puffed sleeves, tight belted waists and frilled bodices. Our catchphrase was 'More is better.' I would spend half the night in the bathroom, sneak drinking. The more vino I drank, the more lipstick I would apply. Gloss over shimmer, matte over frosted and lip liner dangerously close to my nose and chin. I drunkenly and mistakenly figured the more lippy, the better. My friends played charades with me, stretching their mouths and wiping invisible lipstick off their teeth.

In contrast, my coastal life saw me with a clean face, an Afro hairstyle and wearing flared floral Hot Tuna hipster pants or thin corduroy jeans with tight T-shirts and peaked caps. One day Phil, came to pick me up from home. As I was busy in front of the mirror, Phil said, 'We're going to the surf coast Brownie. I hope you're not putting make up on?'

'No,' I said, 'I'm taking it off'.

Our surfie clothes were mostly stolen from our friends' surf shops. In the change room, we put trackie daks over the jeans, disguising them. Back then, I had not one ounce of a conscience. I walked into a friend's surf shop one day and attempted to steal a Jimi Hendrix poster for John who was a dead ringer for the man. As I was walking out, the owner was walking in. He grabbed the poster and whacked me over the head with it. I wet my pants in the middle of the main street. By the time I dried off and arrived back at the 'hot box' the whole town knew what I had done. I heard a chorus of 'what were you thinking?'

~

My relationship with my Melbourne bestie, Sarah, dates back to 1969. We were young and hot to trot and became best friends and even better rivals. We wore the same make-up and clothes and had the same hairstyles. We dyed white Hard Yakka work singlets every colour of the rainbow, which we wore with hipster corduroy bell-bottoms and bare midriffs. She looked like Brigitte Bardot – tall with a glorious straight back and chiselled shoulders. I envied her. I was jealous of her. Maybe I was in love with her.

It seemed my life was marred by envy (my own unreached potential projected onto another) – was that really me?

She was gifted a bright orange Renault on her eighteenth birthday. We took full advantage of our newfound freedom, doing naughty stuff in naughty places. We escaped our boyfriends whenever possible. In Sorrento, we hung out with an older boy, a sexy Geoffrey Rush look-alike. He lived and worked at the Portsea pub. We would sneak into his bungalow, wearing skimpy bikinis, covered in oil, jumping on him, rolling around on his muscly bare chest, giggling. He couldn't wipe the grin from his face. 'Hey girls, what are you doing?' he'd say, feigning disapproval. 'Do your boyfriends know you're here?'

There was no shagging, just a sense of freedom and disobedience. We both shagged him later in the piece though, as did every other girl we knew. He was gorgeous.

We both wanted the security of a boyfriend and yet we couldn't and wouldn't be caged. We were from privileged backgrounds; we oozed with entitlement.

~

When my beau was away, I sought the companionship of the previously mentioned Phil, a reliable, fun-loving, fill-in boyfriend. To his chagrin, ours was simply an emotional affair. He would ideally have loved to be my boyfriend but I refused. I loved him too much to break his heart and break his heart I would have.

Phil was a cool dude, a trendsetter with a wonderful sense of fashion. He was my and Sarah's little plaything. 'Who do you want to be today, Phil?' we would ask.

'I think I want a David Bowie look today,' Phil would say, so we'd dye his mullet red, and paint Zorro markings across his face.

For a Rod Stewart look, we gave him a blonde spikey arrangement with black eyeliner. He so looked the part. Phil was androgynous before it was hip. He wore high-heeled boots, tight paisley Lycra body shirts and flared pants. He spoke with a drawl, had the cheekiest of grins and green eyes that sparkled.

Phil and I were obsessed with Rod Stewart. We spent hours in my bedroom listening to his records; we dressed like him, wearing mullet wigs and strumming broomsticks or mops. We would hang around record stores, gazing at the beautiful vinyls such as *Every Picture Tells a Story* and *Never a Dull Moment*.

Phil and I believed that Rod wrote *I Was Only Joking* about me.

> Susie, baby, you were good to me
> Giving love unselfishly
> But you took it all too seriously
> I guess it had to end …

We attached electric cords to our squash racquets, plugging them into the wall. We played for our friends or empty rooms. In sync, Phil and I would turn our backs to the non-existent crowd, tuning our imaginary amps on the wall, counting to five before we did a one eighty to face the crowd again.

Phil was different. He had a strong feminine side and a unique flair for style. He didn't miss a trick. When I was getting ready for a night out, I would dress to please him, as, unlike my actual boyfriends, Phil would notice. It would make my night when he looked me up and down, his head to one side, his arms crossed over his chest, and in his sexy slow drawl, he would say, 'jeez Sooz, you look really good'. I would beam.

Phil and I made a pact that we wouldn't tell my boyfriend how much time we spent together in his absence as it might upset him. Not long after his return from four months away, while Phil was driving the three of us along Bluff Road heading to Beaumaris, at number 305, he automatically and unconsciously flicked his blinker on! Phil blushed, I giggled, my boyfriend ignored it.

Phil shared houses with his mate, the previously mentioned Geoffrey Rush look-a-like, for thirty years. We called them Felix and Oscar, after the TV series *The Odd Couple*, except they were The Even Couple. They had takeaway for thirty years, with empty containers, cans and bottles filling the place, as well as Phil's squash racquet with its worn-out strings, which, he played nightly, mostly ignored by all.

One night, while sitting on the floor eating fish and chips, Phil spilled an open container of Saxa salt on the cream carpet. He told us not to worry as he disappeared for a time, returning with a bottle of red wine, which he poured over the salt. 'That'll fix it,' he drawled

While nursing disgusting hangovers one morning, we awoke to very loud birdsong. Phil looked across at me and said, 'Can you believe some people like that shit?'

Their letterbox was constantly overflowing with David Jones, Myer, Yves St Laurent, and Tommy Hilfiger brochures. His roomie would throw a stack of them at Phil, asking, 'Who's life are you living, Phil?'

Forward to 1976, when I was in London, I received a telegram from Phil which read, 'BROWNIE GO TO RECORD STORE STOP LISTEN TO ROD STEWARTS NEW ALBUM TRACK EIGHT STOP WILD SIDE OF LIFE FROM ME TO YOU STOP'

The words went something like this:

> You wouldn't read my letter if I wrote you
> You asked me not to call you on the phone
> But there's something I'm wanting to tell you
> So, I wrote it in the words of this song
> I didn't know God made Honky Tonk angels
> I might have known you'd never make a wife
> You gave up the only one that ever loved you
> And went on back to the wild side of life
> The glamour of the gay nightlife has lured you
> To the places where the wine and liquor flow
> Where you wait to be anybody's baby
> And forget the truest love you'll ever know

Sarah and I listened through headphones, our mouths agape and tears in our eyes.

No one has ever loved me like that, nor ever will.

East and West Coasts

Wherever I go, I take myself with me

For a decade, I alternated my summers between the east and west coasts, Portsea and Torquay. When in Portsea, I stayed at Sarah's. Back then I travelled to Queenscliff via the ferry, which was a rickety old boat. Before mobile phones, I would get a message to Mum via the Torquay camp ranger's office, giving her the ferry time so she could pick me up at Queenscliff.

With the Portsea Hotel having arguably the best beer garden in the world, and these days being gin and tonic fests in the sunshine with my favourite people, I found it impossible to leave. My poor mother drove back to the camp from Queenscliff without me so many times.

On this one occasion, my presence was required in the camp for Mum's birthday party, and I was determined not to let her down. There was a chorus from my mates. 'Brownie, you have to get this ferry. It's the last one,' and 'your mum will be waiting'. I knew it. If I didn't get this ferry, my mum would never speak to me again. I said my goodbyes, grabbed my bag, G & T in hand, and ran down the jetty as fast as my legs would take me. I could see the ferry leaving the pier. *Oh no, I'm gonna have to jump. I have to get on that ferry.*

I took a mammoth leap from the jetty to the ferry. *I made it. I made it. Hallelujah.*

That's when I realised the ferry was docking! Back to the beer garden I went, a fresh G & T awaiting me. My friends were crippled with laughter. My mum would be crippled with anger.

On both coasts, I had deep feelings of disconnect, forever thinking there was something missing. What it was I never knew. My anxiety and paranoia became brutal, and the more I drank, the worse I felt. An inner conflict invaded my thinking with a stubborn regularity, like a drum beat that never stops.

~

In 1971, when I was seventeen, Mum and Dad decided to move to Queensland. I was devastated. *Why are they leaving me? What's wrong with me? Now I know they don't love me.*

They put me in a box-like red brick unit in a low socio-economic suburb. How embarrassing. 'I'll never be able to have my affluent friends around,' I moaned. 'I've joined the ranks of the bogan, redneck, plebeian society.'

Dad said I was being overdramatic and that he would pay for me to visit them whenever I so desired.

A mate of mine moved in with me. He was a gay Kiwi known as Champagne Charlie, as his five food groups consisted of champagne. In the third bedroom was an old school friend of mine, however she couldn't keep up with us and moved back home after a month. Her parting words were, 'You need to do something about your drinking.'

'Why? Did I miss a round?' I snarled.

At the same time, there was an incident, which had a monumental impact on me. I was working at a local business as secretary to the industrial relations manager –a slimy German whose name was Heinz Paul Fritz Schneider. I wrote a letter to a friend describing him and his sleazebag ways, which he intercepted and read. He called me into his office, letter in hand, questioning me as to my opinion of him. I remember feeling so frightened that I thought I was going to wet myself. He had a smirk on his face as he said, 'Vell, seeing you think zat I am a sleazebag, now I vill say to you zat if you don't have sex viz me, I vill fire you.'

I left that day. My departure, and the reasons behind it, were ignored by my colleagues and higher management. Apparently sexual abuse was acceptable and tolerated. Go figure.

I wonder now why I didn't question the manager's motives. At the time, though, I felt this was something I should get used to, but there was also underlying shame. *Did I deserve this? Did I bring it on myself? Clearly, I did.*

My appetite for negative self-talk was rampaging.

Events such as these traumatised me, creating strong feelings of abandonment and unworthiness, which lingered throughout my life. I wonder if they were the cause of the eventual abandonment of myself.

> **Diary excerpt May 1974:** *I'm noticing that I am drinking a lot more than the other girls. Once I start, I can't stop. Like some people fake their deaths, I feel like I am faking my life. I am a paradox. A renegade yet a follower, a conformist yet eccentric, conventional, running in accordance with what is generally done or believed, and yet I can be original, commanding my peers. I don't want answers; I want the questions to stop.*

The following event also caused me next-level trauma, exacerbating my sense of uselessness, shattering my faith in humanity and convincing me that trusting anyone ever again was out of the question.

I knew my boyfriend was fond of Sarah. In fact, I was convinced that if she'd been single, he would have been with her instead of me. But we were together and I thought that stood for something. This evening, at a friend's holiday house in Sorrento, I waited in our room for a long time for him to return to bed. Hours went by. I had a sense something was up, so I tiptoed down the hall and peered into the front room. There was my boyfriend with my best friend and another couple in bed. I thought I was seeing things. He ran after me, protesting, 'Nothing happened, I promise. I swear, nothing happened.'

I grabbed his hands. 'You lying arsehole. I can smell her all over you.'

My immediate thought was *why is he lying when it is so obvious?* I heard myself screaming, 'you lying, cheating bastard. Why? Why? Why? Why her?'

I was livid, but more devastated than anything else. In that minute, everything blurred and I was struggling to breath. I leant against the wall for support. *How do I deal with this?* I had no coping skills, no way to calm myself. It felt like the end of the world.

I chased him around the room, scratching his back, drawing blood. I remember him crying for his mother. I couldn't sleep. We both cried into the night. He wouldn't let me near him.

The next morning, I rang Sarah's boyfriend in front of our friends, telling him everything. Sarah was furious. Ha, she was fucking furious! I wanted to kill her.

Nothing was ever the same after that. I felt my boyfriend stayed with me because he pitied me or because he didn't want to get beaten up again. I felt so betrayed, so hurt, and yet my feelings of worthlessness had me begging him for forgiveness. How sad is that? *Did I deserve this? Am I so unworthy of their loyalty?*

I couldn't help but wonder if this is the price I must pay for love? Intense love, powerful love, or at least that's how it seemed. I gave every skerrick of me, my soul, my mind, my body, my spirit to love, to have it all blow up in my face. I felt broken.

We would sit for hours in his Holden, outside my house, he wanting me to leave, me refusing to go, his beloved Ray Charles's 'It's Crying Time Again …' playing loudly, adding to the morbid vibe.

Their joint denial devastated me, as did the consensus among the tribe that I had made it up. That hurt more than the incident. I felt they were all pitying me and my assumed paranoia. Abandoned again.

This is when I came to the realisation that the truth was irrelevant. The truth had no place in our world. If everyone believed lies, then why not just keep lying?

Rod Stewart said it all, when he crooned: *The First Cut Is The Deepest.*

After this betrayal, I figured if you can't beat them, join them. And so I began a clandestine affair with Sarah's boyfriend, whom I will call James, and who had been the previous boyfriend of my sister.

In retrospect, I wonder how on earth I allowed myself to be manipulated by this guy. Adding to my need for numbness, I had come to the conclusion that I had not one ounce of authenticity in any part of my narcissistic self. I was marinating in guilt, but I didn't want to lose him. He was manipulating both Sarah and I successfully, feeding his inflated ego.

My boyfriend, on the other hand, didn't seem to notice. James had some sort of power over me. I hated myself but stopping seeing him was not possible. The sex was sensational and my body ached for him, literally. Because of him, I developed a healthy appetite for sex, experimenting in all sorts of ways. Finally, I got it. Sex was awesome.

There was one night at James's bungalow when we were in bed, naked, and there was a knock on the door. 'It's Sarah,' he whispered. 'Get in the cupboard.'

I grabbed my clothes and any sign of me and jumped into the cupboard, starkers. In the meantime, they had make-up sex. *Perfect!* Much later and with my tits frozen off, Sarah left. I was furious. 'I couldn't get out of it,' he vaguely apologised. 'She was already suspicious. I had to shag her.'

Call it lust, call it revenge. Regardless, I went back for more. At this time, I was so far from realising my truth. If only I saw the path I was heading down and the consequences of this behaviour.

Eventually it became apparent that Sarah and my boyfriend were also bumping nasties. No surprise there. When it all came out in the open, the four of us decided that the sensible, grown-up thing to do was to shake on it and swap partners. So that's what we did, and we all lived happily ever after. Well, not really. Sarah and I didn't speak for a long time until we ran into each other years later at the Oktoberfest, where we hugged and swore we would never let boys get in the way of our friendship. And we never have. She is still one of my best mates today.

Granted, this was a time when many trespasses were made on each other's hearts and many hearts were broken.

Once a player, always a player. When James became my boyfriend, I would constantly be asked questions like, 'so, did you enjoy the drive-in last night? I saw James's car.'

'I wasn't at the drive-in last night,' I would moan.

Along with others, I discovered he was shagging a much younger Firbank girl who I knew quite well. There is something about short men with large egos who are no doubt hiding a multitude of insecurities. Call it 'small man syndrome' – who knows – but he had an insatiable appetite for sex.

I ached inside. I felt unheard, unseen and unloved. It tore me apart. I had no control over the cheating and I was too young to control my own vulnerability, hence it annihilated me. I wondered if I would ever feel safe in a relationship, free to grow into me, while being part of a couple.

In hindsight, I wonder why I would want to be with someone who didn't want to be with me? When James was mine; he was so tactile and romantic. In public, he would pull me into him and hold his lips to my cheek, like Tom Cruise did with Nicole. I loved that. He oozed sex appeal and was a charismatic, captivating boy. What was not to love? Even though I couldn't trust him as far as I could kick him, he had me by the short and curlies. His signature tune, which I'm sure was written for him, was 'The Wanderer' by Dion. '… *well, I'm the type of guy that likes to roam around, yea I'm never in one place, I roam from town to town … yea I'm the wanderer …*' He sang that to me, while dancing voluptuously, with a smirk on his gorgeous face. He was truly irresistible.

His affection however, came with conditions, my outfits had to meet his approval before we left the house, he would say '*your upper arms are too big to wear that halter top, go change*'. I had to carry mints to keep my breath fresh and I had to remove the three hairs from my upper lip. Thanks to him, I was forced to wax for the next twenty years. God forbid I end up like Aunty Ena and Nanna! Interestingly, I thought this was acceptable behaviour. But then again, I would have tolerated any behaviour as long as I was seen with a boyfriend. Sarah was with my ex so I had to hold on to hers. The competition was brutal.

As an aside, James eventually dropped me for Denise Drysdale with the cleavage like a baby's bum! He always was a tit man.

Progressive Disease

When I read about the evils of drinking, I gave up reading.

W.C. Fields

On the booze, I had extreme highs and brutal lows. Alcohol would soothe me and unsettle me at the same time. Drink made everything better, temporarily. It gave me confidence. Fear plus alcohol equals courage.

Alcohol slammed a wide range of confused thoughts, and I didn't question it. Everyone else was doing it, and I predictably did what everyone else did. I didn't have an original thought. I wasn't aware that I had a progressive disease, that I was allergic to alcohol. I wasn't aware that, unlike me, my friends were not dependent on alcohol, nor did they have the 'phenomenon of craving', 'obsession of the mind' or the 'allergy of the body'.

My drinking created so many dramas. At the end of the night, when the girls were obediently following their boys home, I would be begging. 'Come on, guys. Silvers night club is open until three. I'll shout us a cab, the night is but a pup'.

There were constant fights with my better halves, the 'hand brakes'. They wanted to go home and have sex and then sleep because they had footy the next day. Yawn! Such a waste of drinking time! I felt so disconnected from my friends.

I chose drink over anything and everything. *What was an appropriate time to start? Or what was an inappropriate time to start?*

Yes, upon reflection, I was powerless over it, and my life was becoming unmanageable. (Alcoholics Anonymous Step One.)

I was in 'the grip of the grape'. As soon as I had a drink in my hand everything else became secondary. Things would happen around me, but my thoughts were only on the drink, how long would it last and when would my next be coming. *Should I drink faster so I can have my next one sooner, or should I slow down in case the next one isn't immediately accessible?* Drinking consumes our mental bandwidth – we think about drinking, then about not drinking. We drink, we recover and the cycle repeats. Sobriety frees that bandwidth, giving us space to grow emotionally and evolve into who we're truly meant to be. It restores us to ourselves and our own extraordinary potential.

My drinking had become a glamour-less necessity, like going to the toilet. I relished the rituals of drinking. The popping of the cork, the 'glug, glug, glug' sound the liquid made, the crystal glasses, the goblets and the champagne bubbles wending their way to the top. However, cask wine in a plastic cup would also suffice. I wasn't fussed about the nuances of a good wine or the 'cheeky little bouquet'. It didn't last long enough in my mouth to question whether it was aged in wood or not.

This is a disease of greed. Give me more – and then some. Why stop at one when you can have five? Those of us with alcohol use disorder can't imagine life without it. We want it all, all the time, always scheming for the next drink. *Maybe I'll stash a bottle of vodka at Mum and Dad's just in case the wine runs out.*

The hidden vodka would be my insurance, my measure of safety. I was able to relax at dinner while hoping no one noticed how quickly I slammed down my first glass or how I nonchalantly refilled my glass only. And there was always the feeling of disconnect from it all as I hid in my bubble, an invisible chemical layer separating me from the world.

Often, I would excuse myself from social events, taking my large bag and pretending to go for a walk. 'I just need some fresh air,' I'd say, and then I'd sprint to the bottle-o, hiding the bottle in my bag. I made sure I had a coffee cup hidden in every room, including the garage and laundry, and a hipflask in the car, all the time convincing myself that no one knew. One Christmas day at my friend's large house, mum said, 'is there any room in this house you haven't hidden a coffee cup'.

Thinking about having a drink would alter my tiresome day. *I can get through this. Not long now. I'll be fine for the next two hours and sixteen and a half minutes.* Simply the thought of a drink spurred me on.

Even when I was asked not to drink, I drank. For example, one Boxing Day we were invited to the sixtieth birthday of a good mate of ours. Considering he was just out of rehab for alcoholism, his sister asked us not to drink. I had a disgusting hangover and was aching for a 'hair of the dog', but I was determined. *I can do this. I can do this* I chanted to myself. *One minute at a time.*

When I arrived, I noticed everyone was on soft drinks, but before I knew it, I heard myself saying, 'Hi, Rachel. Is it okay if I have a beer? I'll hide out the back.' Her disappointed face said it all. *Why? Why? Why? Why couldn't I just not drink?*

> **Diary excerpt same day:** *I feel like I am living on the outskirts of my life because I am living on the outskirts of my soul. Feelings of hopelessness making it easy to succumb to addiction. Hopelessness is a vicious cycle. It's part of what makes overcoming addiction seem eternally impossible. I am broken. I need to take my power back.*

My drinking was becoming suicidal. In order to shut down the jackhammers of my insecurities and chronic obsessive-compulsive disorder, I would drink to black out. I called it 'time travelling'. Blackout was like untangling a mystery, doing detective work on yourself. *Aha. Lipstick on two wine glasses. I wonder who was here? Full ashtray. Obviously, someone who smokes a lot. Marlboro. I don't know anyone who smokes Marlboro. Clearly, I do?*

My evenings came with trap doors. My hungover mornings were hard to bear. What had I done, what had I said, who had I insulted, whose secrets had I blown? Not remembering how I got home from the party then gingerly ringing the host, 'Hi Vanessa, thanks for last night, gee I think I may have drunk a little too much? I hope I wasn't too badly behaved?'(giggle, giggle) then waiting, dreading her reply, 'Oh no, you weren't too bad'. What the hell did that mean?

Then there were the 'brown outs', the times when you remembered some parts of it. And we cannot forget the blackout sex. This was when my mind was in a coma and the rest of me was at a rave, where I would leave my body so others could enter it. I wonder if the trashing of my body and mind gave others the right to trash me.

Of course, there were also the countless walks of shame, with me tiptoeing out of a stranger's bedroom in their share house, hair like a bird's nest, heels and bra in hand, mouth feeling like the bottom of a cocky's cage, and hearing the tsk-tsks and the snickerings. One of these one-night-stands was with a well-known AFL footballer. After a mammoth night, drinking and drugging for Australia, he took me back to his apartment to no doubt perform the dirty deed but as soon as my head hit the pillow the room began spinning. With no hope of making the bathroom, I leant over the bed and spewed in his shoe.

A nod to the unsung heroes of the inebriated. The barman hunting for your boots and hat – casualties of your bar-top dance. The girl slipping you water as you heave in the cubicle. The friend hauling you into a taxi. The mates acting as human crutches up the stairs to your bed, or the one who quietly nicks your car keys.

The cardinal rule of a lush's life: be kind to the drunken – they're already living in their own private hell.

I try not to think of the articles of clothing I have given away during these times. Whenever I heard, 'Oh I just love that scarf/hat/earrings/vest,' I'd always reply with, 'Really, have it'.

I could kill myself the next morning. *Where's my scarf? Oh no, not again. I loved that scarf. My daughter gave me that scarf!* And let's not make mention of the shoes and phones I have left in cabs.

One night when I was dining out with my friend Tex, she said, 'I love that ashtray. It's so retro. Can you steal it?'

'Sure I can,' I replied and promptly put the ashtray in my pantyhose.

Walking out, I hadn't noticed the ashtray had slipped down to my ankle. The manager did, however, and he wouldn't let me leave until I gave it back. Awkward!

Most mornings, on waking, after eventually finding my specs hidden somewhere in my matted hair, I would marvel at my earrings sitting perfectly placed together on the bedside table and my clothes neatly folded on the chair, and then I'd notice the front door had been left open all night. Despite this, one thing I never failed to carry out was the nightly face cleansing routine. A mate of mine once commented, 'you are fascinating, Brownie. No matter what condition you are in, you always remove your make-up and put night cream on your face.' And to this day I don't think I've ever missed a night.

~

This same mate and one-time partner in crime had turned her life around, as had everyone I knew besides me. Having witnessed me at my worst, she had grown tired of my drunken antics, which included incidents ranging from falling down the stairs at a nightclub and ending up in hospital to wrestling the microphone from a girl on karaoke night, only to knock her off the stage, causing her to cut her head open. In my defence, she was murdering Cher's *If I Could Turn Back Time*. Like a banshee, I screamed at her, 'this is my song. Get off and I'll show you how it's done, bitch!'

Considering the number of times I fell, tripped and stumbled while wearing stilettos (damn you gravity), I'm not sure which is harder to understand – the fact that I drank for that long or that I wore heels for that long.

Over the years, I had confessed all to this mate; I didn't leave anything out. She broke up with me via a letter which read, 'I love you, but I can't worry about you anymore. I can no longer listen, and I can no longer watch.'

The same girl handed me the *Are you a real alcoholic* questionnaire. Do you ever drink to get drunk? Tick. *What a stupid question. Why else would you drink?* Do you drink during the day? Tick. Do you ever black out? Tick. Have you been in jail for drinking? Tick. Tick. Tick. Need I go on?

The exception, and the girl who has stood by me through thick and thin, and is still my most cherished friend today, I will call Kay. Kay and I once shared an apartment, having married at the same time, having had babies at the same time and having left our husbands at the same time. The consensus among the tribe was that she and I had married below ourselves. They may have had a point, however, our decisions to marry didn't come with too much thought or contemplation, as for both of us, it seemed like the right thing to do at the time, and something we should give a go as we hadn't done it before, and we both figured that you've got to try everything once. And there certainly wasn't much thought given to their position, status or rank within society before we said 'I do!' So fuck the tribe and their opinions.

Turns out the tribe was right and those marriages were doomed from the start. The four of us got wasted a hell of a lot and we had a shit load of fun until we didn't. Tuesday nights were pool night at the Sandringham Hotel. We would park the car with the two babies in their car-seats facing the window of the pool room so we could see them at all times. If they cried, we would bring them into the pub, feed them then sit their carry-cots on top of the cigarette machine. Once we were enjoying a 'parmie and pot' counter meal when one of them shat in their nappy. The smell was horrendous so we moved tables.

On one of the many nights drinking at our Mentone home, Kay whispered to me, 'I'm bored.'

'Me too,' I agreed.

We then told the guys we were going for milk, whereby we drove to the bottle-o and then to Torquay, staying the night with some mates. When we got back the next day, the babies were in the same nappies we had left them in and all her hubby had to say was, 'You'll be getting an STD test before you come home.'

On another one of those 'going for milk' outings, when we were actually off to see our favourite band at the local and hiding our Australian Crawl T-shirts in our bags, I heard my husband say, 'You won't get into the Mentone pub looking like that.'

Now grandmothers, Kay and I are still great mates. When I look at her, it seems as if time has stood still, the only difference being our grey hair and laugh lines.

Kay was an exception, but truth be known, most of my relationships, especially with women, were based on drinking. This came with the deep-rooted knowledge that there was a hollowness to them.

I knew these relationships were built on booze, but that was all I knew. I never considered walking away, because that would've meant cutting the drinking thread that tied me to the tribe. As long as I was part of it, I belonged. Looking back now, I see how small my world had become – a fragile bubble built around the bottle.

At one ladies' lunch when our predictable conversation turned from bitching about our husbands to politics, my friend looked at me blankly and said, 'I can't join in, I know nothink about anythink!' And I could relate. I had no idea about world events, politics, the refugee status, global warming, art, nudda, zilch. I have worn blinkers for an eternity. My only concern was 'are we ordering another bottle'.

F.E.A.R. – False Evidence Appearing Real or Fuck Everything And Run

My days began with an unhealthy sense of fear. Fear that mentally and physically tortured me. I relate to this quote I recently read:

'I would hear fear's voice in my ear... have you ever considered that I might be here for a purpose? To remind you that you are alive and that your life deserves to be embraced. There's important work for you to engage in. The more you focus on sharing love, the more I will step back. Fear doesn't have to be a heavy burden; it can be a path toward peace and lightness.'

My addiction created so much internal fear. In my mind, the evidence was real, never false. I chose self-terrorisation over running.

With fear came dishonesty. It became the norm to lie. I lied to avoid appointments, lied about hangovers, lied about how much I drank and how much I hid. I lied for the sake of lying. I lied when a friend would ask me to her house for coffee or tea. I never understood the concept of going to someone's house for coffee or tea. My standard reply was, 'No, sorry, I have an appointment. Are there bubbles? I'll cancel the appointment for bubbles.'

You forget how to tell the truth, and you forget who you are. As Judge Judy says, 'You don't need a good memory if you tell the truth.' With deceit comes defiance and power. How easily the lies caused disassociation from self; it's like you have two lives. And the lies seem to metastasise like cancer until they consume us entirely.

If Nothing Changes, Nothing Changes

*When you change the way you look at the world,
the world you look at changes*

Like all addicts, I went through the Stages of Change Model, including the stage of Contemplation, when I wondered if stopping drinking would change anything.

I would stop for a while, becoming manic and obsessive with something else, like lining up my shoes, colour coordinating my clothes, scrubbing mould off the shower wall with a toothbrush, drinking twenty cups of coffee, turning myself into an over-stimulated, raving lunatic, or trying to kill myself at the gym, all the time wishing it was drinking time. It seemed like everything I did was an addiction. Getting drunk was becoming increasingly difficult and not being drunk seemed impossible.

I was always trying to feel better about myself and so would set rules. *OK, I won't drink at home. I won't drink till 5 p.m. I won't drink on Mondays or Tuesdays. I won't drink on my own. I'll just drink beer. I won't drink on days that end with a 'y'!*

Anyway, maybe I'm OK. I don't drink neat vodka out of the bottle like my friend Martha does. I don't drink in the mornings, well, rarely.

And then there were the rewards I gave myself. If I put the washing out: *Oh well done, you deserve a drink for that.* If I went for a walk: *Oh goodie, you can have an extra bottle tonight.*

I struggled through the day feeling lost, discombobulated and fuzzy. This lasted until I picked up the wine and a ciggie. I was sleepwalking through life while dreaming of drink.

Booze was sending me insane and destroying my health. It had become a wrecking ball, smashing anything and everything in its path. More drastically, it was ruining my looks. Wine had caused me to blow up like a puffer fish. I had red blood vessels hanging out of my face and love handles with their own postcode.

I was questioning everything, especially my sanity. I was batshit crazy. There was only one way to remove these feelings – avoid sobriety at all costs. I justified my constant drinking as essential in my battle against confronting my true self. I became skilled at compartmentalizing my life – the intoxicated version of me, sad, isolated and full of self-hatred, and the sober version – brave, capable and accomplished. I was what is known as a 'high-functioning alcoholic', sparkly and together on the outside, disorderly and desperately secretive on the inside. I wondered if this was obvious to others.

~

Unhealthy people attract unhealthy people. My social bar was lowered as low as it could go and then some. I would find myself in strange public bars, playing pool and darts with random blokes who had their names on their bar stools and personalised beer jugs. I spent hours talking shit to them, my face getting closer and closer to the bar. They became my best mates. If I drank enough our differences dissipated. In those dark, urine smelling, sticky-carpeted dives, we were one. There was no pretence. In one of those joints, I met a guy who I had an affair with for over a year. It took an age for me to realise he was a heroin addict, which explained his constant nodding off.

Behind my facade was a hypersensitive frightened girl who took everything to heart – a girl desperate for an escape from reality. Drinking dulled the edges, sparing me from looking too closely at the reflection in the mirror. And on the rare occasions I did look, what I saw only gave me more reason to drink.

Addiction is so complicated. It's not simply a thing you absorb or engage in behaviourally and then you finish with it and it all goes away. Addiction is spiritual bankruptcy. It's a human problem, a psychic, visceral and many-layered problem. Nothing in the wine glass cures the human condition. Meetings, meditation and yoga won't make us feel worthwhile. The demon drink will remind you, whispering in your ear, '*See you're still not good enough. You are impossible to love.*'

'I am lovable. I am fucking lovable,' I would scream. 'Just give me a chance. I'll show you.'

The high-functioning alcoholic leads a delusional life. We seem relaxed, exuding confidence, but inside we see the truth of our diabolical inadequacies. We pretend that we're not inebriated, that we're absolutely fine. And, in the midst of that pretence, we yearn for a time when we can drink without remorse and love without abandonment, when it will all work out without us having to change the basic nature and essence of who we are.

I managed to surround myself with co-conspirators. You can pick a drinker. We share a certain language. Conversations like, 'Let's have another drink. Come on, just one more.' It seemed so basic. We sustain both the effort and the denial – holding onto hope while protecting the lie. Our lives quietly shape themselves around addiction, built on the silent assurance that the drink will always be there. Alcohol becomes the background hum of existence – everywhere, yet invisible. We know it's there, even as we pretend not to.

You hang with people who are happy to down a dozen litres of wine then hit a pub, people like my friend Mandy. It was a cycle of ladies' lunches that never ended, wine and confession, wine and sisterhood, cascades of wine, oceans of wine. Wine was our lifeline. Our children's birthday parties were a wonderful excuse for a drink. With it, on trend mums like us have Prosecco play dates, never letting the kids get in the way of happy hour.

Drinkers know each other. We have a certain aura about us, an unmistakable vibe. We relate to the ones who ask, 'Where's the fucking waitress?' as they drain their glass; we practise 'liquid lyrics', and we encourage each other to keep drinking. There's a secret relief we feel when the non-drinkers pick up their coats and go home. At those times, you would hear Mandy saying, 'Well, thank Christ we got rid of that riff-raff!'

I remember once an unaware young waitress whisked away Mandy's glass, which contained a minuscule amount of gin and tonic. Mandy screamed at the poor girl, 'I'll have you know I've killed for less than that.'

We see ourselves as competent drinkers, overlooking the unsteady sips taken with trembling hands, the paralysis of our thoughts, and the decline of our ability to cope.

And yet, the underlying feeling through all the drinking and all the co-conspirators in attendance was isolation and loneliness.

What Is This Thing Called Sex?
Sexy is an energy, not a body type

Twenty-one and single, I decided to explore the sex thing. I found that sleeping with random men while drunk had undertones of hostility, aggression and 'fuck you'. The sex was anonymous and irrelevant. Any sense of intimacy or passion was negated by the intoxication, as were my feelings of self-loathing. Inevitably, I was left with shame, remorse and guilt, the alcohol fucking with my sense of authenticity as boundaries collapsed. At these times, I felt powerful, although falsely so. It was power motivated by booze; it wasn't real. Alcohol gives you power as fast as it takes it from you.

I was realizing that women have been objectified for so long that we begin to objectify ourselves. We're so preoccupied with our appearance that we often lose sight of what truly matters. Women understand the desire to be wanted, yet we struggle with knowing what we truly want for ourselves. It seems men and women really are from different planets. Men try to love us with their penises, but women need so much more. Women try to love men with their minds, but men don't understand us.

Generally, women have three lives, a public one, a private one and a secret one. Over the years, I have found that alcohol addiction and sex and love addiction go hand in hand. We think we need that 'person' in order to feel whole, to complete us. Does this mean we are born incomplete, broken? We keep so many secrets, we pretend we want things we don't want, because what we do want is so out of our reach. So we stay in our cage, in our invisible restraints, following the rules, until eventually we succumb to the cage and the boundaries within.

And, as far as the opposite sex is concerned, there's no preliminary research phase. If a boy wanted you, you said yes, feeling extremely grateful to be chosen.

I soon became aware that to be good in bed, I needed a tenderness, a vulnerability, self-confidence, and faith in a higher power, none of which I could lay claim to. I lacked a desire to please my partner. I couldn't make love with the light on, as I was ashamed of my body. My belly was too big (it wasn't); my thighs were too large (they were). They were like stumpy legs of lamb

I sensed that the guys I slept with were looking for more. Maybe they wanted someone more conventional, less predictable – someone who wasn't self-absorbed and didn't think the world revolved around her? Perhaps they wished for someone genuine, who didn't fake orgasms, who wasn't overly focused on body image and who didn't bother with shaving her legs. Perhaps they sought someone more intriguing, more interesting, someone willing to watch cricket with them, someone who actually gave a shit if they were satisfied in the cot. Someone who wasn't an addict? Someone who wasn't me?

None of this mattered when I drank. I couldn't feel emotions, only their imitations. I felt excruciating shame. I didn't know how to love. To be honest, I found sex invasive. Intimacy felt dangerous to me. Mine was an unhealthy attitude towards something that was apparently supposed to be a beautiful thing. I likened myself to Elizabeth Taylor who was reportedly extreme in her 'desire to feel love, not to give love'. My only true love was the bottle. Addiction is like infidelity; it always needs more. Alcohol is a neurological sledgehammer. It's like the beast that continually throws its weight against the cellar door. *Addiction is stronger than a mother's love.*

The bottom line is I couldn't sustain relationships as I refused to show people who I really was in case they didn't like me. As such, my romances were superficial and fake. I began to understand that intimacy requires being comfortable with fear. And that was something I was not.

~

I feel my confusion towards all things sexual was exacerbated by past experiences involving my mother. She once called a family meeting, having found my knickers at the end of my boyfriend's bed, the one he was supposed to sleep in when he had sleepovers. Floundering, I lied, 'Well, he got drunk and passed out in my bed, so I slept in his bed.'

Mum replied with, 'But why did you take your knickers off?' Good point.

Dad interjected, 'Oh jeez, Bugsy. Give her a break. We were doing it at that age, only difference was you had a ring on your finger.'

Another family meeting was called when she found the pill. I was only fifteen but we were all on it. Again, fumbling, I offered 'Because the doctor said it would help with my period pain.'

Dad chipped in again, 'Well, I'm proud of you girl. No teenage pregnancies for this family.'

I had no idea how to kiss my new boyfriend so, when Mardy moved into our house, I asked him to show me. He did, successfully and, I might add, innocently, there was absolutely no tongue involved. As with everything else that occurred, I journalled the incident. Mum, clearly needing more ammunition against me, read my journal.

She called another family meeting. 'Have you any idea what you two have done? You have committed a crime. This is incest and it has to stop.'

Dad, smirking, left the room.

Maybe Mum was right. Maybe sex was a dirty thing, something to be ashamed of.

UK, Here We Come Aye

People don't take trips – trips take people.

John Steinbeck

It was 1976. I was twenty-two years old and struggling with life itself. Confused, I was analysing and questioning everything and everyone. I had a million emotions looping. I was feeling unseen and unheard and irrelevant, when Mary decided we were going overseas. And what Mary wanted, Mary got.

I had as much chance of saving money as stopping drinking so Mary, a clever girl, went behind my back and spoke to my boss at the time, organising a weekly deduction from my wage. We left Australia with no return date and $3,000. I felt like a millionaire.

We travelled for six weeks on the SS *Australis*, a Greek-owned ship, from Melbourne to Southampton. We were in the cheaper quarters, the bowels of the liner, in a six-berth cabin, with the other four girls being 'bible bashers'. As there was no natural light, we didn't know if it was night or day. Mary and I would fall into the cabin at what for us was five in the morning, while the others were heading out for their five p.m. dinner. I never knew whether to apply day cream or night cream. The others put up with our shenanigans until they could stand it no longer, whereby they hung curtains between them and us.

Mary and I dressed to the nines in slinky cocktail frocks, showing as much cleavage as possible. This was our 'Lerve Boat' and we intended to find as much lerve as was on offer. We smuggled a bag of marijuana on board in the base of our suitcase. Following a night at the casino, cocktail bar and disco, we would take a joint to the dungeon, where the laundry and baker boys were working through the night. They were thrilled to see us, '*Yassas kalos* (Hello beautiful).' and were most appreciative of our nightly visits. Chuckling, we would hightail it out of there, barefoot and with make-up running down our sweaty faces, in time to witness the sun rising over the Atlantic Ocean.

We became concerned as we were running out of marijuana. Our next stop was Panama City. 'We're bound to find some there' we enthused. In Panama, we strolled around looking for stoners, when an intuitive local approached us, asking if he could help. We explained what we were after and he said, '*ningun problema, dame el dinero y esperame aqui*', (give me the money and wait here for me). Cool. Job done. He disappeared inside a shop. We waited and waited and waited until we could wait no more as the ship was setting sail. No boy. No dope. Just us dopes.

On the ship, we met two guys, one of whom Mary later married. My ship romance was with a boy by the name of Gerard De Beurs, a young chisel-jawed, six-foot-tall Dutchman with long shiny hair and a gap between his front teeth, which I found so sexy. In a Dutch accent he would say, 'My little *malle meid*, what do we doing *vandaag* (today)?' I had to look up the meaning of malle meid, which means 'crazy girl'. How apt. We couldn't keep our hands off each other, exhibiting massive public displays of affection, which was most unlike me.

After the night's entertainment, Gerard and I would hit the deck for a reefer while listening to the ocean slapping against the ship. Gazing up at trillions of twinkling stars in the black night sky and with the salty air stinging our faces, this was beyond romantic. After a while, however, I realised Gerard was an immature, sulky, misogynistic chauvinist and he started annoying the fuck out of me. So, I dumped him.

I then met a mature English gentleman named. Michael, who owned a European bus line and, from what I could gather, was a millionaire. He looked like Hugh Grant and spoke like King Charles, and he wore Yves Saint Laurent suits and Julius Marlow shoes. Michael had never met anyone like Mary and I – wild, free-spirited, Aussie sheilas. I assumed his sex life was lacking somewhat as when I pleasured him, it blew his mind. Clearly, I was his first. I guess the rich and famous don't do that sort of thing, too messy p'raps!

If Michael wasn't in love with me before, he certainly was after that. He followed me around like the proverbial puppy dog. 'I say, Suzie, do you fancy having breakfast with me? Maybe you would like to promenade on the deck?' I was excited to see where this would go.

Little did I know but the Dutchman had generously shared his scabies with me, and I had passed them on to the English gentleman. Having shared our itinerary with Mike, sometime later, I received a phone call at the Malaga caravan park. He'd tracked me down. 'Hello, it's Michael here. I say, darling, I'm not sure how to put this but it would appear I have a nasty case of the scabies which I unfortunately passed on to my wife.'

'YOUR WIFE?' I screeched.

Michael continued, 'Yes but pay that no mind, and secondly, I was wondering when I might anticipate your return to London as I am looking forward to wining and dining you.'

It appeared the fellatio incident had revolutionised Michael's life, and he clearly wanted more.

Europe

To travel is to live. Life is either a daring adventure or nothing at all.

Helen Keller

In London, Mary and I and two mates from home bought an old run down six-sleeper Commer van before we headed to Europe. Our first stop – Spain.

In Madrid, we were parked illegally outside the post office, and saying farewell to some guys we had met on the ship. It was hot and we were dressed in shorts and halter-neck tops. Having downed a few sangrias, we were a tad rowdy. I don't remember how it happened but the next thing I knew there were police yelling at us in Spanish, then throwing us into the back of a divvy van, where a thin, wire fence was all that separated us from some big, angry canines. I do remember something about pressing my bare bosom up against the van window at shocked policewomen. *Surely that wouldn't be cause for arrest. Would it?* Off to jail we go, with the last words from my mother's lips ringing in my ears. 'Make sure you behave yourself in Spain. If they lock you up there, they throw away the key.'

Perhaps she's psychic.

We were tossed into a cell. *Here we go again*, I mused. The policeman was laughing at us, playing charades, pulling his clothes over his head and repeating, *'estriptista estripista'* (stripper stripper). We were baffled. Well, I wasn't as baffled as the others as I knew what I'd done but there was no way in hell I was divulging that to my mates.

By now we were shitting bricks. The cell was dark and cold with a cement floor. Our Spanish was very limited, and our jailers spoke no English. It was a comedy of errors. They gave us some paper and a pen so, to pass the time, we ripped the paper into squares and attempted to play a game of cards. We were told nothing, escorted to and from the toilets by a guard armed with a machine gun and left to wallow in our rapidly descending hangovers, only being offered a musty blanket and the words, '*dormir, dormir* (sleep, sleep).'

'Excuse me?' I replied. *Seriously?* Still, I had slept in worse places.

In the morning, we rang the Australian Embassy and were put through to our Ambassador. After explaining our dilemma, Terry came to the jail and bailed us out, however, our passports had been confiscated.

Terry took us to a lawyer's office on whose desk were four local newspapers, the headlines shouting 'Madrid stopped dead at ten p.m. last night as four Australian girls bathed semi-nude in the Cibeles Fountain.' *Oh, what the actual fuck. We didn't do that.*

Turns out we were arrested for indecent exposure due to our scantily clad bodies, at least that was the general consensus of opinion, thankfully, but, apparently, they needed a more newsworthy headline. We were dealing with Spaniards. Just saying. Truth be known, we were nowhere near the Cibeles Fountain.

So, our hero, Terry, managed to retrieve our passports. We paid minimal court costs and were set to leave the country, heading first to Morocco. In fact, we were encouraged to leave the country and as soon as possible. To be honest, we were thrown out of the country.

We had farewell drinks with Terry who we had become quite close to and who had saved us from a fate worse than death – life in a Spanish prison. He begged us to behave ourselves for the rest of our trip, pleading on bended knees 'Please don't take drugs in Morocco.'

Meanwhile back in Australia, it's 2 June 1976 – Mum's birthday. Mum and Dad woke to the 7 a.m. news: *Four Australian girls have been arrested in Madrid for bathing semi-nude in the Cibeles Fountain.*

Dad said, 'That'll be Sue.'

Mum replied, incredulous, 'Don't be ridiculous.'

At dinner that night, Mum cried into her shandy, while Dad repeatedly sang, 'Eight boobs in a fountain' to the tune of *Three Coins in a Fountain.*

The story made headlines all around the world. Mary's fiancé rang from London, *is it true? Did you really do that?'*

In Australia, the Herald Sun's front page displayed a photo of me in a bikini on St Kilda beach, taken the year before. The headline read: *'This is Sue Browne, once a happy girl on St Kilda beach, now locked up in a Spanish jail, not knowing if or when she will be released.'* My sister was interviewed by The Herald Sun. She said – and I quote – 'Well, all I have to say is that Sue does love a good time.'

My greatest concern was that they had dragged out that photo of me in the bikini where my thighs looked like humungous stumpty legs of lamb. I cried the first time, now here it was again on the front page, I was devastated.

Our group was now famous for all the wrong reasons, and we were labelled sluts. Young male Spaniards would get excited when they saw us, yelling, '*Quatro prostituta* (Four prostitutes),' chasing the van and grasping for a piece of us, desperate for contact. It was 1976 after all, and we had been warned by an Australian resident living in Madrid, who said, 'With all due respect, girls, dressed in those shorts and boob tubes, in this country you are classed as prostitutes.' Now she tells us!

~

Our van was easily recognisable, and we needed to disguise it and ourselves. On the way to the ferry, we stopped at a campsite where we painted the van, dyed our hair, changed our names and determined to lay low. As we were off to Morocco, I settled on the name 'Fatima'. We decided to ferry to Tangier at the very top of Morocco and relax in the Tétouan camping area before travelling to Rabat, Casablanca and Marrakesh. For as long as I can remember, I had wanted to go to Casablanca to visit Rick's Café. I had watched the movie a million times, and I adored Humphrey and Ingrid. *Play it again, Sam.*

On our first day in Tétouan, we met an English guy called Jesus, a son-of-Christ doppelganger with long flowing hair and robes. He was an Adonis. In a delicious cockney accent, he asked, 'So, girls, any chance you want to smoke some black hash?'

And because he seemed like our saviour returned to Earth, the second coming, all Terry's words and our subsequent promises disintegrated in the stifling Moroccan heat and as good little disciples in a trance like state, we followed Jesus.

We spent the next three weeks lying on our backs in a hash haze, gazing at the deep azure sky and listening to the greater hoopoe-larks singing. We were enthralled by the masses of jujube and poplar trees, swaying in the light breeze. We hung off our saviour's every word, and we giggled a lot. We wore jalabas, which we bought from a travelling salesman and ate donuts kindly supplied to us by a beautiful boy named Mohammad.

You may be thinking that we wasted three weeks of our lives, and I might concur but for a note Jesus handed me which read, 'The Bible says that there is One God and Father of all, who is above all, and through all, and in you all.' I'm pretty sure the 'in you all' was referring to one of ours who had shagged our beloved Saviour, no doubt becoming 'one with God'.

We sent postcards depicting Marrakesh and Rabat back home, pretending we had been there. Before we went back to Spain, we had a lump of hash we needed to dispose of. Mary said, 'OK, *putas*, should we have a vote on what to do with this? If they find it, we go back to jail.'

Jen suggested we throw it out, Liz thought we should hide it, and I said, 'Why don't we smoke it?"

Jen took a video of this hysteria, which was given to me on my sixtieth birthday. It resembled a fast-paced movie – crazies on a mission, packing pipes, rolling joints and frantic passing back and forth in a frenzy. It was absolute chaos and mayhem, but mission accomplished.

At the border, a bunch of gun-packing Spanish cops burst into the van, shouting, '*Quatro prostituta.*'

We were so stoned we couldn't talk. They searched every part of the van. In one of the drawers was a bag of henna we used as hair dye. 'Marijuana! Marijuana!' they yelled, overjoyed.

When they realised what it was, they too began chuckling. We threw the bags of henna up in the air, covering everyone with the dark sticky substance, while we jumped up and down like wild animals.

After Morocco, we ventured to a camping area in Torremolinos where we set eyes on three beautiful young Spanish men. They spent their days lying on their backs, grinning at the sky. After observing them for a while we asked, *'Por que te ries?'*, 'Why do you laugh?'

They explained that they were tripping on acid that came from the beak of a Spanish bird. Seriously? We bought three trips for five dollars each. Jenny opted out.

And so began twenty-four hours in an altered state of consciousness. We were carried beyond the astral, beyond form, stripping away the layers of the mind and delving deeper and deeper into a nova of consciousness and pure energy. We were souls and only souls, and we were one. We lay face down on the grass touching hands with the Spanish boys and each other, in a euphoric state. We discovered later that we all experienced the same trip. Our past, present and futures whizzed through a psychedelic portal created by our minds. It was insane.

After many hours of this, Jenny, the straight one, begged us to eat. In the van, which looked a mile long, were plates of sausages, peas and carrots. I couldn't believe my eyes. 'The carrots and peas are talking to me! They have faces,' I screamed.

Mary looked at her plate, confused 'Oh my God! Mine do too.'

We couldn't enter the public toilets as they were awash with waist high water. We ran to Jenny, 'Help, the toilets are flooded …' She couldn't convince us that there was no water.

I fell in love with one of these young men whose name was Esteban. He was a Spanish version of Mick Jagger. I felt at last I had found the love of my life. I envisaged a future with him, little bambinos running around our hacienda. Esteban and his mates suggested they travel with us to Malaga, advising they had 'business to do' and we all agreed.

At their request, we stopped at banks where they would run, barefoot, returning with wads of notes, babbling excitedly in Spanish. We became suspicious. *Were they drug dealers? Gangsters?*

Us girls left the camp one day and went to town for supplies. When we got back, the boys were gone, as was our money, traveller's cheques and everything else of value. I'm not sure why, but they also took our goggles and snorkels. My future blew up in my face. I became obsessed. I had to find him so, managing to locate his mother in the directory, I rang her. She was yelling and crying down the phone at me, 'Esteban … *ejercito, ejercito* (army, army). Esteban … *narcotraficante* (drug trafficker).'

My suspicions were confirmed; Esteban is a drug-dealing gangster who is now in the army. Maybe I need to let this go?

As devastated as I was, I quickly bounced back. We were off to Italy where the spunkiest boys in the world reside and Chianti is on tap. *Esteban who?* Chins up, *muchachas*. But first, we were meeting our mates at Oktoberfest in Munich for two weeks of drinking beer and having fun. Bring it on.

~

I was excited to be catching up with my tribe of Aussie mates. We set up at Camping Munich, our vans and tents in a circle. Our days consisted of drinking beer in the camp before heading to the camp store for lunch and more crates of beer, none of which were paid for. We ate them out of food and drank them out of beer. They closed their store.

In another van in the camp were three big burly blokes from Melbourne. They had professional jobs back home but you would never know it as, on holiday, they morphed into crazy, drunken lunatics. We nicknamed them 'The Zoo'. They showed me how to shotgun a can of beer, after which they would crush the empty cans in their hulk-like hands. At one point, next to our van, three good-looking Irish girls were attempting to erect their tent, but with no luck. The Zoo asked if they could assist, which they did, and the girls graciously watched as their tent magically appeared up and ready to go. Next thing, one of The Zoo came flying out of a tree, landed on top of the tent and demolished it.

Our newest recruit from Oz got bored in the camp as she didn't drink beer. We said, 'OK, today we'll take you on an excursion. Get your trackies off and put some lippy on. We're going to the zoo'. She was excited. She'd heard the Munich Zoo was a beauty. I can still see the look of disappointment on her face when we walked her three metres away to the lunatic camp.

Our campsite looked like something out of a Tarantino movie. We were more like animals than humans. No wonder Aussies get such bad reputations overseas. We were irresponsible, feral bogans.

At six p.m., we headed into the Hofbräuhaus for bratwurst, mit mayonnaise mit pommes frites, and more beers, after which we went on the scariest fun park ride – the Magic Mountain. If you didn't throw up, you had your beers bought for you the remainder of the evening.

One of these times, we were waiting for the train to take us to the festival. Busting for a wee, I spotted a rubbish bin attached to a pillar. 'Hey, guys,' I said. 'Can you hoist me up and block my view?'

My friends complied. Next thing, they were gone, having jumped on a train, leaving me on top of this very high bin. Turns out there were holes in the bottom of the bin and my wee was running down the spotless platform. Frozen in time, I watched as impeccably dressed ladies lifted their stilettos to avoid the steaming stream of urine.

We drank in the Aussie tent at the Hofbräuhaus and mingled with the Germans, fascinated at how much they drank. Copying them, we would smash our steins on the table, yelling *'Prost prost'*. The queues to the toilets were mammoth so we wore ponchos and squatted over the empty steins then stashed them under our table. This worked well until one of our team passed out under said table and woke up thirsty.

~

Due to copious amounts of beer and bratwurst, we left Munich shattered and fat. We also left with scabies. Considering the van swapping, none of us avoided those dirty little mites. I couldn't tell anyone that it was I, compliments of Gerard de Beurs. I wondered if they were Dutch-speaking scabies.

Sarah and I headed to the closest pharmacy and whispered to the chemist, 'A bottle of Scabiol please?' He ran from us, yelling loudly 'Scabia! Scabia!' This was followed by a mass exodus of screaming Germans.

We arranged to meet the Aussie tribe in Rome; Oktoberfest does Camping Roma. By this stage, we were experts at doing nothing. We lay on the grass in the stifling heat, listening to the Rolling Stones Black and Blue album, on an 8-track cassette tape, while smoking joints and drinking the local grappa. *Oh, Cherry, oh Cherry, oh baby ...* and *Memory Motel ...*

We ventured into central Rome one day to ring home. Loaded with grappa, I thought it would be funny to wrap my legs over the railings at the top of the bus and hang upside down, imitating a monkey, scratching my underarms, screeching 'oooooh ooooh aaaah aaaah'. Sadly, my legs gave way. I don't remember much after that. What I do remember is my good mate Gavin looking down at me as I lay motionless on the floor of the bus, tears welling in his eyes, stifling his mirth. 'Oh God, Brownie. I know you are in pain but I have to tell you that was the funniest thing I have ever seen.' I considered myself lucky that time, because if my head hadn't swung forwards when I fell, I would have broken my neck.

I thought the pain would kill me. At the hospital I was fitted with a neck brace as I had cracked two vertebrae. On explaining to the doctors how this occurred, incredulous, they ran around the hospital making monkey noises, yelling '*Scimmia, scimmia, scimmia. Gruppo di cazzi pazzi* (Monkey, monkey, monkey. Crazy bunch of dicks).'

When I returned to camp, I did as I was told. I lay prostrate in the back of the van with my mates feeding me grappa and unpeeled grapes. When in Rome ...

On the same subject, from Rome we ventured to Florence, where we visited the statue of David in the *Piazza della Signoria*. He brought tears to my eyes; he was glorious, magnificent. He was also on a four-metre-high concrete pedestal. Having had a skin full of grappa, I decided I had to get close to David. I said to my mates, 'How much will you give me if I touch David's testicles?'

'If you lick them, we'll give you fifty bucks.'

Game on!

Climbing on top of each other's shoulders, my friends formed a ladder. Once up there, I successfully wrapped my mouth around David's marble balls. Cameras clicked all around me, and when I looked down, I noticed my friends had scampered. Abandoned again! I clung to David's legs for an hour, my head throbbing with the onset of my grappa come down, before being rescued by firemen and fined by the police, who asked, 'What were you thinking?'

~

After Florence, my friends and I hit Venice. We found a taverna on the Grand Canal. Here we met Chi Chi, an Italian Aussie. After unsuccessfully helping us look for somewhere to park our van, Chi Chi suggested we stay at his place. He lived in a palace on the Grand Canal. Once there, he produced expensive wines and home-cooked seafood pasta, followed by tiramisu, joints and cocaine. We sat by an open window overlooking the canal, where the full moon reflected on the water. The musky aroma from scented candles filled the air, and romantic Italian music played. After each course, at Chi Chi's persistence, we threw our plates into the canal with gay abandon. When in Venice!

In the early hours of the morning, I woke with a start to a crazed, naked Chi Chi on top of me, a gun pointed at my head. I was still drunk and stoned, and at first, I thought it was a joke. *A gun?* 'Now you not so smart arse, are you? You think you better than me. Well, cop this.'

Wow. What had I missed?

I tried to scream for my friends but Chi Chi put his hand over my mouth, silencing me as he roughly entered me. By morning, he was gone. *Had I dreamed it?* There was a note asking us to leave the key with the desk clerk.

I was traumatised, I felt dirty, used and abused. I was confused and angry. I berated myself. *This is what happens when you get drunk and stoned. You no doubt came onto him, made him think he had a chance. You probably deserved it. You have to stop getting so wasted. This is out of control.*

Significant, I sense, but not for one minute did I blame Chi Chi. Also significant were the reactions of my friends. They didn't have to express it but, from their sideways looks, they were clearly under the impression that I had no doubt brought this on myself. I remember thinking that I was running out of people who I could trust. The silver lining from this incident, however, was that mein host would now have scabies. Touché, I say.

When I returned to London and developed my films, there were a bunch of photos of his dick and balls. What a charmer.

~

At this point, I left my van and jumped aboard Sarah and Pam's combi-van. Sarah and I were after the same thing – fun and men. In Florence, we met the coolest Italian musicians. Sarah began a relationship with a very handsome young man by the name of Nello. We spent our nights sitting around the kitchen table in their meagre apartment, dipping stale bread in olive oil and salt, the Chianti flowing for us while they drank espressos.

They had never seen anyone drink like we did. They were a one glass of red wine with pasta at dinner type. We sang Italian love songs including *Il Mondo, Ancora Tu* and *Lo Rivivrei* while they played beautiful music on their guitars.

As usual, I was given the boyfriend's best friend to play with. In this instance, his name was Claude and he spoke little English. In the morning, he would say, 'Now we have shower,' and pointing at me, he'd say, 'First me,' then pointing to himself, 'then you'.

We clubbed it out, dancing the night away to ABBA, overflowing with joy and spritzes. I was intoxicated with this country – the architecture, the fashion, the history, the music, the Chianti, the men. *La vita e bella* (Life is beautiful).

During our stay in Florence, my sister came to visit from Oz. When I introduced her to Nello, she went quiet then left the room. I followed her out, asking 'Are you OK?'

'I can't go back in there,' she moaned. 'It hurts to look at him.'

We roamed the cobblestone streets, wandering around piazzas, shops and cafés. We visited the Uffizi Gallery, the Cathedral of Santa Maria del Fiore and Ponte Vecchio, guzzled the regional wines and ate pasta and tapas. Everyone so welcoming and charming. Sarah and I got fat from the wine and pasta. One morning, while gazing into the mirror, she said, 'you know what, Brownie? I don't think I'm getting fat; I think my head is shrinking.' This was one of many hilarious statements from her during our time away. Our friend kept a book of 'Sarah Statements'. She was such a hoot.

It rained a lot in Florence. In the morning, Nello would gaze out the window announcing, *'Merda, piove siempre forte in questa katso de citta* (Shit, it always rains hard in this shitty town).'

I had to leave Sarah there as I was meeting a new recruit from Oz, Millie. I hated saying goodbye but I was determined to come back one day, maybe to live.

~

From Italy, some of our group went to Egypt while Millie and I chose the Greek islands. My first night in Greece, I drank so much ouzo that I poisoned myself. I was dry reaching green bile for forty-eight hours. I thought I was going to die. To this day, I retch if I smell that toxin.

We found the most exquisite place in the Greek islands – Lindos, a village on the island of Rhodes. It was tiny, serene and idyllic. Here, we befriended a local boy, nicknamed Lefty, who became our tour guide, drinking companion and gigolo should we so desire. Some of the incredible sites we visited included the Temple of Athena Lindia and the Church of Panagia, which was built in 1300. We were blown away by the 15th century frescoes and the ancient history of these countries as opposed to our own. We baked ourselves on the white sandy beaches, dining on fried octopus and sardines and drinking retsina at the beachside tavernas and bars, wafts of garlic and hyacinth in the air. There were no cars on the island, the local transport being donkeys. We 'befriended' said animals and they were most accommodating, as, when it was time to go, we would throw ourselves on top of them, removing their straw hats for our own heads and riding sideways home.

Having met up with some of the tribe in Mykonos, as a group we dined at a taverna under the bright red setting sun. Blissfully plastered, a decision was made to hit and run. Everyone scampered but my high heels were hindering my escape on the already hard to negotiate cobblestones, when suddenly a furious Greek waiter had me in a headlock, holding a knife to my throat and screaming '*Kleftis! Kleftis!* (Thief! Thief!)'

My first thought was *not another jail cell in a foreign country*. My friends were nowhere to be seen. *Abandoned again.*

When the angry manager arrived, I pleaded with him in broken Greek. He relented, removed the knife from my neck, scolded the waiter and told me I could go if I promised to bring the cash back tomorrow. And that I did.

What were we thinking??

London, Again

> When a man is tired of London, he's tired of life.
>
> **Samuel Johnson**

After Greece, we went back to London, broke and looking for work.

We found a two-bedroom apartment in Earl's Court, sixty-seven steps up and housing seven of us, the lounge room floor doubling as a dormitory. We took it in turns to take a bath, topping up the grey slush with hot water from the kettle.

We worked at our local, The Abingdon Hotel, near High Street in Kensington. Out of necessity our shoplifting continued, and our flat was stocked with food from the pub fridge. We donned our oversized multi-pocketed overalls, which were perfect for the job. There were twenty-five of us in our little flat for Christmas day, including my mum, sister and Aunty Gladys who had flown in from Oz. We had a feast fit for royalty and costing only eight quid due to that particular item being impossible to steal. Let me tell you though, the person who spent the eight quid was severely reprimanded. Millie put the turkey under her dress, pretending to be pregnant.

We couldn't afford gifts so one of our mates wrapped up a random Volkswagen bug, which was parked in the street, in reams of crepe paper and ribbons, 'gifting' it to us on Christmas morning. The owner of said Volksie was fuming and spent Christmas morning ripping crepe paper from her car, cursing, 'Bloody Aussies!'

We were longing for a white Christmas but it was unusually warm in London this year. However, suddenly there was snow falling! *How can this be?* It turned out our boys had spent hours ripping up tiny pieces of white paper, which they let fly from our rooftop. We were elated.

We met a bunch of gorgeous Pakistani boys at our local. One of them, Martin, became my boyfriend. He wore fitted lycra body shirts, suede vests and bell-bottoms over platform boots, which had a three-inch platform on one boot and a five-inch platform on the other due to one of his legs being shorter than the other. He had luxurious black shiny hair, which was carefully styled and sprayed into a bob with bangs, a perfectly manicured moustache, big brown eyes, caramel skin and immaculate white teeth. He reliably had a fag in one hand and a Southern Comfort and Coke in the other and he reeked of cheap after-shave. He was delicious!

We commandeered The Abingdon Hotel, and organised dart and pool competitions, pinball tournaments and karaoke nights. The jukebox would be blasting songs including Sherbet's *Howzat*, Chicago's *If You Leave Me Now* and Dr Hook's *A Little Bit More*. So much hilarity, raucous out-of-tune singing and smashing of beer steins. I never wanted it to end.

Friday nights were spent at the Lions Head Hotel, watching an Australian group called The Bushwackers, a bunch of crazy musicians who wore long beards, flanelette shirts, trackie dacks and thongs. They sang Aussie bush songs and played homemade instruments including a lagerphone. We would drink for Australia and dance ourselves into a sweat then pile onto the Earl's Court tube, somehow pulling each other up the sixty-seven steps to our apartment. I have a photo of one of our mates pushing my sister home in a wheely bin.

These were some of the best days of my life. There was no anxiety, no shame and no guilt, as my drinking seemed to be on a par with my peers. On the surface, everything was fine as long as I ignored the ever-present nagging feeling that everything was not fine.

My roomies and I discovered we could make international calls from the local phone box. I would make collect calls to Mum and Dad, giving them the number of the booth. Dad was thrilled, putting on an English accent 'this is grand, lassie. Here I am standing in a phone box at Sandringham Station at seven a.m. in bright sunshine, talking to you at night in freezing cold London.'

He was so proud of me.

After a while, we had to stop this sham when a voice came on the phone, 'we are the police and we know what you're up to.' We scampered, leaving the phone cord dangling, like in the movies.

Not to be deterred, we then found a way to ring home by breaking into newly vacated apartments in which the phones hadn't yet been disconnected. We thought we were so clever. I would slap us all now.

While in London, we orchestrated an Aussies vs. Pommies Guinness drinking championship at the World Trade Centre. I was the adjudicator. At the last minute, one of ours fell ill and pulled out. 'I'll fill in,' I announced.

The Poms looked doubtful, 'With all due respect, love, this is way out of your league.'

My team, however, knowing me as they did, had full confidence. Eleven hours later, the Pommies were passing out and throwing up. Our team members were disappearing – one went to sleep in the dunny. The final tally was Pommies – most drunk by an individual: thirteen pints. Aussies – most drunk by an individual: fourteen pints. Most drunk by a sheila: thirteen pints. I was one of the last men standing. I sure showed them. My mouth, tongue and teeth were dark magenta, and my poo was black for a long time, but so what! I was victorious. My team were so proud of me. Mind you, my drinking at this stage didn't need to be encouraged or celebrated! Just sayin'.

Not long after my return to London, Michael contacted me, dying to catch up so I invited him to our mad house for lunch. He arrived in his designer suit, laden with flowers and Ferrero Rocher chocolates. Here's the thing, we had been living like travelling gypsies for a long time, and whatever private school class or finesse we may have once laid claimed to pre-Europe was well and truly gone, gone, gone. We were like a bunch of newly released mental patients, psycho dancing to ABBA and Leo Sayer's *You Make Me Feel Like Dancing*, shot gunning cans of Foster's, passing the bong, playing spin the bottle, removing our clothes, screaming raucously.

'By Jove, this is jolly good fun, ay?' said Michael. 'I feel like I haven't lived until now.'

Mary being Mary was concerned for my financial future or lack thereof. 'Come on, Brownie. He's a millionaire, for God's sake, and he adores you. Hang on to him.'

If only I was that sort of girl. Again, I didn't feel worthy of someone like Michael, anyway, what would I do with him? He wasn't a damaged surfie who needed fixing. And he was married! Also, he did nothing for me sexually. He was awkward in bed, leaving the work to me. This was an untenable situation as I had made an art form of imitating a starfish and I'll be buggered if that was going to change.

Not long after Michael's visit, he rang me. 'Hello Suzie,' he said. 'I was wondering if you would be interested in accompanying me on my tour bus around Europe for three weeks?'

'Yes please.'

The bus was luxurious but, to my chagrin, smelled of Brussels sprouts and was full to the brim with loud Yanks in hibiscus shirts. Our accommodation was also swish.

On our first night in Liechtenstein, we dined at an Art Nouveau restaurant with domed ceilings, arched windows and sunken and raised dining rooms. A gypsy trio played in the corner of the room, which had painted pink walls covered in elaborate white mouldings and enormous chandeliers hanging from the ceiling. The food was outstanding. We dined on hot crusty rolls with herb butter, fish soup with a spicy paprika paste and tender grilled venison fillets with an apple and plum sauce. Dessert was a dense wedge of ricotta-like cheesecake laced with raisins and topped with a rich apricot sauce. Michael ordered a three-hundred-dollar bottle of the local Burgundy, which I drank 90% of. He wasn't much of a drinker. Praise the Lord.

If I chose not to do the tour bus with Michael, which was most days, I was given a daily allowance and free rein. So, what does a lonely girl with wads of cash do in central Europe? I took myself to lunch, met the locals and shopped till I dropped. I felt like a prostitute, and I loved it.

We travelled through Finland, Sweden, Norway and Denmark. Michael was easy so long as I was home for dinner and sex. However, towards the end, boredom was setting in, and I was drinking from morning until night with whoever I could find to join me. I found myself in some sticky situations, relishing the thought that I would never see these people again. Sadly, most nights, by the time Michael returned to the hotel, I would be passed out. No bump and grind for that little black duck. And still, he spoke of leaving his wife for me.

I had to let Michael go eventually. He was way too polished. I often wonder what my life would have been like had I stayed. I would be rich; I would have nice clothes and an expensive car; I would have an endless supply of cocaine and Dom Pérignon; I would live in a palace with a maid. Honestly, I'd rather eat my own head.

~

Back in London, while working for a temp agency, I had a secretarial job at a contract cleaning company, working for a sexy older dude who went by the name Robbie Robinson, real name, coincidentally, John Robinson. I noticed he wore a wedding ring; however, this didn't stop him flirting outrageously with me. We would go for drinks after work then he'd drive me home and we'd snog in the front seat of his car. He was a good-looking man with a ponytail, sideburns, a goatee and a deep velvety aristocratic voice.

One night, Robbie picked me up from home, blindfolded me and said, 'I am taking you on a mystery tour.'

When the blindfold was eventually taken off, I found myself on a clipper-style ship, surrounded by interesting bohemian people, all of whom gushed over my clearly famous date who they called 'The Admiral'.

I was introduced to Dave Lee Travis, who looked disappointed when I didn't recognise him, as he was clearly famous. He took my hand, leading me to a table abundant with lines of coke and flutes of Dom Pérignon, whilst filling me in on the importance of my date Robbie, who also went by the name of Robbie Dale. Turns out he was the chief DJ for the offshore pirate radio station

Radio Caroline, the first station of its kind and which was operated from this ship. He was called 'The Admiral' because he wore an Admiral's uniform and liked the boat to be shipshape. Robbie recorded a single, *Soul Mama*, which was released in 1969, and he wrote a single called *Soul Entertainer* for the funk-soul band Respect. He is a member of the Pirate Radio Hall of Fame.

This was a party like no other. We boogied all night to a fabulous tribute band who performed covers of The Troggs, Gerry and the Pacemakers and The Who. We were entertained by belly dancers, magicians and jugglers We slept in a single bunk bed in the bowels of the ship. That night, under the most spectacular show of fireworks, Robbie swore his undying love for me.

Our clandestine affair lasted for quite some time and would no doubt have continued had I not been summoned back to Australia by my dad.

I recently googled Robbie Dale. He died at age eighty-one in the Canary Islands, Spain.

I'm not entirely sure why I have included this recollection, but the whole idea of pirate radio, which, like our affair, was clandestine, fascinated me and I felt privileged to be a small part of it.

Return to Oz

You can never go home again.

Thomas Wolfe

Around this time, I was beckoned home by my dad for a pending court case involving suing the Herald Sun for defamation of character following the Madrid incident and the subsequent printed retractions. However, there was no court case. It was Dad's cunning way of getting me home. He was paid $8,000 in compensation, the equivalent of $50,000 in today's terms. He gave half of the money to me, the bulk of which, as mentioned earlier, I spent in the Torquay Pub beer garden on John Robinson, (the original one).

Back home I had no idea what to do with myself. I had been away for so long and felt lost and vulnerable. Where would I fit in back here? Where was my tribe? My addiction had grown to monumental proportions. I was obsessed with alcohol and the subsequent mind-numbing sensation that came with it. I didn't know how to survive without it. I felt as though I was *almost* living, *almost* breathing, *almost* surviving. *Almost, almost, almost.*

Fortunately, my dad knew the general manager of advertising agency SSC&B Lintas, and so began my fifteen years in this industry – and, along with it, fifteen years of hard-core drinking.

I was an account executive/secretary and worked at several different agencies. I lost all those jobs due to my extended lunches. After one such lunch, my boss at the time came for a chat. 'OK guys, the new manager is arriving soon to meet us all. Brownie, can you please try to behave?'

When the manager arrived, I was hanging by one arm from the second story landing making monkey noises. He didn't see the funny side, sacking me on the spot. My boss, exasperated and sad I was going, simply asked, 'What were you thinking?'

Again, because my dad was good mates with the managing director of Monahan Dayman Adams, I landed another agency job, this time working for the one and only Phillip Adams who I admired and adored. He was compelling, charismatic and oh so cryptic.

It was a tough gig, but I was determined to please. Under my desk I had a thesaurus, atlas, a Who's Who and a dictionary. Also, on call, I had my mate Mandy, a clever and learned journalist. Phillip was in awe of me and couldn't believe how smart I was. One day, he sat down with me and said, 'So Brownie, tell me about yourself. You appear to be knowledgeable and intelligent and yet an enigma.'

I smiled and nodded like I knew what that meant. Out of Phillip's sight, I looked up the meaning of enigma: *a person who is mysterious or difficult to understand, puzzling, a conundrum, paradox, a question, and a quandary.* Me, all that?

I was given my marching orders from there as well. Not by Phillip but by a previous boss of mine who was coming in as the new managing director. I didn't like him the first time around so, during Friday night drinks, I wobbled up to him, holding on to the bar for support, with the intention of saying hello, so good to see you again, when I heard myself say, 'So, are you still a superficial, talentless, up yourself cunt?'

As an aside, Phillip Adams gave me an outstanding reference, praising me, my intelligence and my work ethic. I still have it.

My party trick was to flash my boobs. I know, how tacky, but for some reason it went over a treat. It seemed everyone loved looking at a good set of bare bosoms, and I loved the attention. Coincidentally, the previously mentioned new Director's wife, who was a well-known journalist at the time, wrote an article, which appeared in *Advertising News* asking why it is that the only girls who flash their boobs always have good ones. I'll take that.

I acquired several nicknames during my time in advertising. On one occasion, when running late for work, I noticed the fly on my skin-tight jeans was buckled so I put the jeans on, pressed a very hot iron onto my crotch and pushed the steam button. Whoosh. Ah. Shit. Such pain! Not only did this successfully flatten my fly, but it also left a perfect impression of the iron on my pubic area. When I got to work, my boss asked me why I was walking strangely so I showed him the iron imprint. He began to cry with laughter. While at lunch that day at a popular pub in South Melbourne, having had a couple of bevvies my boss suggested I show my colleagues. I stood on my chair and bared all. It brought the house down. As one of our clients at the time was Kambrook, an electrical goods company that produced a very efficient steam iron, my nickname became 'Suzie Shot-of-Steam'.

'Squatter' was another nickname given to me and an appropriate one at that, as I still had an annoyingly weak bladder. When I had to wee, I had to wee, wherever I was and whoever I was with. When a girl's gotta go, a girl's gotta go. There was absolutely no holding it in. I weed on lampposts, bumper bars, fences, trees, in gutters and in milkshake cartons at the drive-in. Alcohol plus an unreliable bladder was a deadly combination. To this day, I still get called 'Squatter'.

Other terms of endearment bestowed upon me were Suzie Slab and Boozie Suzie.

One of the highlights of working in advertising were the numerous and always memorable awards nights which were held at luxurious establishments, with everything laid on for our benefit. On one of these occasions, while imbibing with the creative director in a luxurious hotel bathroom, I dropped a bag of cocaine on the plush carpet. Unfazed, the director handed me a rolled up one-hundred-dollar note and said, 'here, you go first, leave me some.'

On our hands and knees, we snorted every skerrick of that stuff. The rest of the night was a blur, although I do remember having trouble breathing, possibly due to the number of carpet fibres I had hoovered up my schnoz.

At another awards ceremony, this time at the Hilton Hotel, John Cleese was the master of ceremonies. Our general manager had to negotiate the huge room multiple times in order to reach the stage to receive award after award after award. Eventually, John Cleese began tossing the awards across the huge room to our table, saving our manager the trip.

Following the awards, John Paul Young's band held the after party in their room. At yet another attempt at groupiedom, I made out with Rockwell T. James who had the most beautiful eyes I had ever seen. The next morning naked and in a daze. I thought I was going to the bathroom but instead went through the main door, locking myself out. As I was bashing on the door trying to wake a comatosed Rockwell, John Paul Young appeared, and while unlocking the door for me, and trying not to look at my body in its *au naturel* state, he began singing, 'Love is in the air'!

The same night, I had borrowed a pair of expensive Atelier black leather pants from a colleague. I was tearing up the dance floor, busting some crazy moves, when I felt a gush of air entering from behind. I had split the borrowed pants from crotch to waist.

I was accompanied to this awards night by a guy I met on a blind date. He suggested I come to his flat for cocktails beforehand. When I got there, I realised I needed to do a poo. Unfortunately, it turned out to be a large heavy solid log that stubbornly refused to flush. To make things worse, the toilet was an old-fashioned chain-style one which took ages to fill. I was in there for an eternity. God knows what he was thinking. I decided there was only one thing to do and that was to remove the log from the toilet, wrap it in toilet paper and put it in my handbag. I must have asphyxiated my date and the cab driver with the amount of perfume I sprayed.

I'm not sure if it was the poo in the handbag or the bare bum peeping through the ripped leather pants, but he disappeared without saying goodnight.

I was becoming a pathological first date fuck up. At yet another one of these events, dining in a classy restaurant in the city and looking stunning in a cerise silk frock and dangerously high stilettos, I was descending the spiral staircase from the loo when I spotted some people I knew. I stopped midway and smiled and waved like the Queen, thinking how gorgeous I must look to my new date who, no doubt, couldn't take his eyes off me. When I sat down, he quietly whispered, 'Your dress is tucked into your pantyhose.'

I was lucky enough to find myself in the advertising industry at its peak. It was a magical time. Anything went; there were no rules. This industry was known for its debauchery. Friday night agency drinks were a classic example. People came from near and far and it was expected of me to entertain the troops. Not to disappoint, I would jump onto the boardroom table, grabbing a wine bottle to sing into, and there I channelled my hero, Cher, belting out her signature tune *If I Could Turn Back Time*. This always went over a treat, with everyone singing along and waving their arms in the air. Back then I looked a bit like Cher, and I dressed like Cher, not wearing much more than she wore in that video clip on the cannon. The only difference was that my legs started at her knees. As an aside, that very expensive solid oak table was ruined due to holes caused by my heels.

The ad agency I worked in was full of gorgeous guys. Most of them were married but that didn't deter me. At one of our staff meetings, the subject of sexual harassment in the workplace came up. Apparently, there was way too much of it – from me. The manager finished the meeting by saying, 'Suzie, you have to stop sexually harassing the men. You are making them uncomfortable. This is your last warning.'

I had a crush on my Brad Pitt look-alike boss, but alas the feeling was in no way mutual. In fact, I was a constant source of frustration to him. On one occasion, he announced to all, 'If you want any productivity out of Brownie, make sure you grab her in the morning as she's fuckin' useless after lunch.' One night, at our local, a night of copious amounts of vodka and mega- toilet-cistern- coke –snorting- sessions, I must have blacked out. My next memory was waking up in my boss's bed with a hangover you could photograph. *Oh my God, had we done it?* While he was in the shower, I snuck out. When he arrived at work, as I desperately avoided his gaze, he handed me a sealed envelope, inside which was a pair of my Bridget Jones big girl undies.

There was a well-known muso, the leader of a popular band, who joined me in the Friday night entertainment. I will call him Grant. We did a great rendition of *You're the One That I Want*, impersonating Olivia Newton-John and John Travolta. As we had rehearsed, during our performance I took a running jump at Grant, attempting to wrap my legs around his waist as he threw me back 'Grease' style, but because he missed his cue, I went flying off the table, landing in a heap on the floor.

Cocaine. What can I say? On coke, I was funnier, prettier, wittier, wiser, taller, more knowledgeable and totally invincible, and therefore, I believed, justified in my outrageous behaviour.

'Good old Brownie, she's at it again,' they would sigh, shaking their heads and looking at me with sad eyes.

Why didn't anyone want me? I was loud, entertaining, told outrageously inappropriate jokes, had a gutter mouth and could drink anyone under the table. I had the constitution of an ox. I was like a cockroach, built to survive a holocaust. What's not to love? And did I mention self-denigrating, insecure, clingy, needy and constantly seeking validation?

Our work Christmas parties were epic fancy-dress themed affairs that saw our offices turned into dens of iniquity with live music and an endless supply of lethal punch and marching powder. Polaroids were the go back then. There was one of me, which also appeared in *Advertising News*, in a blue crocheted mini dress with my nipples poking through the holes. Another photo showed the general manager snorting coke off my bare boob, our faces distorted with glee.

Our Creative Director had put together a reel of our award-winning ads to the soundtrack of Tina Turner's *Simply the Best*. As I watched it with my colleagues, brimming with pride, I was amazed at how powerful and sensational this all was. Granted, we were blessed to be part of the best Advertising Agency in Australia and yet I was constantly aware of the euphoria dripping in hedonism, egoism and sensual self-indulgence. We measured brilliance by how brazenly we could stretch a slogan past the truth; the more we could airbrush reality, the faster we climbed, as we convinced the general public that happiness could be bought in six easy payments. The status symbols worshipped by the top executives became addictive and their desire for more toys overtook the desire to tell the unvarnished truth.

This couldn't possibly last. I was aware of how shallow and superficial it all was, as it contradicted my deeply ingrained core beliefs. I wasn't brought up this way. I was faking it, desperate for acceptance. I was a superficial pretender.

These people wanted me working for them because I was fun. I efficiently organised the agency's social activities, booked lunches and generally entertained all and sundry. The downside was that I was predictably unreliable and never at my desk when I was supposed to be. At lunch, I had an uncanny knack of tricking myself that one more drink would always be okay. It never was. EVER!

After one of these crazy Friday nights, with only the dregs left, my girlfriend made a poor decision, following a highly recognised married authoritarian figure upstairs to do the dirty deed. Much later back at hers, I heard gut-wrenching screams coming from the toilet. I ran in, 'Whaaaaaaat?'

'I've got crabs,' she screamed back.

I thought I was going to pass out. 'Look,' she wailed, holding a large one in a pair of tweezers. 'There's daddy crab,' and then a smaller one, 'there's mummy crab.'

Guess we knew the whereabouts of baby crab and his siblings; they were no doubt doing cartwheels in my boss's pubic region.

If there was ever a moral compass, and that's debatable, it was obliterated in this industry. Drinking and drugging was an occupational hazard. The most important part of our day was deciding which client job number the French champagne and beluga caviar would be charged to. We were such wankers. That's when the booze worked and worked well. It was the solution.

One of our favourite lunch haunts was Leo's Spaghetti Bar in Fitzroy Street. The owner, Sergio, loved us and our lucrative five-hour lunches and exorbitant tips. Standing pride of place in the foyer of the restaurant was a magnificent marble statue of David, who I was still passionate about. I rearranged him daily, adding a hat, scarf, lipstick or jewellery. Sometimes, I hid him in different parts of the restaurant, sending Sergio into a tailspin trying to locate him. One day, I wrapped David in my coat and walked out with him. I can still see Sergio running after me down Fitzroy Street, his apron flapping, yelling, 'Brink him back! This is not funny. Brink him back now!'

That being said, at times my irrational mind, coupled with my ever-increasing anxiety, would rear its ugly head and I would decline lunch, choosing instead to don Lycra and run four kilometres around the Tan Track or slam a squash racquet for an hour with a colleague. This would inevitably be met with incredulity from my co-workers. It was unpredictable behaviour at its best.

~

In 1979, Bill Armstrong of Armstrong Studios sent our advertising agency a flyer, which announced that Bobby Bright, of Bobby and Laurie fame, was available for voice-overs. A bit of background, when I was fourteen, I was besotted with Bobby and Laurie. They played at our local church hall in Hampton, performing *Hitch Hiker* and *I Belong with You*. I was pretty sure Bobby looked straight into my eyes when he sang, 'When I hear a love song, then I know where I belong, wo wo wo – I belong with (*Sue*).' My friends and I were screaming and crying. I found Bobby backstage, swore my undying love and asked him for a souvenir. He grabbed a pair of scissors and, cutting his tie, gave me half of it while kissing me on my tear-stained cheek. Then and there, I had an epiphany; I was destined to be a groupie.

So, when I received Bill Armstrong's flyer, I returned it with the words 'Are voice-overs all Bobby is available for?' Bill rang and told me to meet him at a hotel at seven p.m. and he would introduce me to Bobby. I was nervous. *Would he remember the little girl he gave half his tie to?* When I arrived, there was Bobby, solo, without Bill. The bastard had set me up. Bobby was no longer in his Thai silk suit with drainpipes and pointy-toed shoes, but instead he had long greasy hair and wore suede bell-bottoms, a tie-dyed shirt and a huge peace symbol around his neck.

'Hi,' I said. 'Remember me?'

Bobby had no idea who I was or what I was referring to and he certainly wasn't here to discuss same. He was here for one reason and one reason only – to shag me. And in case I wasn't convinced, with a sleazy grin on his face, Bobby passed me the flyer I had returned and there, staring me in the face, were my words in black Texta: Are voice-overs all Bobby is available for? In my defence, I was sort of joking, but no matter, in front of me was an extremely stoned dude who was champing at the bit.

I drank myself to numbness, searching desperately for conversation with this stranger. For every vodka I drank, Bobby nipped outside and had a joint, his mull kept in his bum bag attached to his person. His head was getting closer and closer to the bar and his eyelids were fluttering. I'm not sure if it was me joining all my words together relaying the story of the church dance and the tie from twenty years ago, twenty times over, or the part where he ran out of dope but, eventually, he suggested we hit the road. We jumped into a cab, arriving at the sleaziest motel I have ever laid eyes on. There was an orange chenille bedspread, broken tiles in the bathroom and a ripped shower curtain, which had a foot of black slime on the bottom. The only refreshing aspect was that the toilet roll had a neatly folded point. 'Oh Bobby, you shouldn't have,' I quipped.

I couldn't wait to get out of there. When he passed out in the wee hours, I snuck out and hitchhiked home, the words of his greatest hit *Hitch Hiker* ringing in my ears. Another fine mess I'd gotten myself into. *What was I thinking?*

Years later, at a 60s music night at the Sheraton Melbourne Hotel, I spotted Bobby. He was in a wheelchair and looking a tad worse for wear. I approached him, again saying 'Hi. Remember me?'

He gave me a blank look and so I reminded him. 'Oh,' he said. 'Yes, I remember. "Are voice-overs all Bobby is available for?"' We both laughed.

Around 1979 my friend, Mandy, and I went to see Gerry and the Pacemakers at a local venue. This was possibly the fourth line-up of the Pacemakers, with the only original member in the band being Gerry, now almost fifty, fat and bald. Also on the bill were Brian Poole and The Tremeloes. Brian Poole was also approaching fifty, fat and bald. The Pacemakers played the best of the best, including *Ferry Cross the Mersey* and *You'll Never Walk Alone*. The Tremeloes sang their only hit *Do You Love Me*.

We boogied like lunatics, singing thunderously, our arms flailing and drenching each other with sticky cocktails. At one point, I ran at Mandy and wrapped my legs around her waist, sending her flying backwards, and landing on top of her. At one o'clock in the morning, Mandy wanted to leave. She thought it was fair enough; we had come in a cab together, we were sharing a house together, it was a school night and it made sense that we left together. But, alas, not to me.

I had wormed my way backstage, met the band and gushed all over fat little Gerry. 'Ohhh, Gerrry, Gerrry. I aaam sushhh a biiig faaan!'

Gerry ignored me but the seemingly twelve-year-old drummer thought I was a bit of alright and invited me back to their hotel in the city for a party. As all sensibility of any sort evaporated, I jumped gleefully onto the bus with thirteen male musicians. I was sitting behind Brian Poole who was mumbling nasties at me, so I clipped him across the back of his head, 'oh you shut up, you one-hit wonder'.

When we arrived at the hotel, everyone disappeared. Guess what? There was no party. Anticipating the offer of a cocktail of sorts and maybe a joint, I was instead pushed down on the bed by the adolescent drummer, who was rapidly removing his clothes. 'Well, come on then,' he said. 'Get ya gear off. Come on then.'

I headed towards the door when he aggressively grabbed my arm and pulled me towards him. He was starkers, and in his hand appeared to be a doorstopper which he swung around and around in circles. On closer inspection, I realised it was his penis. I couldn't believe my eyes. He had a maniacal grin on his dial, as he was getting closer, with his donger rotating so fast it was making me dizzy. I had to get out of there. I ran as fast as my drunk little legs would take me, with him in hot pursuit, yelling in a cute cockney accent, 'What the fuck did you come back for if you weren't gonna shag me then, ya fucking nutter?'

There were so many doors in this hotel; the place was like a maze. I eventually found a lift and jumped in, slamming my fists on the number panel like in the movies and shaking like a leaf, while he and his verbal abuse followed hot on my heels. I watched that penis swinging away, praying to God the lift doors would close on it and cut it in half. Even then it would be too long.

It was three in the morning in the city on a foggy Tuesday, and I had no money for a cab. I'd done it again. *What was I thinking?*

Tex

A friend is someone who knows you and loves you just the same.

Elbert Hubbard

This seems like the perfect time to fill you in on the notorious Mandy, nicknamed Tex, my BFF and godmother to my daughter, Greer. We met at Firbank; she was a friend of my sister's and a couple of years older than me. We clicked the moment we met. I had more fun with Mandy than anyone ever.

The name 'Tex' came from a cartoon of a naked girl who resembled Mandy, cowboy hat on head, wrestling with a pair of cowboy boots, the bloke in her bed asking 'So tell me, why do they call you Tex?' I had this cartoon stuck to our shared fridge.

Her voice was low, resonant, with that faint velvet rasp that journalists earn from years of deadlines and late-night coffee and ciggies. She had the most contagious laugh – and oh, how she laughed. I have visions of her, mouth agape, dabbing away the tears of joy, before they smudged her mascara. She dressed with style and class. She had an obsession with shoes, expensive shoes. She had more of them than Imelda Marcos. Traditionally, our children also wore expensive shoes, compliments of Mandy.

Mandy was a champ; she was well connected in Melbourne social circles. Her brother was Richard Zachariah, known for his media presence and coupling with Maggie Tabberer who, I may add, was a delightful woman. Mandy was the package. Glamorous, passionate and with a razor-sharp wit, Mandy's presence could light up a room.

We would fall into the local Brighton nightclub after an all-day lunch, pushing the DJ out of the way, ripping off his disc and replacing it with The Pointer Sisters *Slow Hand*. We'd then jump onto the dance floor and perform our well-rehearsed routine, making slow hand movements. Most times we were thrown out. Her dad, who was the headmaster at Brighton Grammar School, was incensed. 'How dare they throw you out,' he said. 'Don't they know who you are?'

Hitching a lift to the club from the city after one of our extended lunches, Mandy and I found ourselves in the back of a panel van. Struggling to get out, she slurred, 'Hey, do we really wanna go in there? I shink we too washted?'

I meant to say 'is the Pope a Catholic?', but instead I replied with, 'Is the Pope a cunt?' Well, that was it. We were paralysed, shrieking.

And believe you me that line never got old.

We had a unique shorthand, Mandy and me. We cracked ourselves up. For a while, we shared a house in Sandringham. On Monday nights, traditionally, we cooked a roast for my mum and dad and then it was off to the Underground nightclub, followed by Mickey's all-nighter on The Esplanade.

Dad thought we were insane. 'It's Monday night girls. It's a school night and you're off to the Dug Out *(his name for the Underground)*. Are you mad.'

I wondered if secretly Dad wished he was coming with us. Never trust a Monday.

Tuesday mornings were a nightmare. We would take it in turns ringing work. 'Hi, this is Suzie's flatmate. She won't be in today. Her grandmother died.'

My boss replied, 'Her grandmother died a month ago.'

'Hi, this is Mandy's flatmate. She won't be in today as she …'

'Hey, Mand,' I called out. 'What's the excuse today?'

Mand, ice pack on head, chewing Panadol and sculling Berocca, called back, 'Tell them I've got gastro.'

'We used that last Tuesday.'

'Find one we haven't used.'

'… Hello. Sorry to keep you. Mand won't be in today as she was run over by a tram last night and lost a leg.'

'Good one,' was Mandy's reply.

We shared a love of The Beatles, Rod Stewart, and all things country, including Brenda Lee and Connie Stevens. The song that reminds me most of Mandy, is Billy Joel's *Just the Way You Are*. Mand would say, 'All I want before I die is for someone to sing that song to me. Is that too much to ask? And Peggy Lee's *Is That All There Is*. 'If that's all there is my friends, then let's keep dancing.' Mandy and I would waltz to that one, holding each other up. She requested those words be on her tombstone.

At times she had a deep mistrust of the world she interrogated so fiercely, times of disillusionment, having been let down by men. Her catchphrase was, 'I'll tell you who fuckin' cares Browne … fuckin' nobody'.

She had a heart that loved unreasonably hard, and she craved love in return. She had therapy for years, desperate for relief from her thoughts of unworthiness. Eventually she married a man who had pursued her for a long time, and who she had rejected for a long time, as she didn't trust herself to commit. I offered to do the catering for the wedding. I got drunk and stuffed it up, letting her down big time. She was understandably furious.

Mandy was a huge Dusty Springfield fan, and she managed to share a bottle of Dom with Dusty during an interview she had cleverly wrangled. This was nine months before Dusty passed, and possibly Mandy's greatest claim to fame.

We had a red-hot go at being Mental as Anything groupies. We followed them around town, never missing a gig. Two well-known facts: when in Amanda Zachariah's company – one, you never pay to get in; and two, you're always a VIP. We made sure we had a bird's-eye view of Martin Plaza's crotch as he sexily pelvic thrusted, we believed, at us. '*How can you see looking through those tears, don't you know you're worth your weight in gold …*' We would salivate.

Greedy, a mate of Mandy's, invited us to the after parties, which were a hoot. Tex flew in from Sydney one evening, arriving at the Golden Gate Hotel, suitcase in hand to see the Mentals. The crowd was massive, so, imitating Pogo sticks, we used the suitcase for leverage. In the cab on the way home, we noticed the suitcase had hundreds of little holes in it and shampoo and conditioner were all over her clothes.

Mandy and I were bad, bad, bad for each other, with our midweek lunches being the most predictable. 'We should go back to the office, we're already late,' one of us would say.

'Yeah, we should. How about just one more?'

'OK, but just the one and then we must go.'

'Yep. You know, it's much cheaper to get a bottle.'

'Oh, I so agree.'

Inevitably on her arrival back at the office, Mandy's boss would take one look at her and call a board meeting, sitting her on a very high stool where she would teeter, trying not to fall off.

Ours was a decadent life, which came with so many perks. *It's not what you know but who you know.*

I'll Be Home on a Monday

We're not groupies. We're here for the music. We are Band Aids.

Pamela Des Barres

It was 1978 and the previously mentioned musician, Grant, the 'John Travolta' to my 'Olivia Newton-John', and his wife invited my colleague, Shazza and I to join them on tour in America. I was beyond excited. Here was my chance at professional groupiedom. It seemed I had been training for this role, albeit unsuccessfully, for an eternity. The band were huge in America, more so than in Australia at that time.

Grant met us at Los Angeles airport, LAX and the first thing he said to me was, 'Brownie, I have one piece of advice: don't shag the roadies.'

'As if, Grant,' I said, somewhat offended.

We stayed at the Sunset Boulevard Hotel, Los Ángeles. Also staying there was the Blondie Band and The Robert Palmer Band. One evening, Shazza and I heard a come-hither whistle from Robert's room as he beckoned us to enter. In his dark glasses and glitter suit, he offered us lines of cocaine bigger than his ego. It was prime gear. At one point Shaz whispered, 'do you reckon the folks back home are going to believe we did coke with Robert Palmer?'

Among the crew on our bus were Molly Meldrum and John Dick, the band's manager, et al. Like in the Eagles song lyrics, *'there were lines on the mirror, there were lines on our face, we pretended not to notice, we were caught up in the race …* At the back of the bus was a large round glass table and an extensive bar. I felt out of my depth hanging with these rock stars, so I went hard, trying to keep up, at times too hard. One night, I overindulged and passed out.

The next day Shazza told me that Molly Meldrum had carried me to my room. I guess I was safe there.

Grant was an excellent host. We were given VIP treatment wherever we went. With his arms enveloping the three of us, he would announce to all, 'these are my girls, and they are to be looked after at all times'. We travelled in limos with an abundant supply of champers, had front row seats and VIP all areas access passes. We watched so many Arena concerts, blown away by the extent of their popularity. I knew every word of every song by the end of the six week tour. It was such a blast. One night, a band member emptied a bowl of fruit salad over Molly Meldrum's head. Good old Molly wiped the syrup from his face, continuing the interview. He is such a trooper.

And, not to disappoint, I slept with a roadie, didn't I?! Paddy was his name. I should have known midway through the act that there was something up, or not up more like it, but in my condition, it was not to be. The next evening, Shazza and I had dinner dates with her man, the sound engineer, and my Paddy but surprise, surprise, my Paddy was a no-show. And still I didn't twig.

~

After the tour, Shazza and I flew to Jamaica for some well-earned rest and recuperation. We landed at a cool little town called Negril. It was hot and steamy. The blue mahoe trees were magnificent with their broad green leaves, the scent of the hibiscus-like flowers wafting in the ether.

We had a couple of constant companions whose names were Barclay and Fritz. You could only see them at night by the whites of their eyes. They were the coolest dudes and eager to show Shazza and I a good time. On our second day there, the boys asked us if we wanted to smoke the local gunja. I think maybe we would have answered differently had we known what was coming. I had one puff of the joint, which was rolled in a massive shiny leaf, and woke up seven hours later. Shazza and I decided if we were to remember Jamaica, we couldn't smoke any more gunja. And who needed gunja when there was exquisite Jamaican rum on tap?

Prejudice was monumental in this country. I remember being confused and horrified. Our boys whistled from the street to announce their arrival, as they weren't allowed on the property. We spent hours with them on the exquisite beach, playing backgammon, topless. For once mine weren't the only breasts out. Our nights were spent at Rick's Café where our boys earned the tourists' dollars in exchange for diving into the water below from a ridiculous height. We watched, amused, while we drank rum and ate banana chips, goat curry and jerk chicken, listening to Bob Marley wailing. *(See what I did there?)*

We were determined to take some gunja home, as it was too good to waste. So, Shazza, having bigger balls than me, decided to put it in her knickers. We arrived at the airport modestly dressed in cowboy boots, distressed jeans, silk fringed shirts and Stetson hats. After looking us up and down, the Customs guys told us to open our suitcases. I started to sweat. In mine was a Polaroid of us snorting a mountain of cocaine through straws. It was a staged shot to us but evidence to the already suspicious Customs dudes. We decided heavy flirting was the go, distracting them from the task at hand and hopefully avoiding a strip search. It worked. They eventually told us to close our cases and be on our way. We high-fived each other with our sweaty, trembling hands. We had done it. We crucified our friends back home with that gunja. They were well pleased we risked a jail sentence.

~

Back home and on a camping trip with my loyal, devoted much younger boyfriend, Lewis, my suspicions were confirmed when he announced, 'I don't know what's going on but I have a dribbly dick.' God bless him. Seems I had been given the clap I so richly deserved. Grant's words resounding, 'Brownie … don't shag the roadies.' *What was I thinking?*

I sat my boyfriend down and said, 'well Lewis, I'm not sure how to say this but here goes. The reason you have a dribbly dick is because I shagged a roadie who gave me a venereal disease, which I, in turn, have given to you. Duh.'

We went to the doctor, who reprimanded me for my infidelity and who I reprimanded back for 'not minding his own fucking business'. He told us to lie on our fronts on separate beds, explaining, 'now I will administer a 10cc shot of penicillin in your buttocks.' As we lay on opposite sides of the surgery and with the needle going in, I looked at the love of my life and sang the 10cc song, 'I'm not in love, so don't forget it', thinking I was so awfully amusing and Lewis thinking I was an unfaithful slut.

I have run into Grant many times over the years, and every time, without fail, grinning, he asks, 'so Brownie, have you heard from Paddy?'

Brighton Hilton

It's very democratic. It's all kinds of colours. All kinds of sizes.

Truman Capote

After Lewis forgave me, he and I moved into a block of flats, lovingly referred to as the 'Brighton Hilton' or 'The No-tell Hotel'. All the residents knew each other, often intimately. Here, there were some real characters including flamboyant gay boys, 'Toorak cowboys', Torquay surfers and Melbourne Mafia. My friend Cassie, a model and a single mother of four children, also lived here. Living with her, much to my chagrin, was my ex- boyfriend John, who had, temporarily kicked the smack. He always did have a penchant for older women, especially ex-model blondes. Another resident was Jane, an ex-crim's moll, and her two sons.

Cassie, Jane and I frequented Silvers Nightclub. We dressed in sequined boob tubes, floral hipster bell-bottoms and platform boots, our midriffs bare and our hair big. When the lift door opened, we would hear the manager, Johnny Wheeler, yell, 'the girls are here,' and on would go our song, *When Will I See You Again* by The Three Degrees, as we danced out of the lift, resembling Charlie's Angels, all eyes on us. We were so damn hot. We boogied with the rich and famous, never opening our wallets.

At three a.m. we would jump into Cassie's green VW beetle and hurtle along the beach road, our arms and heads hanging out of the sunroof, off to the all-nighter, Mickeys on The Esplanade. There we were served Pernod on ice, whooping it up on the electronic dance floor, trying unsuccessfully to coordinate the flashing squares as they changed colour.

Cassie was a firecracker; she was courted by some of the richest dudes in town. She was unaffected by money and fame and was simply enjoying her freedom from her ex. I once watched her smash her high heel through the windscreen of a Rolls Royce which was owned by one of her wanker boyfriends after she caught him cheating.

We threw fabulous daiquiri parties on our large lawn around the hills hoist, our blenders whirring all day long, pureeing strawberries, rum and crushed ice, a massive vintage silver boom box belting out songs by Barry White, 'Can't get enough of your love baby', 'You're my first, you're my last, you're my everything ...' and Labelle, Lady Marmalade. During one of these parties, Mandy played Barry White all day. When the album finished, she would play it again, and again. Her boyfriend at the time, hated Barry White, and after hours of this, he ripped her LP off the turntable, threw it on the driveway and ran over it with his car.

People would come from all over the place. Anyone who could play a musical instrument would do so. Jane usually had some underground peeps in attendance. One of those dudes mentioned that he had a dead painter and docker in his boot. We quickly escorted him off the premises. At this stage, John was manager of three Rip Curl surf shops. His briefcase never left his side as it contained the Brighton Hilton's supply of the best cocaine money could buy.

This was a solid community. We shared everything and I mean everything – boyfriends, girlfriends, clothes, cups of sugar, cars. One morning, Cassie asked, 'Can I please borrow your car, someone must have mine?'

I replied, 'Yes, sure.'

I then hear her shouting from outside, 'Hey, correct me if I'm wrong, but I don't think this is your car?'

Apparently, I had driven someone else's Volkswagen home.

The gay boys made spectacular punches for our wing dings. They would hide condoms full of liquor in the punch bowl, almost passing out with glee at the reactions.

Another resident was a cowboy who I had a brief affair with. He was tall and skinny with bleached blond hair. He slept with his cowboy boots and hat on. I was twenty-six, and he was twenty. My girlfriend was dating his best friend, a doctor's son. Their Brighton parents called us the 'old aunties'. A trust fund baby, he would pick me up in his dad's canary yellow convertible Ferrari. We hammered it around the Great Ocean Road, lunching at top-class restaurants and drinking Galliano, which co-ordinated with the colour of the car. I thought I was in love with this dude, or maybe it was simply my love of anything country. He made me laugh; he was carefree and a bit mad. He serenaded me with Billy Joel's song *You May Be Right*, singing, 'You may be right, I may be crazy, oh, but it just may be a lunatic you're looking for.' He was right. I was.

Of course, this all happened behind the back of my on again, off again boyfriend, Lewis. Ah yes, I was at it again. I was such a disloyal bitch. I would abscond with his car for days, never telling him where I was. Lewis would have done anything for me. Could I harm this patient, devoted boy anymore? Yes, I could.

Not long into the affair, I discovered I was pregnant. What to do? My looseness in that department should have rendered me up the duff many times in the past and yet here I was. To be honest, I didn't think it would ever happen for me. This may be the only chance I ever have. There was no doubt it was the cowboy's baby. I had so many questions. What a moral dilemma this was. I had strong Buddhist beliefs. *Thou shalt not kill anything with a nervous system.* But what were my options? Giving birth to a little John Wayne with foetal alcohol syndrome, fathered by a fly-by-night hedonistic cowboy?

I told my boyfriend Lewis, who was so understanding. After days of deliberation, he drove me to the clinic for an abortion. I fell into a deep depression. I had destroyed a life. I apologised to that baby over and over again. I was in so much pain. I was full of shame and, of course, guilt. Oh, the guilt. I knew then that I would never be free from the memory of my baby that would never be. I prayed for forgiveness. I prayed for his or her soul. I prayed they had joined my baby sister in the next life.

When the cowboy heard, he arrived at the door, swilling out of a bottle of bourbon, screaming at my boyfriend, 'How dare you kill my child. I should have been given a say in the future of my baby.'

Then he punched Lewis fair and square in the jaw, knocking him backwards. Crying and ranting, he stormed into my bedroom grabbing his cowboy boots and hat, berating me, tears and snot flowing.

In 1984, I ran into the cowboy in the local supermarket with my one-year-old daughter sitting in the trolley. He looked at her, then at me. Nothing was said.

Lewis broke up with me, surprise, surprise. He said I had broken him. Der. I always want what I can't have, and I wanted that boy back at any cost. He had moved on and into a share house with his schoolmates. He ghosted me and wouldn't answer the phone. 'You need to leave me alone now, Suzie. I have had enough.'

'Oh, you don't mean that, Lewis. I promise I will change. Pleeease give me another chance,' I begged.

He wasn't budging.

I wasn't settling for that. *I will change his mind. I will lure him back with sex.* I began stalking him. Drunk one evening, I drove to his house and climbed up a tree and into his bedroom window, falling on top of him and his new girlfriend in bed. He begged me to stop. I couldn't stop. I became obsessed.

I followed them in my friend's car, peering through trees into cafés, pub windows and at their place of work. She was so young and so pretty. What did she have that I didn't? Why didn't he want me? I was so self-absorbed; my obvious delusions were in full swing. The shame was eating me alive. I had to let it go. I had broken this boy's heart. I was a narcissistic monster.

Where's the Cheese?

Come and get it... come and get it... with Peter... G'day... Russell... G'day... Clarke!

In 1982, I scored a job at Masius advertising agency, where I became Peter Russell-Clarke's personal assistant. My role was preparing the food for the filming of the *Come and Get It* television series and collaborating alongside the stylists and cameramen producing his many cook books. It was a cushy job. I taxied him around in his Jaguar XJ-S, which had one of the first car phones; it was the size of a shoebox. Peter was ambassador to the Egg, Dairy and Meat boards, an author, artist, television and media personality, cook and shareholder in Masius. He owned several houses and a farm.

Peter was a great bloke with a wicked sense of humour. Our drinking sessions were epic. After one extended client lunch, we had a screaming row, whereby he up-ended the lunch table all over me. Covered in food, stale beer and cigarette ash, sobbing, I ran from him, swearing, 'that's it you bastard. I quit.' His wife and I were close and shared a birthday. I would ring her, crying, 'that's it, I hate your husband, he is a monster, I quit. Come and Get Him'.

Most Friday nights, after our long drinking sessions, he would fire me. Monday would arrive and, because I was sacked, I didn't turn up for work. He would ring, asking, 'where the fuck are you?'

'You sacked me,' I'd reply.

'For fuck's sake, you never listen to a fucking word I say. Why would you listen to that? Now get in here. We've got fucking work to do.'

After yet another booze-fuelled lunch, we were having a scrap in his office. He was throwing things, and I was fretting. I rang my new husband, sobbing and asking, 'can you come here? Pete's going mental. I don't feel safe.'

'I'm in the middle of a game of pool. Can it wait?' was his reply.
'Noooooo! Get here now!' I yelled.

When my husband arrived, Pete and I were on the Veuve Clicquot, and I was dancing on the table and flashing my boobs, which was my foolproof way of calming Pete down. It never failed. My husband was furious.

One of my jobs was to keep Pete's private fridge stacked with wine. Good wine. When he was out of the office, I would invite my colleagues to his office for a 'tea party'. The 'tea' referred to Pete's precious bone china tea set, which we drank the wine out of, everyone talking like the Queen, raising our little fingers as we drank. Pete was constantly baffled as to why his fridge was always empty. Everyone knew it wasn't tea. The receptionist whose job it was to supply the wine eventually put a lock on Pete's fridge and hid his bone china tea set. Bitch.

Even though ours was a volatile relationship, Pete and I were great mates, and we adored each other. We were a good team, producing many excellent TV shows and cookbooks. My time with him came to an end when the Agency decided to cut back on costs, advising all managers that if they wanted an assistant or secretary they now had to pay for them out of their own pockets. Guess he didn't value me that much! Despite my round-the-clock drinking, I managed to hold down some awesome jobs and worked for some amazing people. I must have done something right. People often asked me, considering my drinking problem, how I managed to keep getting jobs. My answer, 'Drinkers pick the right jobs.'

~

This same year, while working for Peter Russell-Clarke, I married a guy I'd known for a long time. When we were fifteen, sitting on the hill next to the Torquay surf club and overlooking the ocean, he told me he loved me and would marry me one day. 'Ha, dream on,' I scoffed. 'I'm gonna marry a rich man.'

So, fifteen years later, marry him I did. My father, clearly doubtful, agreed to pay for the wedding if I promised the marriage would last a year. The courtship was short, just six months, and most of it was spent at Phillip Island where he lived in a share house. Considering my penchant for surfers and party people, this pairing was a monte. We were a perfect match. We were both hedonists and united in the eternal pursuit of a decadent, fun-filled existence. What could possibly go wrong?

He had an eclectic taste in music and introduced me to bands such as Mink De Ville, The Amazing Rhythm Aces, Steve Miller and Jimmy Buffett. He also loved the Goons and Monty Python, repeating their lines word for word. I found him breathtakingly funny. He was intelligent, knowledgeable and a prolific reader. He had a unique way of dancing, a cheeky, crooked smile, long blond hair and a suntan. Tick, tick, tick. Honestly, I was dubious about this from the beginning. I knew I needed to get married and have a child. At thirty years of age, this was the done thing, and everybody else was doing it. I didn't want to be left behind. Maybe this would slow me down? Maybe this would make me feel normal?

When it came to saying 'I do', I was freaking out. *What am I doing,* I screamed internally. I knew it was wrong, and the knowing wasn't going away. I tried to imagine we would live happily ever after but the knowing trumps imagination, every time. I couldn't help but wonder, was I using a marriage to right my wrongs?

Our wedding reception was a spectacular cocaine-fuelled event, held at the Sandringham Yacht Club. At one point my mum was knocking on the locked ladies toilet door, while Phil and I, standing on the toilet, racking up, were 'shooshing' each other, snickering, when her head appeared under the door, 'what the hell are you two doing in there?'

Our wedding waltz was to Monty Python's *Always Look on the Bright Side of Life*. My dress was vintage Gatsby flapper style, made from antique cream lace and I wore an Isadora Duncan scarf around my head, secured with a red rose and white daisies to match my posy. He wore a coordinating cream suit and silk scarf. We looked fabulous. It was a wonderful night. We refused to leave, with the car waiting and Mum holding up my going away outfit, pleading with me to change. 'Nope. We're not going anywhere. More champers, more coke, Guv'nor. Party back at the Sheraton!'

The sun was rising when we finally slept. I awoke at noon to no hubby. Searching through our huge suite, I found him in the spa bath covered in bubbles. 'Aren't I supposed to be in there?' I enquired.

We hungrily devoured the continental breakfast, after which I asked, 'hey, didn't we order bacon and eggs?'

He rang reception, saying, 'excuse me, we are in room 103, the honeymoon suite, and we haven't received our bacon and eggs, and we are starving. Could you please get it here asap?'

There was a pause, and then I hear, 'What's that you say? It's on the bottom of the trolley, under the tablecloth? Gotcha.'

With the help of his folks, we bought a house in Mentone that backed onto the Mentone Bowling Club. It had a large lounge/dining room with polished floors and a 'Happy Days' booth at one end, bay windows and an open fireplace. This was a magnificent party house. Greer's (more on her later) first birthday was a doozy. The following morning, the lounge room floor was covered in adult bodies, the beds were full of hungry children still in their clothes, the house looked like a bomb had hit it and Greer's birthday cake was still in the fridge. The last part I think I get from my mum; she never remembered the birthday cake – ever.

We had a lot of fun initially. We shared an unmatched commonality of interest. We had a network of good friends, all with the same goals – raging, drugging, drinking and avoiding reality. Life was exhilarating. We spent hours at the local pubs, playing pool. My husband was the best, and he won all the comps. There were Bloods football matches on Saturdays, with his position being 'half full on the fence'. We threw dinner parties at our big house, spent Easters camping on the Murray, dined at good restaurants drinking expensive wines and holidayed at friends' houses in Sorrento, Phillip Island or the Torquay camp. I loved his parents and he loved mine. I thought this was a match made in heaven.

Our drinking sessions were predictable. In the beginning, we were as eloquent, witty and deep as drunks can be. Alcohol was so efficient – stimulating every sense, from the first seductive sip to giddy intoxication, then on to belligerence, anger and inflated confidence, followed by melancholy and solemn self-pity, and ending, always, in self-loathing and loathing of the other.

> **Diary excerpt June 1983:** *I am pregnant, and I need to drink. I swore I would stop once I was with child, but I cannot. I am researching. There are several different schools of thought. I'm going with my gynaecologist's point of view which was that it's okay to drink, as long as you don't get so drunk that you fall over and harm the baby. That'll do. He was a father of eight children and had delivered hundreds. He must know what he's talking about. I am worthless. I am potentially putting my baby's life in danger.*

Greer was born on 12 September 1983. We were overwhelmed and in awe of this delicate little thing we had produced. She seemed perfect, which was a surprise as I was surely expecting a child with two heads. I was determined to breastfeed sober, although I was hearing that stout, brought on the milk and helped the baby sleep. I never liked stout but if it meant I could drink I was sure I could grow to love it. I have a photo of me with bub on boob and stubbie in hand. What a clever little multitasker I was.

I had no idea how to conform to marriage; no matter how hard I tried – not that I tried that hard. I was always looking for something else, someone else, something more. Monogamy was out of my reach.

How are we expected to only be with the person we marry? It didn't make sense. We should be able to spread our wings, to share each other around, commune-style. I took everything for granted and nothing seriously, except of course my drinking.

You're in My Heart, You're in My Soul

I've been around so long that I've come back into fashion.

Rod Stewart

When Greer was three months old, I was working at The Wheatley Organisation with Doris Tyler, Rod Stewart's ex-tour secretary. Rod was coming to town and doing seven stadium shows in Melbourne.

'Doris, I have to meet him, I absolutely must meet Rod Stewart. Help me meet him!' I begged.

She suggested I ring every hotel in Melbourne, using her name, asking to speak to Robin Le Mesurier, the lead guitarist for Rod Stewart and a good friend of hers. Not believing for a minute this would work, I made the calls – with no luck – and about to give up when suddenly Robin Le Mesurier was on the line. I panicked and, unsuccessfully attempting an English accent, stated that I was Doris. 'No, you're not,' he said. 'Who am I talking to? And by the way, you have a really bad English accent.'

I had been busted.

'Hi, Robin. I can't believe I'm talking to you. Thank you, thank you, thank you. You see, my mate and I have been in love with Rod since we were kids. He is the soundtrack to our lives. We know every word of every song. We even dress like him and sometimes we even sound like him …'

'Okay, okay. I get it,' he interrupted. 'Meet us in the foyer of the Hilton, back bar, at five p.m. tonight before our show, and you can meet us all.'

Just like that. I slowly replaced the receiver. Screaming and shaking like a leaf, I rang my friend Phil, my fellow Rod Stewart worshipper, telling him to meet me in the foyer of the Hilton Hotel at five p.m. that night to meet Rod Stewart. 'Bullshit,' he said. 'Bloody bullshit.'

So, there we both were at the Hilton, not believing for one minute that this was going to happen. We went to the end bar, which was a boutique affair, and there were the band members minus Rod.

We introduced ourselves to Robin and the conversation flowed, but, to Phil's horror, my head was turned towards the door. *Where was he? When would he get here? Maybe he's going straight to the show and he's not coming?* Phil was content. Why wouldn't he be? This, in itself, was mind blowing. 'Stop looking at the door,' he snapped, 'This is the fucking Rod Stewart band! Chill.'

I drank for Australia to calm myself down, and then he appeared. I thought I was going to faint. Having just returned from Bali, Rod was tanned and wore a skin-tight white T-shirt and faded blue distressed jeans, his hair blonde and spiked. I was paralysed. Robin introduced us to our idol, our God, our inspiration, our reason for breathing.

Rod was so friendly. I asked him if he wanted a drink. He replied, 'I don't normally drink before a show, but I'll have a port and brandy in a bubble glass, thanks luv.' And there was that gorgeous, unmistakable cockney accent – the one I had heard and connected with since I was twelve, the one I never thought I would ever hear in person.

I bought Rod two port and brandies. I had researched and was aware that he had been to the wedding of the manager of RCA Records. Trying to sound blasé, I asked 'So, how was Alan and Jen's wedding on the Condor?'

'Well, you've got to be fucking bonkers to get married in the first place, I reckon, ay?'

I laughed so hard Phil stepped on my toe. Rod continued, 'So, love, are you going to the show tonight?'

'No, not tonight but we're going on Tuesday, Wednesday, Thursday, Friday …'

Again, my toe was stomped on.

When Rod announced it was time to leave for the show, my heart sank. I had tried so hard to not lose it completely, to not make a dick of myself, and then suddenly I lost it. I so lost it. I started crying and said 'Rod, I know there are millions of women all over the world who love you but no one will ever love you like I do.'

He hugged me and laughed, while pecking me on my wet cheek, and said, 'you know what, love? I believe that.' 'So, it's been great meeting you nutters. Maybe I'll see you again?'

If only he knew.

I watched them heading to the door, and off to their first concert – the only one of seven we were missing.

I had given my three-month-old daughter to my mum for the week so I could spend it with Rod and Phil. She understood completely as she, too, loved Rod. She is ninety-five now and still listens to Rod's Greatest Hits and Rod's version of the Great American Songbook, and she has been to most of his concerts with us, where she smuggles our vodka in her shopping trolley, always undetected.

As soon as Rod and the band left the bar, Phil and I threw ourselves face down on the floor, thrashing our fists and feet, screaming, 'We did it, we did it. OMG, we did it.'

The barman peered over the bar at us and said, 'How old are you guys?'

Phil and I then proceeded to the bar and, while he chatted up chicks, I put pen to paper and wrote the whole conversation down. Rod said … Sue said … Phil said … Every word of our twenty-five-and-a-half-minute conversation was documented in that bar. It was the most important conversation of my life.

After what seemed like no time at all, possibly due to us mainlining cocktails, the doors to the Hilton opened and in walked Rod and the band members with no security. I was gobsmacked.

I watched in awe as they got in the lift, pressing floor 38. I grabbed Phil. 'Come with me. We're going to pay Rod a visit.'

'Nooo!' he wailed. 'What the fuck?'

Still protesting, stating that we should be grateful for what we had and that, if we do this, we'll just ruin things, Phil kept on. 'Anyway, what makes you think they will let you up there? And how will you find his room? No, no, no. Not happening.' Blah, blah, blah.

'OK,' I said. 'I will go on my own.'

Hammered and with a cocktail and fag in hand, I jumped in the lift with a disbelieving Phil following. We got to the 38th floor where I looked over the manager's shoulder at his clipboard, discovering that Rod was in room 28. It was that easy. 'OK, let's go!'

We could hear the hair dryer. 'This is it. He is drying his hair in preparation for a night on the town,' I said to Phil, who was hiding behind me. I knocked on the door and it was answered by Rod himself. He wore nothing but leopard print jockettes and the hair dryer was in his hand. Was this really happening? 'Hi,' I said. 'Remember us?'

'Yep, put out your cigarettes and come in.' he said as he disappeared.

We couldn't believe our luck; we were invited into Rod's hotel room to have him all to ourselves.

When we entered, not only was there no Rod, but we found ourselves in the band room with the manager and band members, who were watching a video. The manager looked at us angrily. 'Do you guys make a habit of walking into people's bedrooms? 'What were you thinking, get out,' he yelled, as he physically backed us out of the hotel room into the foyer.

I wailed, professing my undying love for Rod. 'But you don't understand. We are friends of his. We had drinks with him before the show. We are friends of Doris Tyler who is good mates with Robin Le Measurer who is Rod's lead guitarist. Please just check with Rod. He'll tell you.'

The manager told us that if we wanted to see Rod we had to go down to the Lubritorium disco, just like everybody else. 'But I don't want to share him with everybody else. Pleeease!'

If I wasn't such a mess and if I hadn't been so hammered, we may have gone to the Lubritorium, but I couldn't have Rod see me like this, with my puffy eyes and make-up in a quagmire at the bottom of my chin.

It had been mentioned to me by Doris that Rod's modus operandi was to answer the door in jocks as, after the shows, he had girls sent to his room. Clearly, I wasn't his type; otherwise, I could have no doubt shagged him. I blamed Phil for that. Not that I would want to though; I had a spiritual connection with Rod. He was my soul mate. Sex would ruin all that.

In the foyer was a very old friend of mine – Shirley Strachan of Skyhooks fame. He knew my obsession with Rod, everyone who knew me did. He took one look at me and my wet face, hugged me and said, 'So, you met him.'

To this day, I bore people with that story, so why should you miss out? I must have told that tale at least a hundred times, and I will continue to tell it.

I went for a job once in Sydney at a childcare centre. Question: What has been your greatest achievement in life? I answered: Meeting Rod Stewart. The next question: What has been your biggest disappointment in life? I wrote: Not shagging him. I didn't get the job.

Every time Phil and I saw each other after that we would grin like Cheshire cats, high-fiving. 'We did it, Brownie,' he would drawl. 'We promised ourselves we would, and we did.'

Bucket list – tick.

If our relationship wasn't already set in cement, it certainly was now. We were in love with Rod, each other and life. We could now die happy.

Advertising – Take Three

Stopping advertising to save money is like stopping your watch to save time.

David Ogilvy

I went back to work when Greer was six months old. Financially, I had no choice. My husband was running his father's metal business from the pub. Our mums looked after Greer during the day. Picking her up was my job. We had both stopped coming home. He drank at his local; I drank at the office. Reliably, my ever-patient mum would get my call: 'Hi. I'm running late. Just got a deadline. Won't be long.' Then, much later, another call: 'Hi. Deadline been extended. Nearly there.' Then much, much later, slurring: 'Hi. Can you please keep her overnight?' Some mornings I woke up, head throbbing, having to ring both mums to see which one had her.

This lifestyle wore thin after a while, six years to be exact. I'm pretty sure the clincher was being nearly written off by a speeding car that landed on my roof while I was driving to work in my husband's company Peugeot. Both vehicles were towed away; I had no injuries but was in shock. I rang him to tell him what had happened, and he said, 'Oh fuck, no. How much damage did you do to the car?'

I didn't like him much after that, losing what little respect I had left for him. I could no longer call him a friend.

In hindsight, we were like the same person – immature, selfish, emotionally stunted due to our addictions and not vaguely interested in fixing our broken marriage.

We attempted a couple of unsuccessful reunions, one of which was our thirty-sixth birthday celebrations. I drank to black out or should I say brown out because I could vaguely remember some of it, including taking home a band member. The next day, hubby came to pick up Greer who said, 'Hi, Daddy. Last night, Mummy slept with the drummer.'

Upon reflection, I was so sure I needed to end my marriage. There were no ifs or buts. I believe the energy between us had run its course. He was like a stranger. I had stopped liking myself around him.

Carol King's song, 'It's too late baby' was playing over and over in my head at that time, …'it's too late baby, now it's too late, though we really did try to make it, something inside has died and I can't hide and I just can't fake it …' I believe endings are important as they make way for new beginnings. We both needed a new beginning. I would like to think that we, like Gwyneth Paltrow and Chris Martin, had a 'conscious un-coupling', our primary purpose being the welfare of our child.

He has been with his partner for over thirty years now. We are good friends today, and he has always been a fabulous dad. And there are absolutely no regrets there. From this union came my most cherished gem, Greer – my beautiful forgiving daughter. Everything happens for a reason. I will always love the father of my child.

I might add here that when I left her father, I believed that Greer, at five, was too young to involve on any level. How wrong I was. Not long after the divorce, when things were settling down, Greer said, 'Mum, why didn't you tell me you were leaving Dad? I should have been told. It's not just about you, you know. It's my life too.'

You could have knocked me down with a feather.

~

My ex-husband moved into a share house, and Greer and I shacked up with an old mate of mine, Dorothy, a wonderful, flamboyant gay man. Dorothy was a magnificent creature. This was more like marital bliss, and he became a father figure to Greer who he adored. Dorothy was a fashion guru and worked in the rag trade in Flinders Lane. He had a great group of mates who came for

Sunday barbecues. They were known as the 'Gay Young Bachelors', even though Dorothy was the only gay one, with the others being bachelors because they left their wives at home. Dorothy was unique and such a character. He liked to make an entrance the way Hollywood stars made exits. He would throw his head back and roar with glee. His was an operatic laugh. Holding his empty champagne flute high in the air, he would sing, 'my darlings, what is wrong with this picture?', always with a ciggie burning between two lacquered fingers, his hair perfectly styled and sprayed, his clothes immaculate and stylish. He smiled with his whole body – hips angled, his concave chest forward, lashes batting like stage curtains. Underneath that façade however, was a lonely soul. He would often venture into gay saunas looking for company and return home crying. My heart ached for him. He would have loved someone to share his life with.

In the meantime, he seemed so happy with Greer and I, we became his family.

Greer started school at Brighton Primary with her cousins. A fast learner, she fed and dressed herself, only ever asking me to plait her hair. She was resilient and fiercely independent from an early age. She had no choice considering my chaotic fuzzy mornings, trying to organise myself for work.

In a way, Greer was an enabler; she made life easy for me. She was never demanding, never complained and always had a smile on her face. She was inquisitive, delightfully curious and intuitive. I couldn't believe I was blessed with a child such as her.

However, as expected, Greer began to show signs of insecurity. She was craving my attention, as, even when I was with her, I wasn't present. I was physically there but mentally on another planet. Greer started sucking her thumb and dragging her doona into my bedroom, sleeping next to my bed. We called it her 'doggie'. She'd say, 'Mummy, can I be doggie tonight?'

I knew where this behaviour was coming from, but I wasn't ready to do the work required of me, so I allowed it. Never underestimate the power of denial. Greer needed a sibling. She needed someone to read to her at night. Granted, she was surrounded by love and in the constant company of her cousins, grandparents and friends, but she needed me, and I wasn't emotionally available to her. I wonder if those early insecurities ever went away. *God, give me the chance to do it over, knowing what I know now. It would be so different. Or would it?*

I was seeing a young writer, a work colleague. He, Dorothy and Greer got on famously, and he was a great distraction. The first time I met him, he was in his school uniform. His father was Yugoslavian, and I got on well with him, not so much his mother. She wasn't much older than me, and she referred to me as Mrs Robinson. She was horrified at our relationship as I was thirteen years older than her son and I was also a mother. 'Why her? Why her?' she would cry. You can't help whom you love. He was a sensitive soul, a deep thinker, intuitive, compassionate, a great writer and at times, hilarious.

He shouted us a trip to Port Douglas, sending my airline ticket to the office with a dozen red roses. There, we swam in water inhabited by crocs and stingers at Cape Tribulation, dined at fabulous restaurants and baked until we were chocolate brown. Another dreary couple from work joined us, and one night, bored with the conversation, I excused myself, announcing, 'I am bored. I am off to find some mental stimulation.'

At the Port Douglas pub, I got mixed up with a bunch of troppo locals and later found myself in a house with blankets for curtains and heroin needles sticking out of arms. In the wee hours of the morning, I decided to drive our hired dune buggy home, taking a local guy, Trevor, with me so he could show me the way. Trevor had been in a bar fight and had a busted-up face. It was torrential rain that night, and I don't know how we made it home alive, but, when we did get home, I realised I had no key. I threw stones at the window to wake my roomie. When he opened the door, Trevor and his smashed face fell on him. He looked at me with raised eyebrows, 'So this is your idea of mental stimulation?'

These were impressionable years for the young writer. It was his first relationship, and he grew up fast. I adored him, and he made me feel young and uninhibited. He wrote me beautiful love letters, which I still have. We shared a love of music including Dire Straits, Elton John and especially Jimmy Barnes. He had a smashing voice, and when he sang 'Khe Sanh', you would swear it was Jimmy himself.

Our work lunches together were predictably long and were followed by a short break back at the office before after-work bevvies kicked off. We were excellent drinkers. This looseness didn't affect his job as he was a brilliant writer and the agency needed him. Our affair lasted a long time considering the circumstances. We relished the decadent life and the illicitness of each other. However, we knew it had to end. Delusion must end. It finished when he and a mate of his travelled to Europe to live the life he was supposed to live. He left me at one of the worst times in my life.

New Beginnings

Every new beginning comes from some other beginning's end.

Seneca

One evening, a mutual friend of ours had invited Dorothy, myself and my male companion to dinner. I rang Dorothy to invite him. He simply said, 'no, thanks. I have other plans.'

We arrived home late, sozzled and stoned. I had forgotten my house key so knocked on the front door. There was no answer so I rang the doorbell. There was still no answer. Eventually the door opened and there stood a naked Dorothy. He threw his head back, chuckling, 'ha, it's you. Just in time to watch me die.' I scoffed, using my standard line 'stop being such a fucking old drama queen.'

Dorothy staggered down the hall to his bed. Concerned, I went and sat with him, stroking his hair. He was quiet and pale, his skin clammy. The house was silent; the air seemed brittle and empty, making it hard to breathe. Was he serious? Was he dying? I prayed for him; I prayed to be sober. I felt sick, nauseous …

I held him tightly. 'Dorothy, if you die, I will never speak to you again.'

No joking now. 'I've changed my mind. Help me. I don't want to die,' he whispered. He sounded panicked and was gripping my arm, trying to sit up. 'Look in the rubbish bin,' he whispered.

Shaking uncontrollably, I looked in the bin and found an empty bottle of quinine tablets and an empty bottle of bourbon. I screamed at my friend, 'call an ambulance now!'

We helped Dorothy out of bed, laying him in the hallway. His naked body was covered in purple blotches. I put a pillow under his head and covered him with a doona. My heart was beating so fast, adrenaline coursing through me. *'Please, God, help me keep it together. Please help me save this beautiful soul. Please don't let him die.'* My friend and I avoided eye contact. We were sober now.

Dorothy's breath was shallow so I began CPR, trying to stay calm, begging myself to remember. *CPR. I know it. Heel of hand on centre of chest. Go. Thirty compressions, two rescue breaths. Come on. You can do it. You can do it.* I kept at it even though I knew he was gone. I lay my head on his chest and cried. I cried for this beautiful soul, for the life that could have been, for my loss, for Greer's loss. I cried because we didn't know how to make him happy.

The ambulance came, shone a bright light in his face and told me there was nothing I could have done to save him. The police searched the house, asking accusatory questions. I was incredulous. I couldn't think; my body went into shock. I could feel my pulse racing but I was numb. My body was shuddering, and I could hear strange sobbing noises coming from way down deep inside.

The female policewoman took me aside to counsel me. 'Leave me the fuck alone,' I was screaming at her, out of my mind.

Was this just a bad dream? I couldn't believe my old mate was lying there in a body bag. I became hysterical when they carried him out. We both lay there for what was left of the night staring at the ceiling. *Why? Why?* My mind was spinning. How was I going to tell our friends and his mum, dad and sister?

I started drinking early the next morning and didn't stop for a month. Mum took Greer, now six years old, away from me. When Greer did come home, she asked where Dorothy was. I didn't know what to say to her. I didn't want to tell her how he died. I was heartbroken for her. How was she supposed to process this information? How could she possibly understand how someone who has been in her life every day was now no longer? Another father figure gone. I didn't know how to help her. I was so utterly self-absorbed, full of self-pity, blaming myself for his suicide and playing the victim. I spent my days wagging work, drinking bottle after bottle of 'guilt be gone'.

I thought back to my baby sister's death, which happened when I was the same age as Greer was then, and remembering the lack of support from my folks. I was left to process that tragedy on my own. As much as I tried to not be like them, here I was doing the same.

I found functioning in any form difficult. I couldn't understand why life went on as usual, why the sun still rose and set. Why didn't my boss understand why I couldn't come to work? Why was everyone telling me to stop drinking and to move on? How? I didn't know how? My heart felt like it was stuck in a vice. The grief was overwhelming.

Greer and I missed Dorothy so much. One night he came back to visit. And here's what happened. Greer and I were in the lounge room engrossed in the TV which was showing Cher in that cannon clip singing 'If I Could Turn Back Time', when we heard the kettle whistle. At the same time, Dorothy's pet kitten, which was sitting in the same place she sat every night just minus Dorothy's lap, jumped high in the air, wetting herself. But the *pièce de résistance* was yet to come. That night, when I went to bed, there on my bedside table were Dorothy's 18-carat gold and diamond studs. The ones I had asked him for in his will. Crazy but true.

To deal with Dorothy's death, I needed to find something to take away the pain. My ex-hubby suggested I learn transcendental meditation from the same person he learnt it from. Having grasped this transformational technique, I rose at five a.m., sitting quietly and meditating for an hour each day. I didn't think my scrambled brain was capable of reaching these euphoric levels of nothingness, but it did. I was transcending thought. I stopped drinking during this time to have a clear mind. Of course, like everything else, it didn't last. Having said that though, I have never forgotten how to meditate this way, and I can always fall back on it. It is a unique way of finding the egoless consciousness.

I found a new flatmate, an old friend of ours who was newly divorced. He was unpacking in Dorothy's old room when Greer said, 'By the way, there's a ghost in here.'

He replied, 'That's good. I could use the company.'

At this time, my wonderful sister was taking her two children and Greer home from school for dinner while she waited for me to collect my daughter. Inevitably, I would arrive late and half lit, my excuses for my tardiness were ridiculous and my lies were transparent. I wonder how my sister ever put up with my predictability.

On one of these nights, after an extremely long lunch, I sighted a booze bus in North Road, opposite our street. I was gesturing out the window to the policewoman pointing to our street, mouthing, 'I just live there.' She was mouthing and pointing, 'pull in here.' This continued for quite some time when I heard a little voice from the back, 'I think you're a goner, Mum.' They let Greer blow into the machine, watching it light up. She blew zero; I almost blew it up. Yes, I know what you're thinking. How did I justify drinking and driving with my child in the car? And my answer would be: alcohol – powerful, baffling and cunning.

That time I lost my licence for one year and was sent to 'drunk school'. Drunk school is great, rather than a deterrent, it introduced me to a whole lot of cool people to drink with. Sadly, that didn't stop me driving but I did practice caution at all times. Ha. Not long after getting my licence back, I had another DUI, and losing it for two years

The truth is I have always been of the opinion that I drove better drunk. My mind was more alert, and my judgement and reflexes more accurate. One Sunday morning, I looked out to see a huge dint along the side of my car, exclaiming 'What the hell happened to my car?'

Greer answered, 'Don't you remember running into the lamp post, Mummy?'

All of us drunks are potential murderers. The car we're driving is a two-tonne bomb. That ignition key in our pocket is a concealed weapon. We are a disgrace.

The Next 20 Years

You can never get enough of what you don't want.

Wayne Dyer

In 1988, not long after Dorothy died, I met the man I would spend the next twenty years with. I will call him Greg. We had known each other for years from old Torquay days and through mutual mates. This reeked of synchronicity in the manner defined by Carl Jung as 'an acausal connecting principle'. And here's why. Greg and my ex-husband once shared a house on Phillip Island, Greg worked at his parents' pub, The Beach Hotel, where my ex played pool nightly, his brother was a good friend of my ex-husband's and was a contender for best man at our wedding and his sister, Gen, was the barmaid at his local. After waiting for hubby for hours, I would ring the pub. Gen would yell out, 'Sue's on the phone', whereby he would yell, 'tell her I've just left'.

When in Torquay, hubby and I caught up with Greg for a few cleansing ales. He was still with his wife then. We also ran into him at a friend's funeral in Torquay. He looked me up and down and said 'So, when's the baby due?'

I was mortified; Greer was three months old. That night, after the wake, my husband was too drunk to walk so Greg and I carried him back to the camp, through paddocks and over wire fences. We dropped him a couple of times which amused us greatly. Next day, hubby couldn't work out why he was covered in cuts. On arriving home that same night, my angry mum handed me a screaming, hungry baby. I'd forgotten I was breast-feeding and hadn't noticed my milk-soaked blouse.

After my divorce, I ran into Greg at a party. I found him to be amusing, entertaining and like no one I had ever known. He seemed like a multi-layered soul, confident, bereft of an iota of self-consciousness, and bursting with bravado. I was yet to learn that this was a cover for his many insecurities, none of which I ever understood. He was an enigma. Feral looking with long hair, a beard and a ruddy complexion, Greg was most unlike the classic good lookers I was used to. He did, however, have a lovely smile and an unmistakable twinkle in his eye. After the party, Greg insisted on walking me back to the camp. *How chivalrous*, I mused. He had stirred my interest. The next day, Greg turned up to the camp on his pushbike with a box of beer strapped to it, which Dad, Greg and I murdered, while chewing the fat. I asked Dad what he thought of Greg. He said, 'He had me at slab.'

I enjoyed Greg's brutal honesty and filter-less dry sense of humour. He felt like home.

Greg drove a tractor with a post-hole digger attached to it which he used to build fences on local farms. He was also a mature-age law student and barman at the Torquay Golf Club. Our first date was New Year's Eve. He picked me up on his tractor, and I remember noticing he was super chuffed introducing me to his friends. 'Punching above ya weight there aren't ya, Brownie?' his best mate laughed. Yes, coincidentally, we had the same sir names.

This best mate of his was a wealthy real estate mogul and a larrikin. He was up for anything and everything. One night he and Brownie took his pick up truck, along with a rifle and a bottle of bourbon out to the back of Bells Beach and ripped off a plantation of marijuana, filling twenty large garbage bags of dope which they sold, making a lot of money. Much later we discovered this mull belonged to our landlord, who told us this story over and over. We feigned sympathy but we never confessed.

I was working in Melbourne and spending every weekend at Greg's. I was leaving work earlier every Friday and arriving later every Monday, and it wasn't going over too well with the boss. It came to a crunch when I arrived at work late one Monday, dressed in trackies and ugg boots, my eyes hanging out of my head. 'Oh dear,' said my boss. 'Take a look at you. Bongs, thongs and sarongs.'

After six months of this, I decided it was time to move, making the sea change with the man of my dreams. *Well, Greg would do for now*, I thought. He's another father figure for my daughter, and that means less responsibility for me. He was a good reason to get out of Melbourne, as was the fact that I had no driver's licence.

For the first time in my working career, I got to resign from a job. It felt good. My work mates were sad to see me go. There were shouts of 'Who will sexually harass us now?' 'Whose boobs will we look at?' 'Who will be our social secretary?' and 'Who will put stiletto holes in the boardroom table?'

The going away party was memorable. I chose to dress subtly, wearing a black leather miniskirt, lacy camisole, leopard print fur bolero, over-the-knee black leather follow-me-fuck-me boots and fish net stockings. I was presented with the most beautiful bright pink mountain bike, complete with a wire basket, which, they informed me, was 'the perfect size for a box of wine'. I decided to test ride my new bike, slamming straight into a plate glass wall and knocking myself out.

The seaside change was a relatively easy decision to make, although I had a feeling I was running, hiding in plain sight. *What am I doing? Am I listening to my inner self or am I taking the easy way out? Am I thinking about what's best for Greer?* The anticipation of moving to 'toxic Torquay', the party town where nobody had a job, cheered me up somewhat. And this was where I had spent a huge part of my life. It was like going home.

I was anxious. Small towns were insular and claustrophobic. Greg was not long separated from his 'left-over-hippy-from-the-sixties' wife. We moved into his house, which was a perfectly acceptable beach house. Did I mention that he had three children and a dog? Maybe I hadn't thought this through! Yes, six- and five-year-old girls, thirteen months apart, and a three-year-old boy. Zimzalabim, I am now a mother of one, a stepmother of three, a wife and a dog owner. *What was I thinking?*

With some money left to me, we built a large two-storey extension and I got to work decorating. Like my mother before me, it seemed I had a skill for interior design. My colour scheme was dark chartreuse and teal, coordinating with my one piece of furniture – a vintage lounge suite that was a wedding gift from my aunty. I then chose pink vertical blinds to match. If I walked into that room now, I would vomit.

I created a haven in our bedroom, which, over the years, would become my isolation cell. Greer was happy. She now had three siblings to play with, a dog and a new stepdad. And more importantly, my guilt regarding not giving her a sibling of her own, was relieved somewhat, and I'll drink to that.

We threw all-day barbecues that continued into the night, our kids' staple diet being sausages and tomato sauce in white bread. The eclectic group of neighbours included the heroin addicts, the muso lesbian couple and their five sons, our old mate Pup, who was a joint rolling machine, the local tradies and a plethora or total strangers who would hear the music and come to check us out. They were fabulous days.

The whole Brady Bunch scenario I had found myself in daunted me. Don't get me wrong, his children were great. We had them every second weekend and Tuesday nights, when Greg would cook roast lamb with crispy double-cooked spuds.

Following their weekend visits, I would receive phone calls from his ex, saying 'Do you know where Jimmy's other sock is? I am sick of only getting one sock back. I just bought them!'

'Seriously, was Jimmy here?'

The three girls and I had so much fun, dressing up in my wedding dress, hats and feather boas, jumping from couches to tables and singing loudly to the movie *Dirty Dancing*, playing air guitar with broomsticks. I was unlike anyone they had met and the absolute opposite of their straight, psychologist mother.

They loved spending time at the camp, beaching all day and eating fish and chips on the hill. Greg was a wonderful father, and as the four children got older, they relied heavily on his honesty, knowledge and advice. He was the one they turned to. He was a good friend to them all and was also the one who solved the problem of Greer's insecurities and her need to be a 'doggie'. He sat with her at sleep time, soothing her and making sure she felt safe. I was most grateful. When asked, Greg claimed he had four children.

The three girls went to Matthew Flinders Girls High School in Geelong. When Greg's girls were teenagers, they moved in with us for a time. I became the ugly stepmother, my zero coping skills adding to the turmoil and chaos that was our house.

Putting aside the dysfunctionality of our house, we did have some good times. As the kids got older, their friends used it as an escape. They had free rein at our place, meaning unsupervised freedom. Many a time we would come home to find our garage full of smoke and under-age kids whooping it up, drinking our booze and smoking our dope. They were smart kids. Upon my arrival, I would hear, 'Hi, Sooz, I've just packed you a bong.'

Predictably, Greer started playing up. She went from being captain of her class to refusing to wear the red jumper of the uniform, which she coupled with a penchant for odd socks, also not acceptable. This saw her prestigious position terminated. I was called to the head mistress's office several times, always dressing in full animal print.

Years later, Greer informed me of the many times she wagged school, hanging in the mall in Geelong, smoking with her Torquay mates, not to mention the under-age drinking with her step-sisters and friends. Surprise surprise to all of it. What would I expect I wonder. Fortunately, she could never smoke dope as it made her paranoid. What a blessing! Because it was still a relatively small town then and everyone knew everyone, it was a common occurrence that Greer and her friends would run unto us at the same parties. 'Where's Greer' I would ask her mates? 'She's over there rolling joints,' was the answer. Even though she didn't smoke them, she rolled a mean joint and she pumped them out like a machine.

One Tuesday, my ladies competition tennis day, I got a call from Geelong police. 'Hello, Mrs Browne. I have your daughter here. Would you please come and pick her up?'

When we got there, Greer, in the supervision of the head of police, looked at me in my tennis frock and, with a big grin, said 'Hi, Mum. Did you win?'

She and her schoolmates had stolen a significant amount of clothing. I was impressed. They were fined and put on a good behaviour bond. Apparently, one of them had put two pairs of jeans under her tunic and walked out of the shop! Disappointed, I said to her, 'Greer, if you are going to shoplift, don't do it with idiots.'

To be honest, I was proud of my inquisitive, curious, risk-taking daughter who despised mediocrity. I wonder if she had grown up in the city, would she be different? In Torquay she was surrounded by surfers, hippies and freethinking, alternate peeps. She and her stepsiblings were offered freedom and independence from an early age. They were encouraged to pursue their dreams, whatever they may be.

Note: our four children have achieved amazing things in their lives and have successful careers, in spite of us, or because of us? We will never know?

I also encouraged Greer to enjoy new experiences, under the supervision of adults to be safe, and that is a flat out lie, as I really just wanted her to do them with me.

I waited until she was the same age as I was when I took LSD before I suggested she did. She thought that was a great idea, so with a couple of the loco locals in tow, we had one of the most hilarious nights ever. Greer loved the experience, following me around, licking my face. We were crippled with laughter. I figured we should eat, so I put some sausages in a pan. We were all screaming, grabbing onto each other, buckled over, tears streaming, as we watched the sausages talking to us, their heads with eyes and mouths hanging over the side of the pan.

What was I thinking?

Greg's wife had a problem with child support or should I say, lack thereof. I was sensing a criminal element in my new boyfriend's personality, but like everything, I looked the other way.

I woke early one morning; my head throbbing and my mouth dry, to someone screaming outside my window. I gazed out through the black slimline blinds and saw the ex-wife's Volvo out the front of our house. She was yelling, 'How do you two sleep at night? Look at this house! Where did the money come from? You don't even feed your children!' Seeing red, I jumped straight out of bed, filled a bucket with water, ran outside and threw it over her head. Soaking wet, she jumped into her car. Deciding I wanted to strangle her, I put my hands in the window when she promptly pressed the automatic lock, jamming my arm as she slowly drove off. What I didn't realise, and was later informed of by one of our gawking neighbours, was that I'd forgotten to put undies on, and there, for all to see, was my bare bum.

~

This carefree lifestyle was wearing a tad thin. I was becoming feral, bored and fat. Trying to ignore the morning tremors, I knew I needed a change. I was a thirty-seven-year-old woman living in a sensational state of denial. My all-or-nothing sense of self and my obsessive-compulsive disorder came to the fore. I swore off alcohol, marijuana, cigarettes, food and partying. I became vegan, learned how to cook Ayurvedic food, went to aerobics five mornings a week and did beach walks, yoga, meditation, aqua aerobics, bike riding and step classes. Suffice to say, this didn't last.

Greg decided to join our step classes. He was the only bloke and an un-coordinated one at that. When she said 'step right', he would step left, sometimes off the side of the box. So entertaining.

Brownies Café

These brownies are better than sex.

Local customer

I had to find something to do with myself. Considering I could cook, Greg and I decided to buy a café, and because we had the same surname, we called it Brownies. With a solid local following, we did an excellent breakfast and lunch trade. Most popular was my home-made meatloaf and chutney sandwiches on fresh sourdough bread and our signature brownies were out of this world. We had a BYO licence, and Friday and Saturday nights the camping area crew would book the place out. Being hidden away in an arcade meant our all-night parties and illegal shenanigans went largely undetected. We served Mexican cuisine, and once when the beans were in the pressure cooker, the lid flew off and the beans exploded onto my forehead. For ages I had small burn holes across my hairline. My new nickname – Mrs. Bean!

One year the Torquay pub held its Christmas party at Brownies. It was fancy dress, the theme being Roman Empire. There were many togas made of sheets, home-made crowns of thorns on heads, sashes and thongs. There were buckets of jello shots being drunk and joints being passed around. We couldn't see for cigarette smoke. During the night it began to rain torrentially, and the water streamed in under the gap in our door, causing a quagmire of slime and mud. People were falling over, sliding across the floor, slamming into each other. The potent toxic jello shots were causing people to throw up, adding to the quagmire. At five a.m. the cops arrived and closed us down. I will never forget watching the crew wandering down the main street, arm in arm, as the sun was beginning to rise, covered in mud, sheets ripped, body parts exposed, and destroyed crowns of thorns hanging over their faces. That party was talked about for a very long time.

Greg's and my relationship was a volatile one, exacerbated by our substance abuse. We had outrageous fights. During one such quarrel, I stabbed Greg's hand with a fork. The new chef looked on in horror as he watched blood spurting from the four holes in Greg's hand. Greg snickered like a crazy person. I was worried about his mental health. Our tiffs were comical, quick witted, sharp, aggressive and scathing. Greg felt we should charge extra for the entertainment. We were both fiery characters with a need to have control; we were in constant competition. We loved each other as much as we hated each other. Our saving grace was that we both knew how to entertain. We were excellent hosts – the food was awesome and no one ever waited for a refill.

We broke every occupational health and safety rule and responsible service of alcohol law and got away with it. My obsession with country music saw me frequenting the table top, belting out Brenda Lee and Connie Francis tunes including favourites *Who's Sorry Now* and *Everybody's Somebody's Fool*. All the while, Greg was throwing things at me, yelling 'Shut the fuck up!' and 'Get that shit off.'

Our fights had become unbearable. I decided I couldn't live with him and his psychological abuse anymore, so I moved into Mum's caravan. I hated leaving my daughter, but if I had stayed, I would have killed him, and I'm not joking. Greer was worried so rang my mum, telling her 'Mum's moved out. She's living in your caravan.' Mum arrived, so worried about me she was white-faced. 'How can you do this to Greer? Your roles are reversed – she's like the concerned mother and you're the naughty child. Pull yourself together and go home.' I was traumatised. I thought about moving Greer and I back to Melbourne, but where would we live? What would we do for money? I was a co-dependent addict. I couldn't think straight. I didn't have the strength or the guts to take action.

After two and a half years, disillusioned and exhausted, we sold Brownies.

~

Greg and I decided we needed a holiday to reset our flailing relationship, so we took Jimmy, six, and Greer, seven, out of school. In Greg's beaten-up old green Falcon, with no set plan and no set direction, we headed up the east coast. When we got to Iluka, we stopped to say g'day to an old mate of ours, Dogga, who had mentioned his brother had a vacant flat if we wanted to spend a night. We stayed six weeks.

A petite fishing village, the South Pacific Ocean on one side and the Clarence River on the other, surround Iluka, and life there revolves around the water. We fell in love with the place. Across the river is Yamba, which has a notorious surf break and an outstanding pub overlooking one of the best beaches in Australia.

Greg began to surf again for the first time in many years, and he and Dog went out every morning at 6 a.m.

We had picnics on the river, eating fresh prawns in white bread rolls and drinking icy-cold XXXX stubbies. We fished off the rocks, the delicious fresh flathead tails were on our plates an hour after catching them. Dog had homing pigeons in the backyard, and the kids were fascinated watching them coming in on time. The neighbours were all ragers, hence some crazy street parties. Their kids were the same age as ours and they all got on famously.

I made sure the kids did daily schoolwork and journalling. Interestingly, when they returned to school, they were scholastically ahead of the others. Travelling is an education in itself.

We frequented the Iluka Bowlo – and the golf club, both with pool tables, a TAB and pokies. We got to know the locals and eventually our movements and speech slowed down to a snail's pace along with the rest of the town

I imagined this was a bonding time for the family. We were all so happy being away from the grind. Alas, it was a mere band-aid. We were still the same people with the same addictions. 'Geographicals' never work.

We drove to Noosa to catch up with sis and family who were holidaying there. They offered us a bed but eventually asked us to leave, as they couldn't deal with our fights and out-of-control behaviour.

Jimmy and Greer seemed oblivious to our toxic relationship. They talked about our three-month trip away for a very long time.

~

When we returned, in an attempt to be a 'normal' mother, I volunteered at the school canteen, which thrilled Greer. I also read to her class once a week. I set aside a day to do some cooking for the family, and I even made Greer's lunch the night before, excitedly filling the lunch box sections with yummy treats. *I quite enjoy being a normal housewife and mother*, I mused.

On the outside we looked like an involved, responsible semi-nuclear family. The delusion was alive and well.

I enrolled Greer in the Torquay Calisthenics Club. I sequinned her eight leotards as well as the mayor's daughter's eight leotards. I was also the club's make-up artist, applying ghastly paint to those pretty little faces until they were barely recognisable. Greer was a natural, athletic and strikingly pretty, hence, front of stage.

We travelled throughout Victoria on the Eisteddfod trail, frequenting Ballarat, the headquarters, and staying in tacky motels. This was a wonderful way to bond with Greer, and we had a lot of fun. It was also a perfect opportunity to be sober, focusing entirely on my daughter and the concerts. However, the days were long, with thirteen sets of clubs, thirteen sets of rods, marches, and freestyle and on and on and on. After a while, I realised I couldn't do this sober. On arrival at our destination, I would find the nearest pub, down a few bevvies and fill my hipflask, after which I thoroughly enjoyed the eight-hour days, clapping and whistling madly.

We continued with calisthenics for six years. Greer loved it, and that was what was important. Much later, one of Greer's friends, drinking at my bar, said 'Hey, Sooz, you know we were all aware you were drinking through the Eisteddfods. We could smell it on you!' Bitch.

This same girl's mum and I volunteered to accompany the grades three and four on their school camp to Mildura. On the first night, there was a disco. The teachers stayed sober while we, being the mums and also the judges, drank wine, way too much wine. At one point, I jumped on a very high speaker and was belting out my signature tune *If I Could Turn Back Time* when everything went black, as my highly embarrassed eight-year-old daughter threw a blanket over my head.

That night, I snuck into the room of the cute Greek bus driver where we made out and then swam naked in the hotel pool, doing vodka shots and reefers. I spent the bus trip home throwing up in a bucket. The teachers were horrified; the kids were amused. I was summoned to the principal's office and reprimanded. He kept asking, 'What were you thinking?'

'Clearly I wasn't thinking,' I scoffed.

Not only was I banned from school camps but so was alcohol. The school mums have cursed me ever since.

~

At this time, needing something to do with ourselves, a friend and I decided to put our undeniable culinary skills to use and unenthusiastically began a catering company, therefore calling it The Reluctant Catering Company. We were good at what we did and, as such, became annoyingly popular. We travelled down the coast, catering for dinner parties for the rich and famous. On one of these occasions, cooking on-site, we were told to help ourselves to the wine. Big mistake. I was cooking a whole snapper, Thai style, on the outside barbecue, and because there was no light, not only was I unaware of how much wine I was consuming but I also burned the fish. At one point, an attractive woman in a flowing Camilla gown, was spotted fossicking through the fridges, whereupon we heard 'Gaaawsh. Does anyone know where the chaaaardonnay is, daaahlings? I can't seem to find the whaaat whaaan. Harooold, where have you hidden the whaaat whaaaan?'

After six months, due to being too popular and not wanting to work that hard, we dissolved the Reluctant Catering Company.

This girl in question and I have shared many hilarious times and side-splitting laughs and she is still one of my very best friends to this day. She has stood by me throughout, helping me move from one house to another, scrubbing clean every surface, including the oven. She has buffed me out when needed, her generosity is next level.

She and I shared not only a love of cooking, but also a wildly enthusiastic passion for country music. We belted out those songs at every opportunity – Shania Twain, Lucinda Williams, Trisha Yearwood, the Dixie Chicks (whose concerts we never missed) and our favourite, Kasey Chambers. We saw Kasey live several times, including once at the Bell Post Sportsman's Club, where I found her doing her make-up in the public toilets because the light in her dressing room had blown. I couldn't believe my luck. I left my toilet door open while I wee'd, chatting to her like she was a long-lost friend. She's such a cool chick. She gave me a big solid hug before she left.

At another of Kasey's concerts, this time at the Palais Theatre in St Kilda, I spotted Bill Chambers, her dad and fellow band member, in the foyer. I took a running leap, jumped on him, wrapping my legs around his waist and my arms around his neck, singing, 'Am I not pretty enough'.

'Gee you sound just like my daughter,' he quipped, trying to peel me off him.

In 2000, we saw Kasey again, at The Tamworth Country Musical Festival. My sister, my daughter, my niece and I spent the week dressed as cowgirls, changing our names to Tammy, Sheralynn, Emmie-Lou and Sue-Ann. We threw back freezing cold beers while boot scooting in forty-degree heat and belly laughing. At one point, I looked across the pub to see two burly cowboys holding my sister sideways above their heads. 'So, this is how you get picked up in Tamworth,' she scoffed.

Machello's

Pizza makes me think that anything is possible.

Henry Rollins

A popular pizza and pasta joint on Geelong Road came up for sale and Greg and I decided to buy it. It had an open kitchen and needing to look my best for our regular surf industry VIP's, I cooked in high heels and full make-up with big hair. Greg suggested I wear a hair net. You can imagine how that went down.

I made life as complicated as possible, and much to Greg's annoyance, produced a ridiculously extensive menu. For some stupid reason, I included two different types of stuffed chicken breast – mushroom and creamy avocado. To look at them, you couldn't tell them apart. One evening, in a packed house, Greg was waiting on tables and I heard him say very loudly, 'What? You don't like avocado?' When I looked out, I saw him and the woman who had received the avocado sauce instead of the mushroom sauce, looking at my sweaty red face and the smoke coming out of my ears. The next thing I heard was the woman saying, 'Yes, of course I like avocado. Who doesn't like avocado?'

We became well known for our delicious gourmet pizzas, and we sold hundreds of them. Our best seller was 'The Torquay Tantaliser' – marinated chicken, mango chutney, red onion, cashews and topped with tzatziki.

One Easter Saturday night, the restaurant packed with VIPs, I was called over to one of the tables. Instead of the compliment I was expecting on my delicious homemade minestrone soup, to my horror, I looked up to see Kelly Slater holding his fork in the air –

with a clump of my hair dangling from it. *Oh my God, please kill me.* Everyone was staring, so with a burning face, I said 'Well, just think yourselves lucky it wasn't my pubic hair!'

Like Brownies, this, too, was a place of ill repute. I watched two local sisters, who had recently given birth, standing on a table, squirting our patrons with breast milk. Frankie J. Holden was a regular there. He thought it was the best place and relished the all-night shenanigans. It was a popular hang, and the food was delicious and included barbecued Greek platters with oven baked garlic, herb and pesto breads. One night at 3 a.m. the police rang our home, informing us we had locked a customer in the toilet, and asking us to go let her out.

I put myself under so much pressure. As a result, the fights between Greg and I became worse. I was throwing a lot of pots and pans. Greg became excellent at ducking, as did the staff.

I began noticing a severe disconnect from others, like I was watching my life from afar. My self-destructive nature was overwhelming. I felt depressed and anxious. I was living a little too low or a little too high.

My self-obsession was epic. My deep-rooted core beliefs and values were being bulldozed by the booze. I knew underneath I was a good, kind, loving soul but there was none of that on display. I was flailing.

I was emotionally and physically unavailable to my daughter. She was suffering psychological abuse from both of us. We had forgotten what was important; life had become predictable and excruciating. It was drink, drug, hangover, recover, squirm, rinse and repeat.

Booze was the anaesthetic for my ever-present anxiety. My capacity to recall was failing. My memory was jumping back and forwards like an illegal CD. It was a miracle we were able to manage a business, and a successful one at that. Thank God for our personalities.

My mother was disappointed in me. She suggested she should take Greer to live with her. 'She would be better off with me than living with a couple of drunks,' she sobbed. 'You don't deserve her.' I concurred.

I began to notice that my family had zero sympathy for me. *Oh dear, I'm so sorry you have this terrible addiction and that you are faced with so many challenges. You poor thing. Is there anything I can do to help?* No siree, Bob. It was more like 'Stop this nonsense now! Take responsibility for your life, and hold yourself accountable, for fuck's sake!'

To meet my beautiful, well-adjusted, enthusiastic, delightful, loving, pro-active and compassionate daughter today, you would never detect any signs of the insecurities she no doubt suffered. Most intuitive through it all, from an early age, Greer would say, 'It's just you and me, Mum. There's no one else. We need to stick together through this life.'

Of course, she was right. Life was so impermanent, and people were so transient. But, because I didn't feel worthy of her, I discouraged these thoughts and, like everything else, swept them under the carpet.

~

I wasn't looking for an affair, but one crept up on me in the form of a much younger man – a leather-clad Hells Angel with a ponytail. It was lust at first sight, and before long, we were shagging on the back of his Harley Davidson. Bucket list, tick.

My unhappily married girlfriend decided that two could play at this game, so she shagged his Spanish mate. She said it was the best sex she'd ever had. 'And guess what? He came in Spanish!'

My affair continued for twelve months. Once a week I headed to Melbourne under the pretence of participating in an arts course at TAFE. Lies, lies, lies. Guilt, guilt, guilt.

I suddenly felt alive again, young, pretty and funny. The affair was such a wonderful diversion from my horrid, dysfunctional life. We dined out, clubbed and bar hopped, zipping around the city on his Harley. Our nights were sensational, but the mornings were horrendous. Waking up with the tequila hangover, the reality of the inappropriateness would hit me like a brick to the head. The guilt was overwhelming.

One of these mornings, I woke to a woman screaming at my lover. I grabbed my clothes and jumped into the wardrobe in his room. Yes, I know what you're thinking. Yet again, I find myself naked in a closet because of a forbidden affair. 'I know you're fucking that Torquay slut!' she screamed.

How offensive, I thought from the cupboard. More offensive, though, was that he had neglected to inform me that he was in a committed relationship with a girl called Mary. What is it with these cowardice men?

Eventually Greg worked out whom I was seeing, as he had met this guy at the Torquay Pub one night. I had put Dolly Parton's *I Will Always Love You* on the jukebox and sang loudly and directly to my lover, making sure a furious Greg was watching.

Greg did some investigating and caught me out. I came home to a very sad, broken man who begged me to stop. And I did, for a while, but this boy was hard to let go of. Greg would be off chops, raving like a crazy person, following me around the house, tormenting me, begging to know what I did with my lover in the bedroom, he wanted to know all the sordid details. He was a sad broken man. And I was a sad broken woman seeing what I was doing to him.

Looking back, it is beyond all comprehension how I made my life so excruciatingly complicated, how I hurt so many people the way I did, how the booze caused me to make such poor decisions and what a manipulator I had become.

Our Machello's experience ended sadly. Due to our 'feed the bastards' and 'shout the bastards' mindsets, combined with our penchant for poker machines, which we had put a couple of houses through, we were broke and couldn't pay the rent. We ignored our landlord's threats, like we ignored everything else including our lives being in the gutter. We were escorted out of there by a mate of ours who was a police officer. We took what little belonged to us, and continued drinking to obliterate, numbing the truth. It was over. Everything was over. I didn't think things could get any worse but they did.

How Could This Possibly Happen?

... why did I miss a round?

Dick Browne

In 1994, I was at work and the phone rang. It was Mum, sobbing, 'Dad has stage 4 inoperable lung cancer.'

I thought I'd misheard her. It felt like the walls were crumbling down around me. I thought my gut was going to explode. How can this be? Not my dad; he was impermeable. I didn't think this happened to people like us. I felt such pity for Mum. She was shattered, 'how do I tell dad he's dying,' she cried, 'How do you tell your husband of forty-five years that he won't see his grandchildren grow up?'

Dad was in The Alfred Hospital initially. The view from his hospital bed was of his old school, Wesley College, and the toilet block where he first started smoking Alpine cigarettes at the age of twelve. Clearly, this was not a reminder he needed. He was desperate to get out. 'Sooz,' he said, 'You need to get me out of here. I can't stand looking at that toilet block where this all began. I need to go to the camp; I want to die in the camp. Say something to the doctors, please. I'm begging you.'

I felt volcanic sadness to the core of my being.

The doctors were doubtful about Dad moving to the camp, claiming it was unprecedented. However, they eventually signed the necessary forms, having been reassured by my sister, a triple certificate nurse, that he would be in good hands.

Dad was transferred by ambulance to the camp with his oxygen machine. He was happy being in his most beloved place. He went to sleep at night listening to the waves breaking on 'his' beach, and we wheeled him down to the shore daily so he could look at the surf, and sit in the sun.

Because I was working, I didn't get to see him much so, in the middle of the night, I would sneak into the annex, making myself a bed on the floor, close to him. He woke to the smell of stale beer, giving me a weak smile, and in his private school voice, he'd say 'Oh darling, how lovely to see you, but could you please get off my oxygen tube?'

On New Year's Eve, my sis, Mum and I sat on his bed watching the fireworks. He smiled through tears and said, 'I've had a good life, haven't I, girls?' There were no words.

One sunny day in the camp, surrounded by gum trees, the sound of birdsong and waves crashing, watching the Sydney to Hobart yacht race on telly, Dad looked at me with sad eyes, removed his oxygen mask, and said 'To think I was there once, Sooz. Now look at me.'

I reassured him, 'At least you were there, Dad. Not many can own that claim to fame.

Never losing his sense of humour, he would reliably pass around his urine bottle, asking 'Anyone want a top up?'

You would hear shouts of 'Oil 'ave one.'

On 26 January 1995, I received a call from my sister saying Dad was on his way out. We had been hammering it for Greg's forty-fifth birthday, and I was most unwell. 'How typical,' I said to Greg. 'I can't attend my father's death bed until I stop throwing up.'

When I arrived, Dad was at the Cheyne-Stokes stage. We sat on his bed, holding his hands and feet. Mum, my sister, Blacky and Helen, Dad's four grandchildren and I were there. Greer was eight.

The pain was overwhelming, seeing this proud man in such a vulnerable, helpless state. My dad, my hero, was leaving us. I felt nauseous, a foul taste of anxiety lurking, my hands were shaking, sweat was pouring from my face, as I was trying desperately to keep it together in the stifling annex. *Is this really happening?*

While holding Dad's hand, memories came and went, such as Dad teaching me how to roller-skate. I fell a lot, grazing my knees and bruising my bum, so he strapped a cushion to my bottom and bandages to my knees, holding tightly onto my hand as we circled the block. I adored my time with him. To my mother's irritation, he always had my back. Whenever I doubted or underestimated myself, he would stress, 'Sue, you have to believe that you are number one. If you don't, nothing will ever happen for you'. (Where mum would chime in, 'oh stop it Dick, you'll give her an even bigger head!') Memories of Dad's love of gardening and his cubbyhouse under a large willow tree in the front yard, where he had a table, chair, ciggies, ashtray, a big bottle of beer and the racing form guide, a 'do not disturb' plaque stuck to the tree. It was his haven; he called it 'Richard's Retreat'.

And when sis and I hurt ourselves, Dad would hold us tightly while we sobbed, saying 'Don't cry. It only hurts for a little while'.

I thought about dad relaxing on his lounge in the camp, reading the newspaper, his big brown beer belly prominent. I would ask, 'So what are your plans today, Dad?' He would answer 'not sure yet darl, I'm just waiting for my instructions from the war office', (i.e. mum). And when he retired and relocated to the camp, on Sundays, at about 5 o'clock when everyone was heading back to Melbourne, he would grin and say, 'oh dear, I do feel sorry for the day-trippers'!

I was remembering his morning routine, sitting at his desk smoking a ciggie, a cup of Nescafé on the drink coaster, and a copy of the Age spread out in front of him. He was such a creature of habit. When it was time to go to the office he would stand up and recite, 'comb', as he patted his top pocket, 'wallet,' as he patted his bottom pocket, 'hanky', as he patted his pant pocket, then he would take one last puff and stub out his ciggie, while sculling the last mouthful of coffee, and letting out a big sigh he would say, 'well Sooz, another day another dollar'. And he would be gone. I loved watching him.

The inky smell of newspaper, ciggie smoke and Nescafé will forever remind me of dad.

Dad was a devoted insurance salesman, and he had a plethora of satisfied clients as he treated them like family, personally calling them on their birthdays, which were noted in his shoe-boxes. He not only sold them insurance, he took an interest in their lives and the lives of their children. On several occasions he won AMP Victorian Salesman of the Year. He was one of a kind.

My thoughts returned to the time when mum and dad renovated our house, turning it into two units and taking in a border, Christopher, who asked me if it would be OK to plant some marijuana in our garden. I said OK, as long as the oldies don't find out. One day I was watching dad watering the garden, and commenting on the rapid growth of his tomato plants when in his aristocratic voice, he replied with *'yes dear and your marijuana plants are coming along quite nicely too'*.

Dad was a charismatic, charming, hard-working, hard-playing, complicated deep thinker, who loved to make others laugh; a lover of life who was now at the end of his.

Ever the comic, after hours of laboured breathing, Dad's hand went up in the air, and in a soft voice, we heard him ask, 'Can I go now?'

We caught each other's disbelieving looks. Then Mum replied, 'Yes, darling. You can go now.'

And he did. Dad died with a smile on his face.

After he passed there was an eerie silence, the birds had stopped singing, and the waves had stopped crashing. It was as if time had stood still. I felt overwhelming sadness, yet I couldn't cry.

Mum looked so small, her face drained of colour, almost like she had gone too. I made an attempt to hug my grieving sister, who remained head in hands, ignoring me. I knew why. I was a disgrace. My five-year-old niece stayed with her dead 'Gar' for a long time, staring at his face.

None of us smoked anymore but we all lit up. My shaking hands reached for the lighter as I sucked hard on the fag, my head pounding from a filthy hangover, the taste of smoke bitter in my mouth. Standing separately, grieving alone, (don't let your emotions get in the way of life), the hearse arrived and we watched Dad leaving his dearly loved camp.

King Dick had left the building.

Dad died at 12 noon on 26 January 1995 – Australia Day – the most significant day for the campers. More synchronicity. He was only sixty-six, younger than I am writing this.

I went to work that night riddled with guilt. I hadn't been there in Dad's last days. Instead, my sister and mother had been by his side, caring for him. I was filling my life with shame, remorse and regret.

Greg ignored Dad's death. It was business as usual. I snarled at him, 'I wish it was you instead of Dad.'

My dad's funeral was noteworthy. Mum's comment, 'You're turning this into a bloody circus.'

Held at Wesley Chapel, our muso friend and her band played Frank Sinatra's *(I Did It) My Way,* foot tapping and singing heard throughout the church … 'and now, the end is near, and so I face the final curtain … and did it my way.' So fitting for our dad.

It was a fabulous funeral. The wake was held at the Sandringham Yacht Club. The sun shone brightly on the deck overlooking the bay and its many yachts, including the *Winston Churchill* – the one Dad and Blacky had sailed on during the Sydney to Hobart yacht races. I felt Dad's presence throughout the day, and I felt his contentment. He was free, no more pain. It was joyous.

Needless to say, Dad's death provided an excuse for guzzling, 'Give me a break, I'm grieving,'

I Don't Want a Nice Little Simple Life

I want a complex, extravagant, chaotic, hectic existence, a tumultuous over-stimulated journey…

I was becoming more and more aware that there was something wrong with the amount of alcohol I drank. My hangovers were accompanied by excruciating headaches, which included pixelated eyesight. I feared the future, knowing what my drinking was doing to me physically and mentally, but I was even more fearful of stopping. As far as I was concerned, sober people had grown to accept their lives but not enjoy them. Sobriety was less than. Oh yes, they said they had nice little simple lives nowadays, but I didn't want a nice little simple life. I wanted a humongous exciting liberating one. I drank to ward off boredom, normality, and mediocrity. Life didn't seem so mundane with a drink in your hand.

Friends and family were dropping little hints regarding the amount of alcohol I drank and the changes of mood that ensued. These little bits of truth got lodged in my head. I couldn't unhear them and they continued to torment me.

I loved drinking more than anything. It gave me a sense of safety, certainty, and calm, silencing my fears and doubts and locking them away. It was my spinach – my source of strength – yet it was quietly eroding the very values that defined me, causing me to make poor decisions and shattering my confidence.

The fights between Greg and I became monumental, condescending and patronising. Greg would bait and belittle me in front of people. He was an expert gaslighter. And I fell for it. One day, I threw a heavy crystal decanter full of port at his head. It missed and broke three of his ribs. Another time, I scratched his face on both cheeks and drew blood. His children would cry. I came home one morning, having refused to leave our friend's house with him the night before, and all my clothes, including expensive leather coats and cowboy boots, were strewn over the front lawn, rained on and ruined. I tried to run him over with my car a couple of times. The scary part is I would have hit him, had he not moved in time. I somehow justified this behaviour. *It's what he deserved.* I was so revengeful, so angry. I couldn't look at him in the eye anymore. When I did, I saw the terrifying blackness of my own soul staring back at me. What made it worse was his endless ridiculing of me. It felt like mental torture. I hated him with a passion; I loved him with a passion. It was such a toxic relationship. To this day, I don't understand what it all meant.

Greg's name for me was Eve – the temptress, the one who ate the forbidden fruit even though God told her not to. I would constantly talk him into doing things against his will. And I always got my own way – I was a master manipulator. I wore him down to the point where he couldn't say no.

After visiting his parents on their farm in Goondiwindi, Greg would fly home, tired and just wanting his own bed. Thinking only of myself and what I wanted, I would ring, saying 'Hello darling. My, how I've missed you. I have an idea. Why don't I pick you up at the bus station and we'll spend a night of unbridled passion at the Regent Hotel, have dinner and play the pokies?'

'No. Absolutely not. I'm exhausted and we can't afford to. I just want to go home and sleep.'

Several calls later and there we would be, at the Regent Hotel, with me swimming in the pool, lounging in the sauna and spa, being massaged and ordering room service, happy as a pig in shit, while Greg sulked in the room.

Maybe it was a form of revenge, or payback, but I had a need to control him, assert my power over him, beat him at his game just because I could. I was intimidating, overbearing and domineering, without any form of a conscience and he was a sucker for me.

I didn't care about his feelings as long as I got what I wanted. I blamed him for that side of me, the side I hated. He carried himself with such bravado, and yet he was putty in my hands. At the end of our relationship, according to his friends and family, he was a broken man because of me. And I couldn't help but wonder, how does love go so wrong?

We needed to get as far away as possible from each other or someone would have died. A friend of ours had a container full of Brazilian bikinis he needed to sell. I decided to fly to Queensland to visit an old friend, hire a car and do the markets, selling the bikinis. Greg put the boxes of swimwear on a train to Brisbane. When I arrived, Queensland was having a heatwave, with 35–40 degrees most days. I hired a rent-a-bomb station wagon/bedroom, and began an epic market run from Brisbane to the Gold Coast, visiting friends along the way. Of course, I had limited funds so needed to sell product. These bikinis were minuscule. On me, the top barely covered my nipples, and the bottom disappeared up my bum crack. It is worth noting that, at this time, no one in Australia had even heard of Brazilian bikinis.

In three weeks, sitting all day in hot concrete boxes at markets, I had sold five pairs. Also, the air con in my rent-a-bomb broke down so it was like sleeping in a sauna. Greg refused to send money. Prick. I wasn't giving up.

I visited my goddaughter, Lissy and her friend in Byron Bay. We set up a bikini shop on the hill at Wategos Beach and they modelled the bikinis on their stunning young fully tattooed bodies. Business picked up monumentally. These were such great days, bathed in glorious sunshine, with Eskies full of big bottles of VB, the boom box blaring Bob Marley. '... *'Cause every little thing's gonna be alright!'*

And it always was.

On my way back, I ventured into the Burleigh Heads pub and won $1,000 on a poker machine. Yes! I was ecstatic. I was so ecstatic that I decided to shout the bar, which had a snowball effect that ended in me waking up alone in a strange bed covered in vomit. *Please God, let that be my vomit.* I instantly thought of Jimi Hendrix choking on his spew and dying. I think I would have preferred being dead than facing this hangover. *Where was my backpack? Where was my car? Where was I? Why is it so fucking hot?'* I hitchhiked back to the pub, found my bomb, returned it and got on the first train home.

~

It was 1995. Greg and I had sold our pizza oven to the owners of the coolest place in town, and we were offered jobs there making pizza. *Greg and I working together in someone else's kitchen. This should be good.*

I found a way of stealing wine from the bar which I hid behind the salami and cheese. The beer was easy to obtain as it was part of the pizza dough recipe and one of our five food groups. In fact, it was our only food group. I had a feeling I was going to require total inebriation in order to deal with Greg and these dysfunctional peeps. She was bat shit crazy and her husband was an unpredictable, moody prick.

This, too, ended badly. We arrived one morning to the psycho owner thrusting a dustpan of kitchen floor waste in our faces, calling us pigs. Bitch. It was the first anniversary of my dad's death, and I was heavily self-medicating. I had a meltdown, screaming, throwing full bottles of cordial at the owner's heads and threatening to kill them all, while putting my foot through the plate glass door. They called the police and I was escorted from the premises. Greg stayed, as he needed the money.

For years I had wanted to buy this joint, but we needed one hundred and thirty grand to do so. After exhausting all options, I ate humble pie and asked my mum. Sceptical about whether she'd ever see her money again, she agreed. Her love for me outweighed her feelings of doubt. She was understandably concerned. 'Dad would turn in his grave if he knew I was aiding and abetting your addiction,' she reflected.

I bought my dream bar. I was on cloud nine. Alcohol on tap. You bewdy.

I was nervous, scared and excited all at the same time. As usual, my feelings of doubt lingered. I didn't trust myself enough to deal with failure or success. I feared both. *Were we able to do this justice?*

My anxiety was in vain as we turned it into a place everyone wanted to be. We were a success from the get-go as we had a ready-made following and a reputation for creating good food and good times.

I produced an eclectic menu. We had great relationships with the locals and their children. We invited the kids into the kitchen to make their own pizzas, and on the box I would sketch a caricature of their face. It was free rein in our establishment.

In this town, Thursday night was the party night. Between the hotel next door to us and our bar, peeps partied all night, moving from one to the other. We ignored every law, including closing time, noise decibel level, responsible service of alcohol, under-age drinking and narcotics on the premises. We thought we were invincible, indestructible. And for a time we were. On these nights, our bar was like a pressure cooker, bodies jammed shoulder to shoulder, everyone moving like a single organism, fist pumping to the Chemical Brothers and the Violent Femmes – *Blister in the Sun*, rattling the glassware, beer sloshing over rims. Behind the jump we poured doubles as 'singles', lines of shots along the bar, first in best dressed. Our fines stacked higher than the nightly take. It was perfect anarchy.

On these nights our barmaids were run off their feet. Every hour I would cease service, pour them a Cowboy Cocksucker, yelling 'Skol!' We would then throw the shot glasses over our shoulders and whoever made the sink, got another. When the tune called, the girls would jump onto the bar, Coyote Ugly style, cowboy boots clicking, hips swaying. The crowd went wild, cheering and yahooing. Greer, when she was old enough (actually, not old enough), became one of our most sought-after barmaids. Being well endowed and not afraid to show her perfect cleavage, she was often heard saying, 'I don't know why you're looking at them.

They're not going to pour you a beer!' Inevitably at one or two in the morning the local copper would arrive, fine in hand, looking exasperated, 'not again Sooz,' he would sigh, while I offered him my most voluptuous Mae West impersonation, 'well hello Constable Des, is that a gun in your pocket or are you just happy to see me'.

On Sundays, we stuck black plastic garbage bags over the windows, unsuccessfully attempting to block the sound while we illegally ran open mic days with the multitude of local musicians. More fines.

We had some scary substance-fuelled incidents. On one occasion, at two a.m., having thrown out a local boy for being overly inebriated, I noticed car lights speeding towards our plate glass windows. I knew what was about to happen. I said to Greg, 'Here comes Shane', as a car came flying through the window and landing on our bar. The noise of the smashing glass was deafening. Greg acted quickly, removing the keys from the ignition as Shane sat on the bonnet of his car, inside the building, demanding a beer and a light for his cigarette. 'Yes sir,' I complied as I rang the police. My heart broke for him as the police took him to the divvy van. 'Can I please say goodnight to him and tell him I love him? Please?' I begged the policeman.

'What the hell? Why? He has just destroyed your livelihood!'

Shane was a beautiful boy who sadly suffered with schizophrenia. He would often speak to me of the disturbing voices in his head, the ones that never stopped, including the one that told him to destroy our building. I so related, the difference being the voices in my head were my own.

We couldn't leave the premises until morning when the glaziers arrived at which point most of the town had joined us, looking for the scoop. This was the most exciting thing that had happened in our town in a while. The phone started ringing madly. The local papers were chasing the story, including the Geelong Advertiser who printed a wonderful caricature of a woman who looked uncannily like me with big hair and a big cleavage, wearing an apron and with her hands on her hips, looking at a shattered glass window, with a speech bubble that read, 'Sorry sir, we don't do drive through.'

Not long after the incident at the bar, Shane committed suicide.

~

There was a dark side to owning a bar. I was like a kid in a candy store. I would start work at noon and drink through prep and service. After service. I would take my cook's hat off and put my barmaid's hat on, take whatever drugs were on offer and drink with the patrons until closing time when I would move the party to our kitchen, and then to our apartment which was behind our bar, (more on that later), party till dawn, sleep till noon then do it all over again. Our kitchen and house parties consisted of most of the local population, none of whom paid for drinks.

I knew my drinking was reckless, but I convinced myself that it was still on the 'fun' side. I was extremely amusing when I drank, cracking killer jokes, flashing my boobs when I wasn't getting enough attention, or when Greg was getting more attention than me, insulting people and hating on high achievers. I once yelled at a group of hot surfers, Q: 'Hey, what do surfers use for contraception? A: their personalities.'

Who was I kidding? I was barely holding it together. I was intolerant, judgemental and riddled with 'stinking thinking'.

At times, respected members of the community would pop their head through my kitchen servery window, asking 'what do you suggest, Suzie?'

From me: 'I suggest the pub down the road. I hear they do a good steak.'

And I was the boss from hell. Due to my insecurities and constant intake of booze, I screamed orders at my staff, demanding the impossible, yelling, 'Get me a drink now or you're fired', when I would hear, 'do you want it in a glass or your coffee cup?' What!! How did they know? Once, a new waitress took a meal to the wrong table. I shouted at her, 'What's wrong with you, you fuckwit.' She ran out crying. We had a constant turnover of staff, as they couldn't put up with my shit. As one of them was storming out in tears, she cried 'we all know how good you are at being a drunk. Why don't you try being good at something else?' I have never forgotten that.

I was becoming extremely intimidated by Greg. He hung around the bar most nights, holding the fort, slamming cosmopolitans and rolling joints, his red face sweating, rocking back and forwards on his heels, while his sycophant mates hung off his every word. The most popular quips he directed at me were, 'Fuck off' 'Shut the fuck up' or 'go to fucking bed'. He relished the reaction caused by his constant denigrating of me. He was a smug prick. The paradox being, he loved me deeply.

~

It became imperative that I leave. I couldn't keep up this lifestyle or be surrounded by booze, and I couldn't spend another minute alongside Greg. I employed a chef mate of mine, to replace me, and I got myself a job at a café in Anglesea with a couple who I knew from the past. This chef cost us a fortune which we could ill afford but I was determined.

On the second day at my new job, with a packed café, I was using the mandolin without the guard and lopped the top of my finger off. In a panic, hoping the new boss wouldn't notice, I threw the stub away and grabbed a tea towel, wrapped it around my hand, which was cascading blood. Fortunately, Greer and my niece were lunching there at the time. When Greer saw me, she gasped, 'Jeeezus Mum! Get in the car.'

The doctor looked at the headless finger with the little white noodle nerve endings hanging out. 'I'm sorry,' he said, 'but there is nothing I can do unless I have the top of the finger. That way, I can fuse it.'

Back we go to the café, blood still pouring. I was so embarrassed. 'I'm so sorry, Jen, but I have to find the top of the finger to take back to the doctor.' Thinking she would, or should, sack me, instead Jen quickly grabbed newspapers and laid them on the lawn, emptying the bins onto the paper and spreading out the contents. We all searched and searched for the stub but with no luck. 'Maybe the dog ate it?' Greer suggested.

To this day I have no feeling in the top of that rather short finger. This new arrangement didn't last. Back to 'hell's kitchen' I go. I couldn't stop analysing my circumstances. I was so confused; It became paramount that I look after my own welfare and yet when I did so I was disappointing others, letting the team down.

We had to stop driving home after work. The cops got us so many times, but because they were our friends, they would confiscate our keys. 'Not again, you two, when are you going to get it? Now start walking and pick your keys up from the cop shop tomorrow.'

This was not ideal, staggering through the dark streets abusing each other.

We decided to move into the townhouse behind our business, which quickly became the extension of the bar. We were mates with the crew in the opposite unit; they, too, were lunatics.

On one occasion, I had the previously mentioned crim's moll, Jane, visiting. (For some background, Jane's husband was involved in the Great Bookie Robbery and was shot dead by the Mafia in his driveway, in front of his children.)

Our door didn't lock so people were forever falling through it. This night, a friend of ours, hiding something under his coat, flew in mid-party. Jane threw herself onto his back, shouting, 'He's got a gun! He's got a gun!'

They both fell to the ground. Struggling to remove Jane from his back, our friend revealed a bong.

Another night, again with a party in full swing, our door was flung open and, coming from the opposite unit, two dudes wrapped in a stronghold flew across the room, hitting the opposite wall. The party went on around them.

The town knew where our drug drawer was and would help themselves. Even on our nights off work, with Greg and I craving rest, there would be a constant stream of peeps wanting to hang at our place, helping themselves to our fridge. There was no respite.

In the mornings I would find strange bodies in obscure places. One night, I jumped into bed and there was a naked man in there. I had never set eyes on him in my life. Apart from the international surfers, we had some famous people in our bar including Damien Oliver who was a regular. The first night he came in, I ran up to him, wrapping both arms around his thighs, lifting him up in the air, saying, 'Darren Gauci, I'm so excited to have you in my bar,' to which he replied, 'actually, my name is Damien Oliver, and would you mind putting me down?'

And, of course, we can't forget the famous ex-Cats footballer. This was before he turned to God. This was when he was our 'God'. He drank with his entourage. 'Put that on the tab,' they'd say. On this particular occasion, when the tab reached four hundred dollars, I approached him, asking 'So, when do you think you might pay up?' He looked offended, and one of his mates said, 'Don't you know who he is?'

I said, 'Yep, he is a has-been who owes me a lot of money.'

Quick as a flash he responded with, 'Well, it's better to be a has-been than a never-was like you.'

Touché, I said.

That night he left his very worn-out wallet on the bar. It contained his driver's licence and one single five-dollar note. I rang him to tell him. When he arrived, I hugged him and said, 'Sorry for calling you a has-been.'

He returned the hug ten-fold and replied, 'I'm sorry for calling you a never-was.' I was in the arms of God and I wanted to stay there forever.

There was a moron living opposite our bar who was hell bent on getting us shut down, filming the illegal goings on twenty-four seven. He took us to court several times, showing video footage of unquestionable behaviour. We received more fines and decided to teach him a lesson.

In the early hours one morning, my dishy and I, dressed in black garbage bags and rubber gloves, armed with a can of black spray paint, were heading over the road to destroy his house with graffiti. At the same time, the local coppers drove up. 'What are you up to now, Suzie?' they enquired, sighing audibly.

'Well, Des, funny you should ask. Frank and I are just heading off to a fancy-dress party, the theme being plastic fantastic.'

'At two in the morning?' he questioned.

Soon we were back in court.

This person had a shiny new V8 utility. At dawn, still dark and eerily still, I grabbed a carving knife and, with my girlfriend and my cat, Dick (named after my Dad), ran up the hill to his house with the intention of destroying all four of the six-hundred-dollar car tyres. We stabbed the first tyre, the noise from which almost burst our eardrums and would no doubt have woken the neighbourhood. We looked at each other in horror and bolted, Dick the cat sprinting alongside.

He continued filming and I continued the harassment. I hid a whole snapper inside his car bonnet once during a heatwave. From all accounts that smell tortured him for a very long time.

But he won in the end, as, even though videotaping is apparently inadmissible evidence in court, he was a huge catalyst in our demise.

Getting Serious

Addiction is the hallmark of every infatuation-based love story.
Elizabeth Gilbert – *Eat Pray Love*

Until now, the drug of choice was weed. Greg hid the stuff all over the place. One day I decided to clean out the storeroom. Next thing, I hear Greg ranting, 'where's the oregano? Where the fuck is the oregano?'

How was I to know he was hiding his mull in the oregano? There he was, head in the dumpster and legs in the air, desperately searching for his stash.

By now, we had been introduced to mind-altering drugs of all sorts, including ecstasy tablets, as had ninety per cent of our patrons. These drugs enhanced the senses and created a euphoric state of mind. The 'apple' was the most popular. It was brutal, creating hallucinations, euphoria, insane behaviour and, at times, paranoia. We were not equipped to deal with the negative side effects manifesting in our patrons. How could we? We were on them ourselves.

Apparently, taking these drugs anally was more effective than orally and worked a lot faster. I glanced across the reserve one night to see a line of bare bums into which ecstasy tabs were being inserted.

Considering he had the perfect venue for it, Greg decided to become a drug dealer, his new name being Papa Bling Bling. Our storeroom became the 'drug room', and it was the worst kept secret in town.

I was fearful of what was becoming of us all, and of this untenable situation. We had four children to think about, for God's sake. We now had every drug under the sun on our premises. It was only a matter of time before we got busted. We even delivered pizzas with a four pack of eccies and a six pack of beer.

As an aside, years later, I was in Byron Bay, dancing on the table at the Byron Bay Backpackers with a well-known actor. I gushed, 'well, how lucky am I dancing with a famous movie star?'

'I'm not as famous as you and GB,' he replied.

'How do you know Greg and I?' I enquired.

'Well, Kelly Slater is a good mate of mine, and he still talks about this funny little bar in Jan Juc where you could buy eccies on EFTPOS.' (It should be noted here that Kelly Slater himself didn't imbibe in drugs or alcohol.)

Strangely enough, the cops stayed clear of the drug room. Years later, I asked them why that was and they said, 'we couldn't face the paperwork.'

I must make mention of an iconic three-metre-long unique surfboard-shaped table which stood pride of place in our bar and was lacquered with local surf industry logos. What happened on top of that table is a book in itself! One Easter and with a packed bar, I decided the pro-surfers should be on said table, so I began a chant, 'Get it off. Get it off.' T-shirts flew across the bar, and there, on our surfboard table, was a bunch of half-naked, genetically blessed, six-packed, tanned bods, disco dancing. Just imagine a scene from Magic Mike and you'll get the picture.

From nowhere, I found myself jumping onto the table and pulling down my signature overalls, realising all too late that I had on my ancient Bridget Jones-style big girl undies with the elastic gone. Not to be deterred, I hitched them up my bum crack and bared my buttocks to the bar.

Greg, the good Catholic boy, refused to speak to me for a long time until he relented and grinned, saying 'That was the funniest thing I have ever seen you do.'

That surfboard table had a reputation of its own, and let's just say I'm pretty sure there were some local children conceived on it. At times, there would be so many crazies on that table it would rock on its hinges. How no one went through the plate glass windows, I will never know.

~

My signature cook's clobber were Yakka coveralls, which I bought white and dyed in all the colours of the rainbow. After service, not wanting to miss anything, instead of popping into my house, showering and changing, all way too hard, I would head to the bar, where I would hear a chorus of 'You stink of food'.

Of course, the flashing of my boobs continued, my coveralls being most accommodating for this prank. 'Show us ya tits' was a common request and, not to disappoint, show them I did. Let me add, they were a commendable set back then. If I did that now, I'd get bruised knees. Some say I was insecure, loose and attention seeking. And their point is? Everyone saw them, whether they wanted to or not. If you drank at our bar, you would see my breasts.

One day, I was at the beach with my girlfriends, sunbaking topless, when I spotted a group of young local guys walking towards us. I started to cover up when one of them yelled, 'why would you bother, Brownie? We've all seen them.'

We had our rituals at the bar. When our patrons refused to leave, Greg would squirt them with sticky soft drink from the post mix machine while I jumped onto the surfboard table and to the tune of The Moody Blues *Go Now!* I belted out, 'I don't wanna see you go, but, darlings, you better fuuuuuuck oooooff.'

As they were being herded out like sheep, channelling Elly May Clampett, I would roar, 'Y'all come back now, ya hear?' And they always did.

Twenty years later, I still run into crew from that town who thank me for the 'best days of our lives'. And still today while walking down the street or shopping there, the words 'y'all come back now, ya hear ...' will ring out somewhere in the ether.

~

When Greg and I moved to the townhouse, mates of ours rented our house. One of them was Pat the plumber. He was a little bloke who wore stubbies shorts and wife-beater singlets. Ignoring the part that I was taken, he was determined to have me. He brought his own CDs to the bar – love songs – which he sang to me, like R. Kelly's *If I Could Turn Back the Hands of Time.* Never in my whole life had anyone serenaded me. This dude got to my heart. Here we go again.

I began frequenting my old house. That, in itself, was weird. His roomie was from Brixton, England, and was a little chap with a big belly, and a full head of dreadlocks. He was covered in homemade tatts and piercings and had a sick cockney accent. Both of those guys had awesome voices. The three of us spent so many nights singing, jiving and shrieking with laughter.

When at the house with Pat one night, there was a knock at the door. I opened it to find a very sad Greg looking at me. To add insult to injury, I had spilt red wine over my frock, so I was dressed in Pat's wife-beater and stubbies shorts. Greg looked like he was going to cry. He left me there. I woke up the next day riddled with guilt. I couldn't understand my own behaviour so how could I explain my motives to someone whose heart I was breaking?

For some unknown reason, I found validation and emotional support in these random blokes. I craved Greg's love and yet I wasn't open to receiving it. We didn't know how to fulfil each other's needs. I wanted to punish him, and yet it killed me seeing how much I was hurting him. I felt a deep visceral love for Greg.

I wondered why I was so 'needy', why I craved attention and validation from these strays. It appeared I needed these dalliances to keep me high and functioning.

We had to ask the tenants to leave our house because we decided to turn the place into a greenhouse for marijuana. We gutted the bottom half of it and installed a ten-thousand-dollar sophisticated hydro set-up. Greg moved in, turning the upstairs into a popular, drug-infested man cave.

As instructed, I stayed away. Our relationship had run its course, and I was now living independently of Greg. I didn't need him. I had my own house, bar, friends, and a plumber for a lover.

We began to notice unmarked cop cars in the street opposite our townhouse. They were clearly checking out the constant comings and goings and drug deals taking place. There was a queue of Greg's clients at our door. Our kids decided to give them a post-it-note with a number, so we knew whose turn it was. Greg, still in denial, would react to our concerns, with 'They're only interested in the big guys. They're not interested in small-time dealers like me. I am a mere facilitator. If it's broken, I fix it.'

Greg was living in a drug-fuelled bubble. I was living in a fear-fuelled nightmare. This was a precarious, dangerous lifestyle. I was in denial regarding my involvement with a criminal. The threat of jail was looming, and I was guilty by association.

No drug was off the table. We tried them all. Heroin bongs were fashionable for a time – a short time, as even though they produced a euphoric state of mind, the ensuing projectile vomiting wasn't much fun. Like Charlie Sheen, we got into the 'coco-puffs' where we put cocaine in the top of our cigarettes, causing a massive head rush.

And here's the thing, if there was no drinking of alcohol, there would be no taking of drugs.

> **Diary excerpt April 2001:** *I cannot believe what an insidious disease this is. Alcoholism. Substance abuse disorder. There I said it. I am a hardcore alcoholic. I have lost total control of my life to this toxic poison. It's like a parasite under my skin. Whoever would have thought that a strong determined warrior such as I could become so weak, so powerless, and so vulnerable to this demon? And yet here I am.*

He was at the beach when the police got him. They arrested him on the spot. In his car, they found scales, notes and an over-abundance of drugs. The police couldn't believe their luck as they followed him to our house, discovering sixteen fully grown female marijuana plants, forty-seven bagged up ounces of mull, (for personal use, he stated), scales, more drugs and stacks of notes.

That day, I had a strong sense deep in my gut that something was wrong, so I drove to the house. I couldn't believe my eyes. It was like a scene from Miami Vice – police cars and vans, police, sniffer dogs, and rubbernecking neighbours gawking at a handcuffed Greg who looked like he had seen a ghost. 'Guess I'm a goner,' he mumbled.

I wanted to hug him and never let him go.

The police chief then asked me who I was and did I know this man. 'Know him?' I grinned. 'Yes, he is my partner, and I am his co-conspirator.' I held my hands out, saying, 'Go ahead. Cuff me.'

They didn't. I was disappointed. Clearly, I watched too many crime movies.

I was then handed over to two young plain-clothes cops, who I fondly referred to as 'Starsky' and 'Hutch'. They were given the job of taking me to our place of residence to search extensively for contraband. I offered to drive them in my old beaten-up Volvo with the seats covered in dog hair, our smelly Great Dane, Rove, in the back seat. The first thing Starsky saw was the out-of-date registration sticker. 'We'll ignore that,' he said.

I'd already had several wines, and as the shock wore off, my head throbbed. On arrival, I suggested I would have a gin and tonic. 'No, not allowed. You may have to bail Greg out of jail,' said a stern Starsky.

During the search Starsky's phone rang. It was the police sergeant, telling us that Greg had exonerated me from all charges. 'Just as well or there would be no more sex for him,' I joked.

Now that I was off the hook, in my permanent state of delirium, I realised I had been strangely prepared, almost curious at the prospect of incarceration. Greg was taken to Geelong lock-up and put in a holding cell. Greer and my stepson came down from Melbourne, throwing themselves into damage control mode, sourcing lawyers.

Greg being busted was big news in our little town. The story consumed the front page of the local papers and the Geelong Advertiser. I attempted being the ever-loyal girlfriend, working on his release. The next day was my birthday and I went to visit

Greg. There was a Perspex wall between us but, disappointingly, no phone. He was dazed, confused and in severe unassisted detox. We pressed our palms together. 'Guess I fucked up, ay?' he said, and then, 'Suppose it's a not-so-happy birthday. Sorry.'

Greg was at his most vulnerable. It was surreal. I thanked him for exonerating me and refrained from saying 'I told you so'.

Bail wasn't an option. I was distraught, leaving Greg in that depressing lock-up where he was amusing himself by kicking a pair of socks to another inmate. I took him in books, pens, paper and a change of clothes.

We thought he'd be released and a trial date set. He was there two weeks. This was unprecedented.

The town was in turmoil. Papa Bling Bling had been put behind bars. What was going to happen to the rest of them? Their mobile numbers were in his phone, which the police now had. Greg was doing time for the whole town, a fact that didn't go unnoticed or unappreciated.

What they didn't know yet was that, unseen by the sergeant in charge; a very smart, quick-thinking Papa Bling Bling had thrown his SIM card into the bushes. The town was safe.

Greer and I went to our house. The place was covered in dirt and ripped plastic sheets. We cried. We went to work, getting it ready for my return. Having lost our business and with Greg in jail and me unemployed, I could no longer afford rent.

Our dear friend Bennie, an old mate of Greg's and the guy I have forever had a crush on, offered to help me with the move. Having him to myself, without Greg's sarcasm, was unique. I flirted uncontrollably, laughing at everything he said, blushing and giggling like a schoolgirl. This boy rocked my world.

As Bennie was carrying a box marked 'Kitchen' to my car, I heard an almighty smash and there, on the ground, was my cherished Wedgwood dining set – a wedding gift from my godmother – completely shattered. There was nothing left of the eight-piece set except for one cup. I wanted to scream but, because it was him and because he looked like he was going to cry, I merely laughed it off with, 'Oh don't worry. It was a cheap old set.' When out of his sight I sobbed.

That's when it hit me. *He's the one I want to spend the rest of my life with.*

Greg received a twelve-month sentence, with six months suspended. We couldn't believe it. Had this been in the States, Greg would have been given six years. No one seemed to know what to do with him, including the judge. Due to bullying in the Melbourne Assessment Prison, he was given a second trial, which was attended by Bennie, the staff and me.

Greg's and my favourite TV show, and one we rarely missed, was *Deal or No Deal*, so when the judge offered Greg a deal he looked across at all us supporters, asking, 'Well, guys, what do you reckon? Deal or no deal?'

We actioned 'take the money' with our hands and yelled 'Deal'. The courtroom, including the judge, burst into laughter, applauding madly. Consequently, he was to serve his remaining time on a prison farm in the country. He was happy with that outcome.

I have always fancied being a crim's moll, and I planned to milk it for all it was worth. Hence, my outfit for my first visit to Port Phillip Prison was a leopard-print fur coat with matching cowboy boots and a cowboy hat, with my fingers, wrists and neck dripping in imitation bling.

The prison warden looked me up and down. 'Where the bloody hell do you think you are, love?'

It took forever to get through security, with lots of beeping from the scanners and de-blinging going on. Even though Greg was thrilled to see me – and my coins for the vending machine – I'm pretty sure he was of the impression that these visits were more trouble than they were worth. Every time someone visited, Greg was strip searched, including a finger up his bum.

Despite the huge grin on his face, my heart ached when Greg first appeared in his dark green overalls. He seemed like his old self – humble, vulnerable but with a sense of calm about him. I would straddle him, wrapping my arms around his neck and kissing him on the mouth. This antagonised the warden, who would predictably yell at me every time, 'No touching. Get off him.' This amused us both.

My visits were terminated after an hour. My gut ached as I watched Greg dragging his feet through the security door back to his cell. I blew kisses at him, forever wondering how our lives had come to this. However, I had a deep sense of peace in my gut knowing he was behind bars and safe for now. Strangely in that visiting room and away from the chaos, I felt a deep spiritual connection to him again. He was my soul mate after all. And yet the knowing outweighed the emotions and we both knew it was over.

Get a Real Job

There are no menial jobs, only menial attitudes.

William J. Brennan

Needing to find work after our business folded, I got a job as a trolly dolly at Deakin University. I was part of a team who prepared and delivered morning teas and lunches to the meeting rooms, and we were on constant deadlines. Dressed in a maid's outfit, I had to run down corridors, into lifts and over rough brick paths, pushing overflowing awkward trolleys filled with food and drinks. At times, the glasses would fly off, smashing on the concrete. I carried a bag of speed with me just to maintain my sanity. The boss hollered at me, 'I can't have you here anymore. You are more interested in applying lipstick than meeting deadlines. You are fired!' Oh no not again.

I tried to explain to him that I was famous in this area and needed to look good as I never knew whom I might see.

I was demoted to the counter in the caféteria. My job was to serve the students their pies and Big M's and to make sure I was giving halal food to the Muslims. Alas, I had gone from successful restaurant owner/chef to trolly dolly and now tuckshop tramp, with a shower cap on my head and wearing a black apron that read, 'Deakin University'. *Oh, the shame.*

One lawyer friend of ours was upset when I handed him his lunch, he looked like he was going to cry. 'I'll see about this!' he said in disgust.

Part of my job was cleaning the restrooms and mopping the floors. Joy of joys, I discovered a bar. I became adept at transporting bottles of wine in the mop buckets, and hiding them behind the Big M's. I was proud of my innovative ways in making sure I was inebriated in whatever form available to avoid reality and my tragic life.

I had no desire to face the future or even think about it, so I remained numb, therefore annihilating my inner critic which was doing overtime. My world was so small and it was shrinking daily. I was earning a pittance. I had joined the ranks of the low socio-economic plebeian race. Praise the Lord my father wasn't alive to see it.

But no matter where my head was at, I made sure those toilets and bathrooms were spotless and the aluminium benches sparkling. I was a perfectionist, riddled with obsessive- compulsive disorder, and whether it was a dunny bowl, a plate of food, my lipstick, my outfit or my hair, half measures didn't cut it. I found it was more effective convincing others I had an element of sanity about me when I looked the part. *'Act as if...'* and *'fake it till you make it'.*

My other job was also at Deakin University as a barista to the academics. I wore a little chef's hat and manned a large eight-cup coffee machine. It was nerve-racking and stressful, with frothy milk often running onto the floor and clients returning their cups, complaining, 'I didn't order this. I ordered a one-and-a-half shot three-quarter almond milk in a mug and a double-decaf soy cappuccino, hold the sprinkles.' I was close to tears.

I was playing barista the morning after Greg went to jail. I looked down at the Geelong Advertiser, the front page screaming at me, 'LOCAL RESTAURATEUR AND DRUG DEALER GIVEN PRISON SENTENCE'. There was a large photo of Greg behind our bar, smiling. My first thought was *Gee, that's a nice shot of him.* I watched in amusement as those professors glanced at the front page, at my incarcerated hubby. I wondered if I'd still be employed among these law-abiding, disciplined academics if they knew.

~

As per *The Sopranos*, and considering my hubby was incarcerated, I decided I needed to find myself a lover. I chose a local painter with long curly blond hair, who was a self-confessed bogan with a hippy element.

It was a freezing winter this particular year. My lover and I spent our time drinking cask wine in front of the wood heater, eating 2 Minute Noodles, playing backgammon and singing loudly to Etta James … At last my love has come along … . and … A Sunday Kind of Love … Greg's daughter Clem moved in with me. When cleaning under the stairs, we found eight bagged-up ounces of homegrown mull. We couldn't believe our luck. It had been hidden by Greg and was missed by the cops. I decided to take on Papa Bling Bling's role and it turns out I was good at it. I sold it in one fell swoop.

I was forced to quit the marijuana as it was causing me so much paranoia. I had convinced myself the cops had left it there as a trap and they were coming after me.

Greg rang from jail often, I would hear 'hello, I have a collect call from Port Phillip prison, will you accept the call and pay the charges m'aam? I so wanted to say no, fuck him but I always said yes. He was livid that I was making money from his mull. Didn't he get it? I had an addiction and an out of work lover to feed.

Clem and I got a message from Greg in prison that there was a shipment of cocaine arriving at our post office box in the next twenty-four hours. We were to get rid of it in order to pay his debts. What the fuck? Who does he think he is – Pablo Escobar?

At two o'clock in the morning, when it was eerily dark and quiet, wearing hats and dark glasses, Clem and I hid the getaway car a few streets away from the Post Office and sprinted the rest of the way. Sure enough, when we opened our post box, there it was – a large pink birthday card inside which was an ounce of cocaine. I was shaking uncontrollably, convincing my paranoid self that this was a set-up and at any minute the long arm of the law would appear and whack handcuffs on us. Clem and I, singing the Sopranos theme song '… woke up this morning and got myself a gun …' quietly screaming, sprinted back to the getaway car, tossing the parcel back and forth, filled with excitement at the prospect of the tasting.

Once we were safely back home, Clem said, 'We can't taste this. We are sworn off drugs in solidarity with Dad.'

'Fuck Dad,' I said. 'This is Columbian rocks and, besides, we don't want to sell stuff that isn't up to scratch.'

Clem agreed. And it was exquisite. We jumped on it, not too severely, sold it and paid off the debts.

~

I was at rock bottom, or as I like to look at it, 'cross roads'. I hated my life, and I hated these menial jobs. *It can only get better,* I told myself. *It can't possibly get any worse.* It did.

I found a job at a café in Geelong as a short-order cook. The owners were a notorious, established Lebanese Mafia family who owned half of Geelong. I fell in love with my young boss, Billy, a renowned ladies' man. I talked him into taking me clubbing one night at the hotspot in town, Lamby's. There we were, Billy and his five big beefy Mafioso brothers, and me. Me who came up to their chests and who was old enough to be their mother. I was convinced they were all packing and doing drug deals. It was like a scene from Underbelly. They dressed the same – peaked caps pulled tight over their hoodies, Adidas trackies and runners, in case they needed to scamper from a scrap, I assumed.

They were ignoring me in my miniskirt, lacy camisole and push up bra, exposed cleavage and black leather follow-me-fuck-me boots. Did someone say mutton dressed as lamb? I was amazed at the age of the patrons. I had T-shirts older than most of them.

After doing serious damage to the cocktail cart, I hit the dance floor, showing off, busting some never before attempted dance moves, whilst checking to see if my boys were watching me. They weren't, not one of them blinked my way, not one flinch of recognition at my wild display, so I walked up to the top of a large curved staircase, swung my legs over the railing and slid down the length of it, losing my balance halfway and landing spread-eagled and face first on top of a pair of Adidas runners belonging to none other than my boss. I got my own way home.

There were two shifts at this café. After the evening shift, I would drive down that long, lonely stretch of road from Geelong to Torquay at midnight, freezing, in a borrowed car with a broken window and a door that was attached with an occy strap, home to a cold dark house. I felt so alone, so sad. Greg was in jail, and Greer was in London. I missed my daughter terribly. Of course, there was my bogan boyfriend, but he was rapidly getting on my nerves, demanding I cook for him! 'I'm doing my best with what little I have in the cupboard,' I pointed out. 'Did you even notice I added ham and peas to the 2 Minute Noodles tonight?'

Considering he was a painter, albeit a bad one, I commissioned him to paint the inside of our house which had been severely damaged by the installation and ripping down of the hydro set-up. *How am I going to explain this to Greg?* I pondered.

I then found a job closer to home. I was now a cleaner at the local holiday park. Yes, folks, just when you thought it couldn't get any worse. Now I was cleaning up vomit and scrubbing toilets. I would dry-retch as I removed the mountains of hair from the public shower drains.

One of the other cleaners had a weird obsession with Guy Sebastian, hence a portable tape player blaring Guy accompanied us on our cleaning journey. *Angels brought me here.* My ever-loyal hipflask and bag of speed got me through. At 10 a.m., we would stop work for morning tea which consisted of donuts, sausage rolls and Caterer's Blend instant coffee – yuck. I waddled out of that place. My employment was terminated because I had left a piece of fluff under a couch. Hurrying to get out of the place, I removed my 'Torquay Holiday Park' T-shirt, throwing it in the owner's face and screaming, 'Let me tell you, I've been thrown out of better joints than this! And don't think it hasn't been heaven!' As I stormed out of the place, I wondered why heads were turning and people were gawking, when I realised I hadn't worn a bra.

The Brown Conspiracy
What do you have to do around here to get a 'thank-you'?

Greg and his family had it in for me and that's a fact. I was the scarlet woman.

While in Queensland, I received a phone call from a friend telling me that my Toyota, the one Dad left me in his will, had been seen on the beach, and smashed to smithereens after having been thrown off a very high cliff. *What the fuck?* Apparently, from prison, Greg had instructed his son to get rid of the car for insurance purposes.

Consequently, on my return, I decided to use Greg's car in his absence, until his son was instructed to confiscate it as well.

At the same time, Greg's mum was attempting to render me homeless. 'You need to get her out of the house so you can sell it,' she told him. 'She's half the reason you're in there. She can find her own place to live.'

Apparently, I didn't deserve a place of residence or any form of transport. To add insult to injury, I was getting abused over the phone from prison on a daily basis. Now, I don't want to whinge, I had made my own bed and all, but I had worked my butt off for twenty years in our restaurants and bars, feeding hundreds, menu planning, ordering, cleaning, paying wages and playing mother, stepmother, confidante, psychologist, entertainer, slut when required, and crim's moll, and in all those years, I never got so much as a word of thanks from Greg or his ingrate family. In their eyes, I deserved nothing – *niente, nada, zilch*. Of course, my turbulent mind convinced me that this is no doubt what I deserved, my self-worth at this point being non-existent.

In twenty years, Greg paid me one compliment – to a friend of mine, saying 'I can't believe my luck. When I wake in the morning,

I get to look across at an angel.' I'm guessing that was early in the piece, before I ravaged my pretty face.

~

Greg's son and I picked him up from prison at the end of his time. He was a changed man, broken, quiet and subdued. He quickly became bored and began taking and dealing drugs again. I tried to love him but to no avail. I drove him to see his parole officer and to his anger management and post-prison rehabilitation classes. Greg appeared to be quite robotic, like a ticking time bomb. On noticing the painted house, he questioned, 'I suppose your boyfriend did this, did he?'

I played dumb.

'Well tell him to fuck off. There's not enough room for the both of us in this town!'

When I repeated this to my lover, he said, 'who the fuck does he think he is? The mayor?'

I knew then it was well and truly over. Greg was worried about what he laughingly called his reputation, not about the part that I was having an affair.

Greg's substance abuse had brought out a nasty, abrasive side to this formerly empathetic soul. He had become Machiavellian and manipulative. He had turned his children against me. He was stealing our friend's licences, creating false identities. He was forcing me to borrow money from friends and family. 'Tell them they'll get it back in a week. I need to buy drugs,' he'd demand.

Greg had so much power over me; he frightened me. I couldn't say no to him. I was begging my rich friends for money. They refused to give it to me, saying, 'For God's sake, leave him.'

I moved into my friend Poppy's beach shack up the hill. As I packed my bags, leaving the house, I remember saying to Greg, 'You make my skin crawl.' I'm not sure where that came from!

Determined to leave me broke, Greg began spying on me, stalking me and gathering incriminating evidence. And unbeknown to me, I was giving him all the ammunition he needed and then some. I was making the most of my freedom and the hot local boys, becoming what I had always aspired to be but had never been given the opportunity, until now – the town bike.

One night I was kissing a boy in my lounge room and singing along loudly to Kasey Chambers, '... *you're the Captain ...*' when he says, 'There's a pair of eyes looking at us through the venetians. I think they're Brownie's!'

Not long after this, Greg put the house on the market, having decided to move to Columbia, where, as he put it, 'the cocaine is pure'. After the sale of the house and business, Greg gave me just twenty-five thousand dollars. His explanation for this was that I was a slut and a whore and that's all sluts and whores deserve'.

~

One part of me wanted to go with Greg to Columbia to keep an eye on him, with the ulterior motive of getting my hands on the ninety per cent of our funds he was absconding with. Even though I hated him, he was an object of obsession and I begged him to take me with him. Full disclosure, I was fearful of being without him, but I was even more fearful of being on my own. I argued, 'we belong together after all these years. We are a team.'

Even if he did agree with me, he knew that if I accompanied him to Columbia it would mean less coke for him. I played James Blunt's *Goodbye My Lover*.

> *Goodbye my lover*
> *Goodbye my friend*
> *You have been the one*
> *You have been the one for me*
>
> *I've seen you cry, I've seen you smile*
> *I've watched you sleeping for a while*
> *[You've been the father of my child]*
> *[I've spent a lifetime with you]*

In that moment, he appeared so vulnerable, a broken man, tears welling in his beautiful sparkly eyes, he choked, 'I have to go. I have to go, but know that I will always love you.'

We hugged each other for an eternity and cried. Then he was gone.

Through our passionate, tumultuous, volatile relationship, whenever I told Greg I loved him, his standard reply was 'I know you do, but maybe love's just not enough.' And maybe it wasn't. I felt a gut-wrenching sadness way down deep inside. We had been through so much together – bliss, torment, tragedy, passion, intimacy, hilarity, drama, hate, love – but most of all companionship and a commonality of interest for a time. At different stages, he had been my best friend, my lover, Greer's step-father, my teacher, my producer, my director and my security blanket. And yet, upon reflection, throughout our relationship there had been a feeling of loneliness.

I couldn't help but wonder. Had we failed? Failed at love? Failed in our businesses? Or were we survivors, having been enlightened from the many life lessons slammed into us?

My song to Greg had always been Shania Twain's *You're Still the One*:

> *You're still the one that I love*
> *The only one I dream of*
> *You're still the one I kiss goodnight …*

Standing on the surfboard table with a full bar, I often sang this to Greg. He would try to remain nonchalant, but his joy was palpable, his grin enormous. He loved hearing those words.

Though the substances became the fabric of our relationship, I wonder if we would have survived without them. Now I had to learn to survive without him and I had no idea how. I knew that I would never feel the pain I needed to feel in order to move on and heal if I kept indulging. I had never felt so lost in all my life and yet I had an underlying feeling that from here I could only be found.

Free At Last

I do not wish women to have power over men; but over themselves.

Charlotte Bronte

As mentioned earlier, living on my own at fifty-two years of age, I decided to play the field. Greg who? This town was full of cute boys, and I was going to have me some. I was seeing two much younger boys at the same time; I'll call them Bluey and Bill. Having had a lifelong aversion to rangas, strangely enough, they were both red heads.

Bluey was a musician, poet and artist – a traditional hippy, alternative and anti-establishment. Convinced that 'radiation kills', at bed time my mobile phone was confiscated in case we died of a brain tumour overnight. I was intrigued by this seemingly free spirit. I was also hesitant as I knew he had a girlfriend, the mother of his child, but he convinced me they were no longer an item.

Bluey threw notorious full-moon parties at his ranch involving fireworks, live music, bonfires and hallucinogens. As the setting sun spread a dazzling red over the ocean, a shimmering full moon appeared, creating much howling. Daybreak would reveal a sea of comatose bodies scattered across the grass, sky gazing and wishing the euphoria would never end. I, of course, made sure it didn't end, and finding some willing glassy-eyed participants, we popped again, while settling in for the next twenty-four hours of psychedelic euphoria.

Bluey heard me singing and, impressed with my voice, asked if I would jointly record a song he had written. Finally, a chance at stardom! My backup vocals sounded good, and we were pleased with the finished product. I played it over and over to my friends until they couldn't take it anymore. 'Enough!' they would cry. 'No more, pleeease.'

My time with Bluey was liberating. At six a.m., dressed in a poncho, knitted beanie and ugg boots, we would check the surf. *Whose life was I living? Is this what they call a midlife crisis?*

Bluey asked me for money to produce the album. I stared at him, mouth ajar. 'I don't have any money,' I replied.

'What do you mean? Haven't you and Brownie had a property settlement?'

Aha! The light bulb moment. Until then, I couldn't understand why Bluey was with me as I was clearly used goods. Now it all made sense. It was my money he wanted, not my mind, body and soul as I had imagined.

I have to say, people warned me about getting involved with this narcissist, and now I knew why. It was a shame as I could have imagined a future with him, drinking mulled wine around the campfire and eating mung beans while surrounded by barefoot, snotty-nosed, dreadlocked rug rats. Alas, it was not to be.

For the third time, I was working back at my old bar for its new owners. At the same time, Bill, the other boy I was seeing, was also back there making pizzas. I had déjà vu. To alleviate the feelings of lost power from cooking in my old kitchen – one I no longer owned – I drank copious amounts of the finest wines money could buy. I made sure they were the finest wines by convincing the new owners, who knew nothing about hospitality including food or wine, that I was a wine connoisseur and should oversee everything to do with wine. They agreed – a decision they would come to regret.

I didn't want to put my name to their menu; it was embarrassing to be back there again. But if I didn't do this job, what would I do? Go back to Melbourne and get a real job? Take responsibility for my life? Move from this toxic, godforsaken town that had outgrown me and that I had outgrown, putting on my big girl undies and making some life-changing decisions? Go to rehab? I don't think so. That all sounded way too hard. Instead, I chose denial and pretended this was where I was meant to be. After all I had a rent-free house, a job and no judgemental family close by. The convenience of it all was too good to knock back. Plus, I had two rangas to play with.

One night Bill and I, along with the owners, were having a drink at the bar when in walked Bluey's partner, Avril. As it turned out, she was not an ex but current. Oops.

Avril looked at me and began by saying, 'Hi, Suzie. I'm waiting for a friend of mine to arrive, as we need to have a chat about the fact that Bluey has apparently been sleeping with his wife.'

I said, 'Oh, you don't say,' and moved away.

Before long, Avril's mate Simon arrived and I heard him say to Avril, '… and not only is Bluey sleeping with my wife but apparently he is also sleeping with someone called Suzie who works here.'

Fuck, fuck, fuck.

Avril, shooting an accusing look my way, asks, 'that wouldn't be you by any chance, would it, Suzie?'

I was thinking *Of course it's me, you fucking moron* but, instead, I threw my head back and guffawed, saying 'Oh, daaarling, of course it's not me. Don't be ridiculous. I have just recorded a song with him. Have you heard it? It's very good. I'm doing backup vocals. He is a good songwriter, isn't he? And, if I do say so myself, we sound really good. But sleep with him, goodness no. I wouldn't dream of sleeping with him. Absolutely not.' Blah, blah, blah … Seemingly, unconvinced, she then said, in a rather loud voice, 'Oh, well, that's good to hear because Bluey has genital herpes.'

I will never forget the look on Bill's face!

Furious, he began taking his frustrations out on me in the kitchen. I came to despise him and his stupid round fat freckled Ronald McDonald head. I was sick to death of these boys, of their lies and demands. I decided to dump Bill and Bluey along with their over-inflated egos and little dicks.

At the same time, I was going through menopause, and with it came a feeling of total freedom. I felt keenly alive. Monumental changes were happening within me. I came to the conclusion that I didn't need men and the shit that came with them.

It felt liberating to no longer be conscious of the male eye. I could do what I wanted, wear what I wanted and say what I wanted. I had a tingling feeling of self-awareness and self-approval. *Who was I kidding?*

Having said that, after moving in with my friend Janice, I found I wasn't on my own for long, as it seemed I had quite a few admirers coming out of the woodwork. These were boys who had previously resisted making a move on me until it was safe to do so. Without Greg hovering, now it seemed it was safe to do so. I agreed to any forthcoming advances, hence several one-night stands ensued, including a half-night stand. These situations were awkward, disastrous and regrettable, and all served to plummet what was left of my sense of self-worth to the depths of despair.

I swore off men forever. The only one I wanted was now living in Sydney and no matter how long it took, I would wait forever for my Bennie.

At this stage, Greer was living in St Kilda and had been suggesting I visit her. In my borrowed car, I packed my precious valuable Dr. LeWinns creams, leather and suede cowboy boots and fur coat. I parked my car in a side street behind Luna Park, and Greer and I went to dinner then clubbing.

The next morning, we cabbed to where I thought I had left my car, however it seems there was no car. We walked and walked, looking down every street but still no car. So, off to the police station we went to report it missing. The policeman looked us up and down with our bare feet and mascara-smudged faces and asked 'What make is your car?'

'I don't know,' I answered.

'What model is it?'

'I don't know.'

'What year is it?'

'I don't know that either,' I say.

More disbelief. 'Is it your car,' he asked, 'or did you steal it?'

I had been putting off ringing the owner of the car, but this now seemed inevitable. 'Hi, luvvy. What make, model and year is your car?'

'Why?' she asked.

'I've lost it.'

I eventually bought a wreck of a car from a local mate. I gave him $300 and drove it away. *That was easy*, I thought, until I was pulled over by the cops only to be told that the car was still in my mate's name and the registration was out of date and it wasn't insured. Damn, I have never been good with detail! Greg used to organise that stuff for me. I refused to worry my pretty little head over paperwork. These were all new things I was learning, like how to pay bills and put the garbage out.

As an aside, three months later, I got a call from St Kilda police informing me that they had found my friend's car. It was a couple of streets away from where I had parked it, having been hot-wired for the short trip. Unbelievably, there was nothing missing. My faith in humanity was restored, and my faith in the St Kilda police department shattered.

Central America Here We Come
Off to the land where the cocaine is pure...!

A few months after Greg had left for Columbia, my goddaughter called me from Central America, suggesting I meet her in Costa Rica. 'Don't be ridiculous,' I scoffed. 'I don't do things like that!'

With a bit more convincing from her, I decided to go. Why not? I needed a change of scenery, and I had enough money for the airfare and a little bit left over for cocaine. I was salivating at the thought *Am I really doing this?* I kept myself numb in case I changed my mind; I was full of fear and anxiety. How long would my funds last? I figured when the money ran out, I would go to Columbia and retrieve some of 'ours'. I was dancing around the house singing, 'Do you know the way to San Jose', Dionne Warwick's song, when Janice said, 'If you buy a ticket to that San Jose, you'll end up in the wrong country'.

I did some research, learnt some Spanish and packed a suitcase. I figured I was following the direction from my Higher Power, as I can't imagine having come up with that decision on my own. I was a stubborn Taurean who hated change of any sort, and this was a mega change.

While waiting to board the plane, I had an anxiety attack which caused me to break out in a sweat. I had to talk to someone, so I rang the obvious one, Bennie. 'I don't know what I'm doing. I don't want to go. I'm so scared, I'm in a total panic.'

Just hearing Bennie's familiar voice calmed me. 'Of course you're nervous. This is big for you, but you need to take the risk. This is the best decision you could have made. Go, enjoy, send me some cocaine.' I hung up the phone, head spinning. *When I come home I will marry you, love of my life.*

Going through Customs, my anxiety was exacerbated as I watched them dispose of hundreds of dollars' worth of my Dr.

LeWinn's face creams. I guess I hadn't thought this through. I wondered for the better part of the thirty-hour flight if, in secret, they retrieved it and smothered their faces with the magnificent stuff. What an incredible waste if not!

Lissy and her boyfriend met me at San José airport where we jumped on a bus to Malpais, located in the Puntarenas Province. I was blown away by the heat and the obvious Third World culture differences. It felt euphoric. There, they introduced me to ceviche, a dish of diced white fish fillets, jalapeños, limes, orange juice, honey, tomatoes, garlic, coriander, pepper and salt. This delicious treat became our daily bread.

Their trip was centred around surfing, while mine revolved around sun-baking and watching them surf, which made me so very happy. Our mornings were spent on the idyllic beach doing just that.

We met the dealers straight away. 'Five dollars per gram, buy three get one free.' *I was never leaving.* Every boy on our travels fell in love with Lissy. She is a free-spirited, enthusiastic, positive, energised kind of gal, with a surfer's physique, blonde hair and a permanent suntan. We became known as 'the old hippy and the surfie chick'. I was thirty years her senior but we were mentally the same age. And we had the same goal – absolute annhiliation!

It was thirty-five degrees in Costa Rica. I spent the days lying around our hotel pool drinking sangria and icy-cold beer. I was happy, joyous and free, except for the niggling sense of anxiety looming, destroying what should have been ultimate peace of mind. *What the fuck am I doing here? A fifty-two-year-old in a Third World country with two kids and no money?*

Questions about my future and re-uniting with Greg nagged at me. *Damn that man, hundreds of miles away and still causing me grief. Why couldn't I let him go?'*

I hated going to the office to get my emails but I continued to do so, reading his mumbo-jumbo as he evaded my questions and suggestions regarding us hooking up.

I was reading *Marching Powder*, as you do in a cocaine-fuelled country. Because it was so hot, the glue holding the pages together was melting, so as I finished each page, I passed it on to my American friend in the banana lounge next to me until we had finished the book.

Lissy, and I travelled everywhere on a quad bike, in tandem. We danced the nights away at the open-air disco, witnessing some of the most awesome sunsets.

Costa Rica's catchphrase is *pura vida*, which translates to 'pure life' in Spanish. Costa Ricans (*Ticos*) use this term to say hello and goodbye, everything's great and everything's cool, and it became part of our vocabulary. Skipping down the dusty streets, fist pumping the air, we would bellow at the top of our lungs, 'Pura vida!' It was magical, powerful and spiritual.

In Tamarindo, on the Pacific coast of Costa Rica, we met a local called Spider. He was an imposing character with a spider web tattooed across the entire expanse of his chest. We adopted this young man as not only was he the local dealer, he and his mate were house-sitting a two-story mansion on the beach. We spent our nights dancing to thumping reggaeton at the local outdoor bar, with me on stage playing a tambourine I had absconded with and singing back-up vocals, until I was eventually pushed off the stage.

Next up was a bus trip to Puerto Viejo. Upon arrival, there was a Snoop Dog look-alike who, funnily enough, introduced himself as Snoop Dog. Apparently, Spider had set us up with a Puerto Viejo dealer. We felt like royalty.

This town was woven through with the fabric of Jamaica. The town square blared reggae music, Bob Marley's face was everywhere, market stalls boasted reggae T-shirts, beach bars served authentic Jamaican rum and incense wafted in the air. We shuffled everywhere to *No Woman, No Cry* and *Buffalo Soldier*. We couldn't wipe the grins from our faces.

From there we got a bus back to San José and moved into a central backpacker hostel. San José was the second most dangerous city in the world. That didn't bother us in our hostel love bubble; it had everything we needed. We did, however, frequent a cool bar we had found called, to our joy, Ozzy's Sport Bar. You bloody bewdy.

We carried a hammer at all times as the coke crystals required smashing. Even though I felt like chopped liver most of the time, there was an advantage to travelling with a hot young chick and that was the many free drinks bestowed upon us.

I had an underlying nagging feeling that this was going to end badly. *I'm too old for this. I need to go home to rehab. I need to find Greg. I need my security blanket.* Another line and a vodka disposed of those depressing thoughts. I tried not to dwell on the thought of eventually arriving home as a fifty-three-year-old brain dead, scrawny, broke, unemployed loser. Of course, my mother was disappointed in me, not the first time though. 'I have to hand it to you,' she said. 'You're the only person I know who manages to travel overseas with no money.'

I figured that was something to be proud of.

My melancholy times didn't last long around Lissy. She cheered me up by dancing like a crazy woman, singing Bob Marley's, 'every little thing gonna be alright.' She was a godsend.

We were financially embarrassed most of the time. I rang home begging my mother and sister for money. The ATMs continually flashed *Rechazado no hay suficientes fondos* (Rejected, insufficient funds). But when the notes did appear, we would scream with joy, galloping down the street, high fiving, 'Pura vida! Pura vida!' We met three beautiful Irish surfers in the hostel. I instantly fell in love with Simon who had deep green eyes, dark Irish skin and a prodigious smile. We did a lot of clubbing with these boys, swaying home arm in arm at sunrise, singing raucously and speaking gibberish in Irish accents. I was throwing myself at the unattainable Simon, even though he loved the attention, he explained, 'I think you're grand, lassie, boot I have a girlfriend at home. And besides, you're a fookin nooter.'

Lissy was off to Mexico while I, on the other hand, had no plans. I had come to the realisation that I wasn't going to Columbia to meet with my ex. He was still pretending I didn't exist. However, I was running out of options and thinking of flying home. I felt like I was in the midst of an enormous journey of self-discovery and yet my substance abuse was hindering any potential enlightenment.

The three Irish boys invited me to accompany them to Nicaragua on a surfing safari. I couldn't conceive of the notion. Why would they want me when I was obviously past my used by date? I was hesitant. This was so risqué, and I didn't take risks. Thankfully, those boys did. While I was still umming and ahhing, desperately trying to come up with reasons why I couldn't say yes to possibly the offer of my life, they had packed me and my threadbare clothes onto that bus and the four of us took off on what was to be one of the most memorable times ever. Pura Vida.

We travelled from surf beach to surf beach. My surfie-chick skills instantly kicked in and, without having to be asked, I was waxing their boards and rubbing sunscreen on their gorgeous muscly tanned Irish backs. I thought I had died and gone to heaven before but this time I really had. I sat on those exquisite white sandy beaches, watching them surf, practicing my lines. 'Saw you in the green room, babe.' 'Cool left.' 'Fully sick right.' 'Bitchin' barrel.' I still had it. Surfie molldom was just like riding a bike.

I was living off Liam's money. He said he was flush and that it wasn't a problem. Liam was generous to a fault. 'Ay, lassie, you're not to be boffered. Your laff is well worth the *córdoba*, ya fooking nooter.'

The hostel in San Juan Del Sur was abundant with party animals from all over the world. The Aussie girls were in awe of me with my three boys. We slept in the same room, four bunks. When we arrived at a hostel, Liam would rip up a floorboard, placing our passports in the hole, and then nail it back down. So clever. One night, Simon arrived back from the Internet café distraught as he had lost an important document. He threw himself on his bed, close to tears. I thought I'd capitalise on his vulnerability and whispered, 'Simon, if it would help, you have my permission to take your frustrations out on my body.'

He pretended to be asleep.

We ate tapas and paella at the beach cafés, drinking icy-cold Imperials and laying spread-eagled on the soft sand while gazing at the kaleidoscope of stars. We danced the nights away at sixties-style nightclubs, our white clothes iridescent purple under the fluorescent lights. Vodka and tonics were a dollar each and the white marching powder was abundant. Although I was surrounded by sweaty tanned bare chests, I only had eyes for Simon. Alas, he was unbreakable; it was killing me. When I slept, I positioned myself on my front, naked, with a sheet strategically placed over my bum, Cleopatra-style. I imagined when he saw my lithe tanned body, he wouldn't be able to resist. He resisted. Always.

One night, Liam and Trevor took off, so it was just Simon and I for dinner. I was treating this as a date night and the night I would lure the unattainable Simon into my boudoir (bunk that is). I decided a new frock was in order. The department stores in Nicaragua sold only one style of dress – a fitted mini, embroidered in floral silk. I also dyed my hair for the occasion. Turns out my Spanish failed me that day as the dye turned my hair blue. Halfway through the evening, while dancing to James Blunt's 'You're Beautiful ...', and serenading my date, my too-tight dress ripped down the back seam. Thank God for my tanned bottom. I also had an infected foot, which had blown up like a puffer fish, so I could only wear one shoe. To be honest, I don't think he noticed any of it.

~

It was time for my boys to fly home. Knowing this, I was a physical and emotional wreck, and I had no idea what I would do next. I was broke, homeless and alone in a Third World country. After a teary goodbye and promises of staying in touch always, I went to a bar and met a rich American cowboy, whose name was Earl. I sobbed my heart out on this accommodating man's shoulder, and he consoled me by buying me a million drinks and offering me a place to stay.

I am still in touch with Simon on Facebook, eighteen years later, and he still laughs at my determination to woo him.

My new accommodation was in a basement under Earl's tattoo shop. There were no windows, and it was mouldy, dark and damp, but hey, beggars can't be choosers. Carnival was in full swing in San Juan Del Sur, and masses of people wandered the streets, dancing, singing and yahooing. I heard it all from my dungeon but couldn't join in as I had contracted some sort of mysterious virus and was quite ill.

Earl and his girlfriend, Candy, kindly brought me food and water. There was no toilet, only a hole in the ground, and I had yuck coming from every orifice. It was also that time of the month and I had no sanitary items. I was a broken soul.

I needed to get to the bank in Managua but didn't have enough money for the bus. What I did next haunts me to this day. When I was well enough to leave, and making sure no one was upstairs, I found a pair of Earl's jeans, rifled through the pockets and stole 230 cordoba, the equivalent of a ten dollar note. I grabbed my backpack, pulled my hoodie over my head and ran to the bus stop, hoping to God I didn't run into mein host. I was a monster. I hated the person I had become. I decided my only option was to get a bus to San José and fly back to Australia. I was done.

On the two-day bus trip, I met a lovely Dutch girl named Danielle. These buses didn't have toilets, so we had to pee in a plastic bag. I was a pro at this system by now and walked Danielle through the process. All done, I tied a knot at the top and, as is standard behaviour in these parts, threw it out the window. Unfortunately, the wind brought it back in, covering two cute boys with urine. Thank the Lord they saw the funny side and we partied all the way to San José.

Danielle had recently returned from Confradia, Honduras where she had been a volunteer teacher. The school was owned by an Aussie named Ben, who was looking for teachers, especially Aussies. Problem solved, Another God job methinks.

I rang Ben, introducing myself, and he said he was looking forward to meeting me. I had to wait a week in San José and due to lack of funds, I couldn't afford to leave the hostel. I spent my time lying around on the mattresses in the TV room, drinking tea and chatting to people from different countries. I was helping myself to other people's food and booze. Those people caught me out after a while and, to pay me back, they stole my specs – I was travelling blind on the bus to Honduras. Ben's wife, Mirna, met me at 11 p.m. My blindness was exacerbated by the darkness; I felt disoriented and anxious. Mirna took me to a large white stucco brick two-storey house in the centre of this funny little town. I was shown to my room with the promise of new specs in the morning. I was exhausted, and as I drifted off to sleep, I channelled Scarlett O'Hara – '... *tomorrow is another day, I will think about it tomorrow*. I was pining for the Irish boys.

The next morning, Ben came to the house to meet me and we connected instantly. The first thing that hit me was the cultural difference. No one spoke English, and they made it clear from the beginning that, if I was to teach, I had to learn to speak Spanish and pronto. Unlike everywhere else I had been, this was not a tourist town. There was nothing to see here, and the only tourists were the teachers in the communal houses.

Cofradia is in north-western Honduras, in the Naco Valley. Ben took me for a tour of the town. It was minuscule, and quaint, shaped in a square around a public park. The dusty, unpaved roads were occupied by wandering chickens and mangy dogs. Half the population were living below the poverty line. Tiny little shops dotted the town, selling ciggies for $1 a packet, so cheap that I had no choice but to become a chain smoker. The town had a wonderful vibe; it felt like home.

Ben also showed me around the Cofradia Bilingual School where I was to be teaching. It was made up of bright yellow fibro buildings and a dirt yard and basketball court. There was no grass to be seen. I was to teach grade three English.

That same day, volunteer teachers arrived at the house for the start of the new term. One of these was an extraordinary chap called Frank. Frank was 'loco'. From a wealthy American family, he was the black sheep – a tortured genius who had served time before and was again facing jail upon his return to the States. He was edgy, irritable and restless and talked at a hundred miles per hour.

Six feet tall, with an expressive smile and baby blue eyes, Frank spoke in cryptic narratives. His conversations were deep and consequential; he was searching for the meaning of life. He was twenty-eight and well balanced. He had a chip on both shoulders.

A gifted poet – think Leonard Cohen – but Frank's greatest love was music, in particular the Red Hot Chili Peppers, and that's what he played, day and night, twenty-four seven.

Our house stayed cool in the stifling heat as it had white tiled floors, thick brick walls and fans in every room. The shower was a cold-water hose. None of the toilets flushed so we were always looking at poo.

We were to take this job seriously. Our day started at five a.m. with an alarm that was the cock-a-doodle-doo from the lone Honduran rooster outside my window. Frank and I walked to school mostly in the stifling heat. If we were hungover, which was most of the time, we got a *toot toot*, an open cart costing $2.50, so only accessible when flush. I was reprimanded at school for my mode of dress – a camo miniskirt and black camisole. Mirna frowned, saying '*Demasiada piel* (too much skin),' as she quickly covered me with a flowing floral Honduran frock.

I was in charge of seventeen eight-year-old children. On my first day, entering the classroom, I was shocked. Little Hondurans jumping around from desk to desk and screaming. I stood there, books under my arm, covered in dirt and sweat and cried. What the fuck was I supposed to do with these feral children? 'Pay attention. *Prestar atención*,' I yelled. Nothing, *nada*. '*Tranquillo! Tranquillo* (Quiet! Quiet)!' I screamed. Taking deep breaths, I chanted to myself mentally over and over. *You've got this*, while the children were making paper planes out of my work sheets and torpedoing them at my head.

Calling on my default distraction, I ran outdoors, hanging from a tree by one arm, scratching my armpit, 'Ooh ooh, aah aah, ooh ooh, aah aah.' That got their attention, and they were soon all pointing and laughing, exclaiming, 'Miss Suzie monkey! *Mona, mona, mona* (monkey, monkey, monkey).' They seemed to warm to me after that. Every now and then, they would all stand up in unison and run into the yard, like they had a secret code. I decided to move the classroom outside, where their desks fit perfectly under a ginormous mango tree.

I played my cassette tapes. They came to love country music, and I performed my best air guitar with a broomstick, singing

Do Ya Think I'm Sexy and strutting like Rod Stewart. 'Miss Suzie rock star,' they shouted. Then it was their turn, and they loved it. I encouraged them to sing along in English which was a much more successful way of learning. I was reprimanded for being an 'unorthodox teacher'. They had never before seen a teacher hanging from a tree or playing guitar with a broom. But the kids were responding. I was winning.

I watched Frank teach. He was so professional, and he had those kids under control. This was his third time teaching here, and of course, it helped that he spoke fluent Spanish. I loved this life, and I was beginning to become very fond of Mr Frank. Or maybe I just needed to get laid.

We spent a lot of time at the local John Wayne-style western bar. Dos cerveza, two beers, just one dollar each, would appear on arrival, followed by many many more dos cervezas as we fell out of there, throwing ourselves on a passing donkey for the trip home. The locals were beautiful, simple, chilled people who always had a smile for us. That was until they got to know us 'loco professors'.

There was a young boy Danny who attached himself to us. He adored Mr Frank and Miss Suzie. We were paid US$25 per week, and it was spent before we got it. We had an ongoing tab at the bar and bottle shop. Mostly we were skint and desperate for a drink. Danny knew everyone in town, including the local bottle shop owner who had banned Frank and I from his shop. While I waited outside, Danny convinced the guy to give him liquor. Next thing, the cops were at the door, and off I was hauled to the police station. Allegedly, I had instigated and attended the scene of a crime, the crime being an under-age person accessing liquor. Damn. How was I to know he was fifteen? I flirted with the cops and apologised profusely, avoiding a fine.

The traditional Central American music, Reggaeton, was everywhere, ringing out from speakers throughout the town. On Friday nights, there was a dance in the town square. Little Danny taught me to salsa, and I was a natural. One night, I jumped on the stage and did my rendition of break dancing, spinning on my back, legs in the air like an out-of-control beetle. 'Bravo! Bravo, Miss Suzie!' was the call from my students, as Mr Frank hauled me to my feet.

On Monday morning, Ben called me into his office, suppressing a smile, saying 'Suzie, your behaviour is way too inappropriate considering you are a professor. You have to tone it down. These children look up to you'. Truth be known, they loved loco Miss Suzie.

At this stage, Mr Frank and Miss Suzie were shagging. I guess it was only a matter of time. Frank eventually succumbed, as he was sick of my begging. It was no doubt a pity fuck initially, but then we found ourselves magnificently compatible in the cot and so it continued for the rest of our stay.

The months of drinking their liquor – which was toxic poison – was taking its toll. God only knows what was in that stuff. My brain was scrambled and I was barely holding it together. I had lost more weight, and I was fighting with everyone in the house.

I decided to use what was left of my brain by taking Spanish-speaking classes with one of the other teachers. I walked an hour to her house, in the stifling heat and across paddocks, twice a week for lessons. I became an accomplished speaker of Spanish

~

Realising I wasn't coming home, my daughter decided to come to me, offering an all-expenses-paid month in Guatemala. What a champ she is!

Our Cofradia experience was coming to an end. Frank was returning to the States, via Monjaras, to be incarcerated. I said *hasta la vista* to Ben and Mirna and the kids, which literally means 'until the next sighting' as I knew I would see them again.

I jumped on yet another bus to Antigua, Guatemala, where I was meeting Greer, and made myself at home at the Airbnb pre-booked by her from Australia. It was a lovely place, clean and tidy, with floral curtains and matching couch covers. For the first time in six months, I had a comfortable bed with crisp white sheets and steaming hot water. I had the longest shower, scrubbing myself from head to toe. The water at the base of the shower was dark grey. I ate dinner in the dining room – a feast of authentic Antiguan cuisine including fungi, seasoned rice, saltfish and lobster, all washed down with Rioja red vino. '*Poner eso en la pestana* (Put that on the tab),' I announced, grinning.

Feeling elated and excited, I chatted to the locals who invited me to a nightclub, after which I woke next morning on a beach somewhere, covered in black sand, the dangerously hot sun burning my eyes. I panicked. I had to be at the airport to meet Greer, and I didn't know where I was. I jumped in a cab and, looking like something the cat dragged in and with my head throbbing, arrived at the airport with ten minutes to spare, just in time for a hair of the dog. I was beyond excited, anticipating her arrival. The plane landed, and the people piled off, and they kept coming and coming and then the plane was empty and there was no Greer. I had the wrong day.

I went back the following day and there she was. I didn't realise how much I had missed her until I was looking at her. She looked so pretty, her hair shining, and smelling like daisies. She was so coherent. *I'll soon fix that.* I mused. She couldn't wait to acquire my brain-deadness. 'Bring it on,' she enthused.

The following day, we bussed to Livingston. The first thing I did was teach Greer how to pee in a plastic bag. She picked it up instantly.

Livingston is a town in the Izabal Department in eastern Guatemala, and it sits at the mouth of the Rio Dulce at the Gulf of Honduras. It is a strange little corner of Guatemala that is completely different to the rest of the country. Livingston is noted for its unusual mix of Garifuna, Afro-Caribbean, Maya and Ladino people and culture. The local Garifuna are known for their music and dancing. The only way to get to Livingston is by boat, as it sits on a densely forested peninsula without a road connecting it to the rest of Guatemala.

We found a backpacker's run by sexy young Aussie boys who, after showing us our rooms, offered us a line and a cold beer. Home at last! The manager was an American dude who looked a bit like Julian Assange and who had a constant stream of white powder coming from his nostrils.

Livingston was hot and wet. We were surrounded by water and jungles, and therefore used boats as transport. Even the stifling heat didn't deter my sunbaking. Everyone told me to stop as the grass was full of bugs, but I ignored them. And then it happened. I woke up one morning covered from head to toe in sand fly bites, big, ugly, itchy red welts. 'How am I going to pick up a bloke looking like this?' I cried to Greer. 'They told you so,' she said.

Greer hooked up with the American, and I hooked up with a young English marine biologist named Caleb Munday. He was the iconic ladies' man, however, having no luck with the young backpackers, he decided the old hippy lady would do. All sense of body image and self-respect had flown – I was carefree, loose and loving it. Greer pointed out that, through my having lost weight, my braless boobs were now bobbing up and down around my waist, as I was reggae dancing on the table. Regardless, Caleb and my relationship blossomed. He was funny. 'If you get pregnant, can we call the baby Manic?' he asked. 'Just another Manic Monday.' I assumed he was referring to the Immaculate Conception.

The locals used their rum to make home-brew known as *gifiti*. They pour it over roots and herbs and leave it to soak for a few weeks in the sun, lending it medicinal properties. We went loco on that shit.

No one believed Greer and I were mother and daughter, they thought sisters was more like it. Greer came to me one morning panicked, saying she needed the morning after pill. I was gobsmacked, not because of her irresponsible behaviour – who am I to judge – but because I didn't have a clue how we were going to explain to the *química* (chemist) what the morning after pill was. Thank God it was a woman behind the counter of this tiny little room with its lino floor.

I had researched the English/Spanish dictionary and found the translation: '*Pildora del dia despues* (Morning after pill).' I proudly and distinctly pronounced these words to the química, imagining she would give us a knowing smile, nod her head, go straight to the drawer that contained the morning after pills and send us on our way. Instead, she stood there with a blank look on her face. I repeated the words again and again, trying to avoid the inevitable, but still she had a blank face. It was time for plan B: charades. I squatted down, parted my legs and pretended there was a baby coming out of me, pain distorting my face, pulling the baby out then pushing it back into my vagina. 'No bebe. No bebe. Pildora for no bebe'. Still the woman had a blank face. We were buckled over, shrieking. Eventually, I fetched an English-speaking local to do the job. Fortunately, there was no baby. We were relieved. Can you imagine arriving home with a cocaine-addicted Julian-Assange-look-alike baby? We would have to request a package deal at rehab – three generations of us.

Needing a break from the mayhem, Greer and I got a boat to Utila in Honduras. Utila is known for its coral reefs, dive sites and, more importantly, nightlife. We found a cheap two-bed B&B. There were bars all along the foreshore. We went deep sea diving in the Mesoamerican Reef, which stretches seven hundred miles from the Yucatan Peninsula to the Bay Islands of Honduras. It was teeming with life – sensational. That day, I discovered that this reef is the second largest reef in the world after our own Great Barrier Reef.

We hired a motorbike, that Greer rode with me on the back. Channelling Evil Knievel, she took a corner rather sharply, hitting a tree and denting the bike. We took it back to claim our deposit, stating in earnest that the dent was there when we hired it. They were most amused, and it cost us a packet.

We returned to Livingston to get our stuff and say goodbye to each other. Greer was flying back to Australia, and I was returning to Cofradia, to do what, I had no idea. It was beyond sad saying goodbye to Greer. We had shared a memorable experience like no other, one that only the two of us would ever comprehend.

Caleb decided that, as it was our last time together, he would shout us to a romantic weekend for two. We found a cute little Airbnb in

Antigua. What started as a summer romance had grown, and here we were on a sort of honeymoon. We ate local food consisting of barbecue corn, rice and pork, beef and chicken tortillas. We drank Gallo beer and locally distilled rum. On our last morning, Caleb drove me to the bus. He held my hair back as I vomited into the gutter; sick from months of substance abuse combined with the mysterious medication I was taking for my ever-present red welts. He politely declined a kiss, but we held each other tight, swearing our undying love and promising we would meet again. I slept all the way to San Pedro Sula where Ben picked me up. 'Oh no, not you again,' he sighed.

Back in Cofradia it was school holidays. I didn't know what to do with myself, so I convinced them to let me run cooking classes for the teachers. I taught them how to make meat pies, pasties and Bolognese sauce.

~

I was missing Caleb more than I thought I would. Maybe there was a future for us? After all, Dustin Hoffman and Anne Bancroft made it work in *The Graduate*. Perhaps we would end up together, living happily ever after in a little cottage with a white picket fence in the English Midlands with sheep on our rolling hills. I would cook roast beef and Yorkshire pudding for him when he came in from the farm, exhausted, hungry and thirsty, helping him take off his gumboots, while rocking little Manic in his cradle.

I wasn't sure if my post-menopausal apocalyptic body could get knocked up but miracles do happen. It seemed the six months of petrol drinking was causing a fair amount of delusion.

Not long after my return, I received an email from Caleb. I was so excited opening it. *This is it. He is going to ask me to marry him.* With hope and anticipation, I opened the email from my future husband. It read, 'Hi, Suzie. I was wondering if you saw my passport and cash, as they went missing from the Airbnb.' What the fuck? I returned an abusive email as my future blew up in my face.

I was staying in the other teachers' house by myself. I had a month to go until the date I was due to fly home, and I was determined to stay until then. I couldn't go anywhere or do anything. There were lots of books in the house so I spent my time reading. I read Johnny Cash's biography, sunbaking in the stifling heat and morphing into a lizard. There was only one cassette tape in the house – it was a James Blunt album with the song I sang to Greg while begging him to never leave me, *Goodbye My Lover*. Perhaps it was a sign.

There was an avocado tree in the back yard which I ate from. I was sick from unassisted detox. There was no alcohol, and the local bottle shop wasn't an option as I still owed him from the last time I was here. In fact, he had made a habit of abusing me whenever he saw me. '*Me debes dinero, gringo perra* (You owe me money, gringo bitch).' I gave him my standard answer, 'for the last time, I'm not a gringo bitch. I'm an Aussie bitch.' We were all the same to them.

I thought of asking Danny to help me acquire some liquor, but he wasn't talking to me as, in the big house one night, in a drunken psycho rage, I slapped one of his friends hard on his face, knocking his glasses off his head.

The only accessible booze was at the one-horse bar. I set about picking up poor unassuming locals whose ears I would whisper sweet nothings into and they, in turn, would fill me full of cervesa, with the occasional bowl of Cajun fries thrown in.

These were awkward situations as obviously they wanted payment in kind, no doubt. I would excuse myself on the pretence of visiting the powder room – the hole in the ground – whereby I would slip out the back, finding a donkey to gallop home on, dust consuming me. Thank God no one knew where I lived. Everyone knew of the 'loco Aussie professor'. I had developed quite a reputation for myself.

I decided to become a recluse. I stole alcohol from the other residence when the occupants were at school, topping myself up with sleeping pills, fifty pills for three dollars. Turning my one tape up loud and dancing like there was no one watching, throwing myself around like a crazy person.

Diary excerpt August 2006: *I have never been alone this long in my entire life. This should be a time of empowerment, enlightenment. If only I could utilise this time to go within, 'find myself', meditate, deep breathe, and yet I am still filling myself with substances, anything I can get my hands on.*

When it was time for me to leave, Ben and family came to say goodbye. I had become close to these people, and was sad leaving them, especially knowing that this wasn't a 'hasta la vista' scenario and that I would never see any of them again. I have a feeling they were glad to see the back of me.

From Playa Jaco to Australia

I still call Australia home...

Peter Allen

I decided to spend my last night with Mr Frank – the lunatic – so I bussed down to Playa Jaco on the central Pacific coast of Costa Rica. Frank and I went to a bar, followed by a beach party. The last thing I remembered was smoking a joint. We woke on the beach, the hot sun torturing us. I felt like my head was in a vice. Apparently, there was heroin in the joint. Great! I was in a bad way. I had to get to the airport for my flight to Australia and it appeared I had spent my last cent on smack.

Thank God for the pending thirty-six-hour flight with free booze and food, compliments of Qantas. Frank came with me to see me off. That was tough. It blows my mind how close you can become to someone from another decade, country and upbringing. In the real world you would never cross paths. There are no coincidences in life. I was devastated leaving him.

I was amused reading my diary from this time:

> **Diary excerpt – flying home:** *Debilitated as I am, I feel empowered in a way. I no longer doubt myself. I look and feel different. I am tough and resilient. I take on life and situations with enthusiasm and gusto, I take risks. I have a sixth sense and deep-rooted survival techniques; I have nine lives. I am still an addict and totally brain dead, but hey, I am the ultimate survivor.*

Strangely enough, I was ready to go home. I'd had enough of these low socio-economic countries and the poverty, cultural differences, smell of sewerage, language barrier and oppressing heat. I was excited to return to the best country in the world.

I was furious with myself for spending my last cent, as my throbbing head was screaming for a beer. While I was checking in my luggage, I was told I needed forty dollars for airport tax. What the fuck? I temporarily stopped breathing. Crying and shaking, I asked for help at the desk. All she had to say was, 'No tax, no flight. Why don't you sell your jewellery? That's what every other Aussie in this situation does.'

How dare she liken me to every other Aussie.

I decided to weigh up my options. I could offer my body for sex but was this dishevelled, leather-skinned, undernourished, drug and alcohol addled feral worth forty dollars? I doubt it!

I begrudgingly took off my engagement/wedding ring – a valuable diamond and sapphire estate piece from Kozminsky and worth a lot more than forty dollars – and began walking around the departure lounge, asking if anyone wanted to buy it. One woman told me to email home for money. 'Excuse me?' I replied, gobsmacked. 'My flight is leaving in one hour. And besides, if I asked them for money, they would tell me to stay here!'

I was pouring with sweat, panic gripping every part of me, when an Aussie guy, clearly sensing my pain, handed me an American fifty-dollar note. 'Here, take this,' he said. 'I have been in the same boat. I know how it feels.'

I hugged him, insisting I would give him the change. He wasn't fussed but said if it made me feel better, he would gratefully accept it. 'God bless you,' I cried.

Of course, hiding in the corner of the bar, hat pulled over my eyes, I drank his change.

I can't remember much of the flight. I do remember being thrilled about the complimentary slippers and the vodka on tap. Unfortunately, I also remember a cringe worthy part that I have tried unsuccessfully to forget.

For reasons beyond my understanding, I decided to sneak into first class to have a look. Who should be in there with his wife, both in wheelchairs, but the one and only Mickey Rooney! My mum and I loved Mickey Rooney. I ran to him gushing, 'Oh Mickey, oh Mickey, I'm such a big fan. I so loved you in *National Velvet*.'

Mickey glared at me, and in a slow grumpy Brooklyn drawl said, 'you have got to be fucking joking. I have made three hundred and forty-three movies and all you can talk about is National fucking Velvet? Hey hostess, get this fucking idiot out of here.'

As the hostess was escorting me back to my seat, I was trying to explain to her that my mum and I were big fans and could she please, please get me an autograph. She came back with one. Well, in reality, it was more like a scribble, and it probably read 'fuck off loser'.

After going through Customs and having my hand luggage and passport examined, the Customs officer gazed over the top of his glasses at me and whispered, 'This is a warning and nothing more, but you can throw this passport away. It's riddled with chemical powder.'

~

I knew Mum would be thrilled with Mickey Rooney's autograph. And that was the only thing she was thrilled about as she greeted me at the airport, a look of disbelief on her face. She made me throw away my clothes. I was sad saying goodbye to those grafts and the memories within. She bought me a pair of black jeans; size six, and a cardigan. A cardigan! I didn't argue though. She was shouting; I was wearing.

We went to lunch in South Yarra with my daughter and sister. I felt so out of place in that classy restaurant. Where were the donkeys? The streets were paved and everyone spoke English. I wanted to order tortillas and vodka shots, but no one was drinking so I ordered a strong latte – what a treat that was!

I felt like everyone was watching me. Or was it my addled brain paranoia? I moved in with Mum. She took me to the bank to send money orders to those I owed from my trip. I swore I'd pay her back one day. She wasn't fussed; she was glad to have me home in one piece.

Back home, I felt alone, discombobulated and disconnected from life itself. I missed the heat, the anonymity, the chooks on the dirt roads and the freedom.

I was receiving convoluted, abusive emails from Greg, talking gibberish, speaking in tongues, telling us we're all delusional and we should take lessons from the Columbians.

Greer offered me temporary accommodation at her apartment in St Kilda. I found a job as a housekeeper at a mansion in Toorak that was owned by a Jewish family. I was required to arrange the flowers, make the beds, vacuum, clean the six bathrooms and do the washing and ironing. The wife was a stunning looking, silver-haired woman who was immaculately dressed in labels, of course. And yes, she was a fundraiser for Jewish charities. The husband was a moneylender. They had a massive cellar and a pantry the size of a bedroom, both fully stocked with kosha goods in case of war, I gathered.

The wife had kindly written lists of my chores for me which included diagrams demonstrating the correct way to stack the dishwasher and make the bed. The bedding was heavy Egyptian linen. The bottom valance had to be one inch from the ground, the overlay three inches from the ground, the top coverlet four inches from the ground and the doona cover six inches from the ground. She gave me a tape measure to make sure I got it right.

My grandfather was Jewish, and I know it only counts if it's on the mother's side, but I was proud of my Jewish blood. After the wife explained that her ancestors were holocaust survivors, I dared to indulge in conversation. 'You know, I'm quarter Jewish. My grandfather's name was Lionel Barnett, and my great aunts were Myrtle and Selena Levy. I know it only counts if it's on the mother's side, but I still have Jewish blood in me.' I waited anxiously for her reply, wondering if I had spoken out of school, when suddenly her beautiful face distorted with anger and she spat the words, *'it didn't matter how much Jew you had in you, they still threw you in the ovens'.*

I was taken aback. *Don't mention the war.* I think I got away with it!

I needed a knee replacement badly. I was in pain and popping Voltaren tablets like lollies, desperate for relief. I knew a drink would fix the situation. I had scoured the huge house for an open bottle with no luck and, disappointingly, the cellar was locked. The wife asked me if I cooked. 'Yes,' it just so happens I am a cook'

She was delighted. I instantly pondered recipes that required wine and announced, 'I make a mean osso buco. I'll need a cheap bottle of red, if that's OK?'

She looked at me quizzically, 'Daaarling, in this house there is no such thing as a cheap bottle of red.' She went on, saying 'And surely you would never use wine in the food that you wouldn't drink yourself?'

I nodded furiously.

So finally, on my own, I proceeded to make my renowned osso buco. I opened the wine and poured some into the rich Napoletana sauce and then some into my mouth. It was like liquid velvet. I finished the bottle. The osso buco was delicious.

The following day I got a call from the employment agency saying they no longer required my services. I was confused. I thought after tasting my food they would want me to move in. Greer was also confused. I explained the situation. She said, 'Mum, you know those houses have cameras?'

My daughter, God bless her, was becoming impatient with her mum living with her. She was a single and social being. One night she met a boy at a club, and in a 'your place or mine' discussion, he said his place was unavailable. 'I live with my mum,' he moaned.

Greer replied, 'I sleep with my mum.'

Home Is Where the Heart Is

My therapist told me to confront my demons, not to move back to where they came from!

I was determined not to return to Torquay, and I was being discouraged by everyone – 'Too much history/ghosts/bad memories/a toxic town of substance abusers' – bring it on! Poppy once again offered me her house. What an amazing friend she was. So, after deliberating over my options, which didn't take long, off I went back home, back to where my heart lie. Miraculously my car started. I found employment at our old café, again, with new owners. Fuller circle.

My friend Janice offered me my room back, but I decided I needed to live on my own and to drink whatever and whenever I wanted to without being judged. Don't get me wrong, Janice loved a drink, but her drinking was a piss in the ocean compared to mine. And, as she was a vegan, there was to be no cooking of chops in her house. I had so missed grilled chops with crispy tails, mash and peas. Janice was a health nut. Her day began at five am, cross-legged, 'omming' on the yoga mat, followed by a kale smoothie, beach walk and swim, all the while wanting to chat about the meaning of life. Ouch to all of it. Even though this was a lifestyle I totally aspired to, I had planned on a lot more suicidal drinking before I made that commitment.

Eventually, I took up Janice's offer and moved in. Living with her was wonderful – cheap box wine in front of the Coonara, playing Led Zepplin, AC/DC and The Beatles. We understood each other. Janice was a well-known musician and a member of two bands. She played electric guitar and taught guitar at the Melbourne Juvenile Justice Centre. And she was a very funny girl. While out for dinner, she would put spinach on her front teeth and grin, saying stone-facedly, 'What's the matter?' or she'd suddenly hold her eye, exclaiming, 'Oh oh, my eye, my eye! It's my eye!' I adored her.

Eventually I joined her on the mat in the mornings, and besides the occasional crispy tailed chop, I became an aspiring vegan.

~

As mentioned previously, I had been in love with Bennie from the first moment I set eyes on him twenty-five years earlier. He was a surfer and a tradie – my favourite kind. He was tall and gorgeous looking with a mop of blond curly hair. Bennie and Greg had been mates for a long time. They shared a love of golf, surfing, techno music and, of course, me. From the get-go Ben and I would sit up all night talking. Greg would become furious, resenting the closeness between Ben and me. When Ben's car would pull up at our house, a young Greer would run to me and say, 'Quick Mum, Bennie's here. Put your lippy on.'

One night Greg saw Ben and I on the couch, our legs draped over each other. When Greg asked, 'What's going on here?' we blurted out in unison, 'We're in love.'

Unfortunately, Bennie had high morals and would never back door his mate. 'As long as you are with Greg, you will never be with me.'

My heart would miss a beat when I saw Ben. Wherever we were together, we would be watching the other. Even though I hoped and prayed we would end up with each other, I wasn't confident.

When Greg was in jail, Ben and I spent a lot of time together. After visiting Greg, we would go play the pokies. I wondered if he felt the powerful sexual tension growing in his loins as I did in mine. We were denying the inevitable but, as far as he was concerned, I was still with Greg even though he was behind bars.

One morning, at Janice's, there was a knock on the door and there, standing in front of me, was my knight in shining armour, the love of my life. Finally, Ben had come for me. All that was missing was the white horse?

In that moment, twenty-five years collapsed into a single breath and my life was changed forever. Our eyes met and butterflies slam danced in my tummy. We both knew this was it. No guilt now, no chains – only the sweet astonishment of timing that at last aligned.

This was a sliding doors moment. I had returned home from overseas, Greg and I had officially broken up, and Bennie had moved back to Torquay to tend to his ailing mother. This reeked of synchronicity. Ben had a casual girlfriend who worked at the health food shop and had an annoying high, squeaky voice. She was no threat to me, but I got rid of her anyway. No, I didn't kill her if that's what you're thinking but threaten her I did.

Up until now I had never believed in destiny with its mystical nuances. In fact, I had scoffed at it and treated it like a cliché, one that made no sense. But I was destined to be with Bennie, and I had never been so sure of anything in my life.

We had shared a bed several times as mates; 'spooning' was all that took place. But the night we consummated our relationship, it was electric – spooning became forking and sparks flew. I'm pretty sure I levitated. Finally, I had reached nirvana. We were both in shock. The years and years of pent-up sexual tension had finally exploded in a night of unbridled passion. That night, Bennie said, 'you know, I have always loved you but I never thought I would be "in love" with you.'

Of course, I had underlying thoughts and feelings of doubt. *I'm not worthy of this gem. I wonder how long it will take me to fuck this up.* I had put him on a pedestal for a long time. Now, I felt like I had won the lottery.

I know I have spoken before of soul mates, but I take it all back. Ben is my one and only soul mate.

Hooking up later in life is a bonus – me at fifty-three and him at fifty-one, which makes me a cougar. We already knew each other inside and out, and neither of us had one inkling of desire to change anything about the other. Praise the Lord. I felt free, free from pretence. Hallelujah, I could be myself. It was a liberating feeling and one that was so foreign to me. Our friends said as a couple we glowed. Maybe that's what happens when soul mates finally step into the sunlight meant for them all along. Strangely,

Bennie was over a foot taller than me but it was never noticeable to either of us.

We decided to break the news to Greg who was still sending complex emails preaching to us ignoramuses. From Machiavellian to Messiah. We sent off a rather long email announcing our coupling and received a one-word email in reply: 'Der.'

I knew I needed to live with my new boyfriend, so with a tinge of sadness, I moved out of Janice's. In our new place, Ben and I had our own rooms and shared when needed. How people sleep in the same bed is beyond me. I use the whole bed as I snore, kick and thrash in my sleep due to sleep apnoea and insomnia exacerbated by my middle-of-the-night histamine alertness due to too much red wine. Ben also snores, thrashes and farts, and therefore both of us in one bed was an impossibility.

I got stuck into decorating this rather drab house, hanging prints, filling it with plants, candles, incense burners, a buddha shrine and on our bedroom doors I stuck wooden letters spelling our names. When Janice came to visit she commented on the kitsch letters, which she knew cost $5 dollars each and said, 'lucky your name wasn't Rumplestiltskin!'

Ben was a good drinker and loved a party but as previously mentioned, he was more of a doof-doof-eccy man. I began to notice that he would have a few drinks and then stop, usually making himself a big cup of Milo, who does that? While I, on the other hand, would be opening yet another bottle. I did this even when I didn't need or want to drink, like when we were simply relaxing and watching TV. I didn't get it and he didn't get it, but he knew better than to say anything.

~

It was October 5, 2008, Ben was working in Sydney, and I had just had my right hip replaced and was staying with my friend Poppy in Windsor. I was bedridden and in excruciating pain.

One evening, I heard the landline ring and Poppy yelling, 'It's for you.'

Who would be ringing me on her landline? I felt a wave of nausea envelop me and I couldn't understand why. On crutches, I hobbled down the long hallway and hesitantly picked up the phone, saying 'Hello. Who's this?'

It was Greg's ex-wife. 'Hello, this is Laura. Greg is dead.'

And there it is. I tentatively replaced the receiver, as the cold dark room seemed to close in on me. I noticed soft rain falling outside the window. It was so eerily quiet, you could have heard a pin drop. Poppy was staring at me, asking 'What? Whaaaaat?' 'Greg's dead' I whispered.

Even though I had been expecting this call, I wasn't prepared for it or for my body's reaction of a racing heart and a cold sweat drenching every part of me.

Mixed emotions ensued including sadness, disbelief and, most of all, guilt. *If I hadn't broken his heart, he wouldn't have gone to Columbia. This is my entire fault. I'm the reason he's dead.*

Greer arrived. I hadn't cried until then, and once we started, we couldn't stop. We tried to make sense of it, but how? We slept together holding hands, reminiscing in the dark and crying, laughing and sharing memories. I felt so close to her, so grateful for her. She adored her stepdad and we were bonded in grief. We eventually dozed off to the dulcet tones of James Blunt:

> *Goodbye my lover*
> *Goodbye my friend*
> *You have been the one*
> *You have been the one for me*

The next morning, social media exploded and our phones were on fire. *Papa Bling Bling has left the building.* The town was in mourning.

The guilt took over my whole being. I had once emailed him in Columbia, in a moment of resentment and anger writing, 'you are so fucked up, nothing you say makes sense. I hope a Columbian savage cuts your head off with a machete!'. *How would I live with this?* It was paralysing.

There were front-page headlines: *Drug dealer dies in Columbia.* Greg's family accused me of informing the press, but I had nothing to do with it. When Mandy and her husband, also a journalist, begged for the exclusive, I turned my phone off. I wasn't surprised at Greg's family's reaction; they also thought it was my fault he was over there in the first place and would surely blame me for his demise.

Greg's son organised a memorial service at a friend's house down the coast. On crutches and still in a lot of pain, I travelled horizontally in the back of the panel van of my old mate Dick. It was a memorable wake. Greg's son spoke, sharing amusing stories of his dad detailing the uniqueness of the man, how he was one of a kind, eccentric, erratic, outlandish, amusing, honest and out of the ordinary. He was a man who fought mediocrity until the day he died. He was admired by the locals and was their shoulder to cry on, their guru, their Papa Bling Bling.

Our local musos jammed and we reminisced. It was a perfect send-off as we watched the bright red sky over the ocean as the sun set. RIP Papa Bling Bling.

Ben was still in Sydney, and I felt so alone. I was mixing booze with painkillers, a deadly combination for someone in the mental state I was in. The four children were ignoring me, no doubt blaming me.

As soon as I got home, I became hysterical, throwing up and sobbing. One of the greatest loves of my life was gone. For twenty years, Greg had rocked my world inside out and back again. I didn't know how to deal with these emotions.

In the morning, Greer and her sisters left for Melbourne with barely a goodbye. *How had our lives come to this?* Those girls were finding it hard to cope. They were in so much pain having lost their dad. I didn't know how to help them, and they didn't want my help. We were mourning on our own like ships in the night. I felt so distant from my baby girl. I wanted to hug her, make it all better, but I didn't know how. I was so self-absorbed, so in my head, hobbling around on crutches, in pain, mainlining painkillers with vodka and pining for Bennie. It was all about me. This was crazy really. Considering how much I hated myself, I spent a lot of time thinking about myself.

Our friend and former waitress came to see me with a bag of Greg's belongings, which included his exercise book with documentation of his drug dealings, a T-shirt, a pair of shorts and his sequinned 'Papa Bling Bling' hat I made for him.

Apart from the memories, this was all I had to remember him by, as his weird, very wealthy family refused to pay the $10,000 to bring him home. It was five years before they had him cremated.

~

I knew my time in that town was over. There was nothing left here for me besides a whole bunch of bad memories, brain cells and dregs of my messy love life. I needed a change. I also needed to get the hell out of Victoria. I hated the cold.

So, when Ben asked if I wanted to move to Sydney, I jumped at the chance. We organised for our mates up there to find us a unit in Dee Why in the Northern Beaches, also known as the 'insular peninsular', which they did. It was five minutes from the beach.

I decided this was my chance at anonymity, a chance to drink myself to death without comment or notice from family and friends. No longer would I have to look at their sad, disappointed eyes. No longer would I have to lie, to pretend. No longer would I feel I had to change.

Forty-eight hours later, we were on our way. We hired a trailer for Ben's floor sanding equipment, beds, the boom box and a fridge, attached it to Ben's station wagon and off we went up the Hume Highway to Sydney, singing loudly to the B-52's *Tell It Like It T-I-S*, my *head* out the window, screaming,

'Good riddance, toxic Torquay! Don't think it hasn't been heaven!'

Steak and Kidney here we come, ay!

I had cousins in Sydney and a few old Torquay surf club mates but that was it. I was excited and unsettled at the same time. I had an overwhelming sense of 'dis-ease', my depression and anxiety ever present. Fundamentally, I knew that 'geographicals' never work because you are taking yourself with you.

On arrival in Sydney, our car broke down in the main street of Dee Why. Not wanting to leave Ben's valuable floor sanding machine, we took it and a bag of mull in a cab to the Dee Why RSL, the place that would become our second home. Hours later, at our new and sparse unit, we realised we had left the sanding machine and marijuana in the cab. Sitting on empty milk crates, we maniacally searched the yellow pages for the cab company. Eventually we found it, and when the driver arrived, we offered him a milk crate and a joint. He got so stoned he ended up sleeping on the lounge room floor.

We became friendly with the peeps in the units around us. In unit 3 there were two cute young surfie-tradies, Fish and Chook; in unit 5 lived a cool English couple, whose autistic son I would come to babysit; and in unit 16 was 'Jerry the Janitor', the longest-serving resident and grumpiest man on the planet. We were ignorant as regards unit living etiquette and had outrageous parties, one of which included my daughter and friends visiting from Melbourne, along with the unit 3 boys.

We were draped in sarongs and playing charades when we heard a violent bang on our door. There stood Jerry the Janitor with two pretty policewomen. Jerry, shaking with rage, said 'Have you any idea what time it is? It's three in the morning. This is unacceptable behaviour. What sort of impression do you think you're making on the other residents? What about unit 3? How are they supposed to sleep?'

With that, Fish popped his head around the door. 'It's okay, Jerry. We're here.'

Ben and I met a guy who worked at the local bar on The Strand. He became our new BFF. He was a hedonist like us and lived with a bunch of surfers and substance abusers. We went to rages at their rooftop apartment, and we spent New Year's Eve there. That night, I watched one of his mates shoot up two grams of cocaine. Fascinated, I forced him into a conversation. It was like listening to the Road Runner on steroids. We left the party at 7 a.m., the oldest ones there and the first to leave.

I pondered our motives hanging out with these tragics. There was something fundamentally wrong with it. We were in the thick of the Northern Beaches drug culture – Sydney's answer to Torquay.

It's So Not Fair

Grief is the price we pay for love.

Queen Elizabeth II

Not long after we arrived in Sydney, I got a phone call from Janice informing me that she had been diagnosed with stage four inoperable lung cancer. Her mum died at forty-nine from lung cancer. Janice was forty-nine. The crazy part was that Janice never smoked cigarettes – it was second-hand smoke from playing in pub bands that was the culprit.

I flew down to visit her in palliative care. I was heartbroken, anticipating the final goodbye. Nervous about offering my last words to this magnificent woman, I stupidly went to the pub for vodkas and Dutch courage. By the time I got to the hospital, I was too befuddled to say what I wanted to say. When I was leaving, Janice held my head, kissed my forehead, looked directly into my eyes and said, 'Goodbye darling girl. Don't be sad, I will see you again.'

Janice passed a week later on 26 June 2011.

She had organised her own funeral, and as she had a regular gig in the Gershwin Room at the Hotel Esplanade, that's where it was held. The day resembled a rock concert. Her handmade, hand-painted eco-friendly coffin was carried in to AC/DC's *For Those About to Rock* and lead out to Led Zeppelin's *The Rain Song*. On arrival, we were presented with a lanyard on which was a photo of Janice, with her arms in the air, her guitar around her neck, both hands in a peace sign, looking radiant with her long blonde hair, sparkly blue eyes and beautiful smile. Printed on it was 'Janice Jason – Goddess of Rock 26/09/1962 – 26/06/2011, Farewell Tour

Access All Areas'. There was live music throughout, and we all wore odd socks, as was her passion. It was a magnificent day. RIP Goddess of Rock.

~

Around the same time, Mandy rang me to tell me she had been diagnosed with pancreatic cancer. To this day, I feel shame and guilt for not being there in her final days. In my defence I was in Sydney and she was in Geelong but why I didn't visit her to say goodbye I will never understand. Also, in my defence I was in denial and couldn't face her nor did I know how to say goodbye to my dearest mate. This death was too tragic to comprehend.

Tex died at age 58. A close friend and I were honoured to be invited to do the eulogy at her funeral. We tried to keep it light-hearted and humorous. We had to.

Chosen by Mandy, the music was fitting: Dusty Springfield's *If You Go Away*, Billy Joel's *Just the Way You Are* and her personally recorded version of John Lennon's *Stand by Me*, her absolute favourite. She had a great voice.

I remember Mandy for so many things but mostly for her default statement, and the most truthful of all. 'Isn't that why we're here Browne, to love and be loved?'

I still feel like there is a Mandy-shaped-hole in the atmosphere moving around me. A space where she should be but isn't. She is a permanent photograph in my psyche and there she will remain.

~

Not long before Mandy died my sister left her husband of twenty-five years for Kelly, who she is now married to. My sister's ex-husband was comforting Kelly's ex of twenty-five years and they have been together ever since. One of my ex-brother-in-law's mates said, 'Gee, you're good, dude. First you turn a straight woman gay then you turn a gay woman straight.'

As you can well imagine it was rather controversial.

At the same time, the husband of one of our good friends died. At his wake, my sis was busying herself in the kitchen for obvious reasons. I said, 'Gee, sis hasn't come out of that kitchen all day.'

Mandy said, 'Give her a break. She's just come out of the closet.' It was at that point my eighty-five-year-old mother said, 'I just don't get it. All my friends have such normal families and just look at me. One of my daughters is an alcoholic and the other one's a lesbian. My family is so Jerry Springer.'

~

Not long after Mandy and Janice died, I was sitting in my car outside work when I received a phone call from Phil. 'Hey, Sooz. I've got pancreatic cancer.'

I sat for a long time, staring into space, trying to comprehend. There were no tears, I was beyond it. I was shattered, overwhelmed. *Not my beautiful Phii.*

I made a couple of trips to Melbourne. In the Alfred Hospital, out of sight, I watched him flirting with the nurses, a lump in my throat. My heart ached for him. When he spotted me, he grinned, and in a drug-induced drawl, slower than usual, he said to the nurse, 'Here comes the love of my life. Unfortunately, she didn't love me quite as much as I would have liked'. I choked back tears, wondering how I was going to survive this one.

At their home, because of the meds, Phil couldn't sleep. He would wake me in the early hours and I'd fetch Marlboros for him, red wine for me, the boom box and Rod Stewart and Rolling Stones cassettes and head over the road to Port Melbourne beach. The ocean and the sky were pitch black, and the only light came from the streetlights and distant liners, the salty air biting into our faces. We had the beach to ourselves, and it was still and eerily quiet.

Phil and I had deep conversations, the soul-searching type. I asked him how he felt about dying, and he said, 'I would have loved a few more years, Brownie.'

I cherish those times when it was just the two of us. I felt in harmony with him in his vulnerable state.

The day came for me to return to Sydney, and I knew this would be the last time I would see him, ever. How do you say goodbye to your lifelong friend – someone connected to your soul, who loved you and believed in you unconditionally? Someone who made you feel beautiful, and special, always with a compliment? Someone who listened to you, who warmed every cockle of your heart? Someone you laughed with, cried with, were completely honest with – someone who shared your passionate love of Rod Stewart.

It was the worst day of my life; I was racked with sadness. I drank myself into oblivion and could not remember getting to Sydney.

Phil died two months later on 24 July 2013, one month short of his sixty-first birthday. His funeral was unique – a Rolling Stones banner draped over his coffin, Rod and Stones tunes playing in the chapel, *You Can't Always Get What You Want* drifting through the speakers, photos of all of us with him rotating across the screen. I was asked to speak. I wrote a rendition of Rod Stewart's *You're in My Heart*. It was so fitting.

> **Diary excerpt at this time:** *My friends are dropping like flies. I feel an underlying sadness that is difficult to describe. The grief inside me is like a living thing, tightening around my heart as if it's trying to squeeze the life from it. I pretend at normalcy while inside an endless echo asks. Why them? Grief has no clock.*
>
> *Before I remove their names from my phone, I listen to their voicemails over and over. Now in the ether, a memory, another one I can ask for help. I'm sure they have more power once up there. Or down there. I feel their energy around me, sending messages. I will never let them go. I continue my relationships with them all; it's the only way. My Dad, omnipresent and transcendental, is always with me. The imprint of my love for them all remains. In order to heal, I need to let grief lead the way. I need to sit with the pain. I need to see a professional, talk it out. Instead, I drink.*

Living in Heaven

I would rather have a bottle in front of me than a frontal lobotomy.

Tom Waits

Ben and I lived one block from the absolute best beach. I had trouble finding a job, probably because I wasn't looking. I had other plans, which involved a serious career in lunching and tanning. Up from the beach was The Strand, a strip of restaurants and bars. It was my idea of paradise and the reason I insisted we live in Dee Why.

I spent my days on the banana lounge overlooking the ocean, gazing at the Norfolk Island pines and reliable glorious blue sky, listening to Adele on high volume. I lunched daily with my companions, Prosecco, Who magazine and Words with Friends on my iPhone. I couldn't think of a nicer person to drink with, and that was fortuitous as there was no one else to drink with. I was living a champagne lifestyle on a beer budget. The dole was barely cutting it.

I developed a successful system. Knowing I had no funds, I would pay with my EFTPOS card, and when the inevitable 'declined' flashed, I would look at the sky and say, 'Gosh, isn't it the [such-and-such date]?' They'd reply, 'No, that's tomorrow,' and I'd laugh and say, 'Gosh, silly me. No wonder there's no money in my bank. Look, why don't you keep my card and I'll fix it up first thing,' A week would pass before I had money, and by the time I paid my Strand debts, I was broke again.

My new mate Tom and I threw all-day dance parties on the beach. We were never short of takers – no one seemed to work in

Dee Why. The sun was always shining and the surf was always up. I loved my new life, and I never wanted to work again.

Ben, however, wasn't so thrilled. Ultimately, he would have enjoyed coming home from a long hard day sanding floors to a home-cooked meal, but in my defence, and as I pointed out to him on several occasions, 'When would I have time to cook?'

In hindsight, he must have really liked me as he was sponsoring me in my unemployment and paying the rent, I wasn't cooking dinner for him, I was never home to greet him, sex was well and truly off the table due to the post-menopausal thinning of my vaginal walls which caused a sensation of a bull-ant nest, accompanied by an excruciating itch, I was a really annoying, predictable and cliché drunk, and I refused to get a job. Go figure!

To be honest, Ben and I both had seriously low libidos and after a time, sex became non-existent which suited us both. We had so much more going for us and besides, who could be bothered?

Many a night, in the 'grip of the grape' as I was heading out the door with car keys in hand and making sure I was as far away from Ben as possible. I would call out light-heartedly, 'Just popping down to Woollies, can I get you anything?' I would then hear a monotone reply; 'There's a bottle in the laundry cupboard.' *Phew, saved again.*

Ben hated being an enabler, but it was better than waiting for the phone call from the police station or the morgue.

I flew to Melbourne frequently for family functions. I would return miserable and with a hangover. I'd drink on the plane and then sample the wines at Sydney airport, ordering a box, forgetting I'd done so and having no money to pay them upon delivery! Meanwhile, Ben would be circling the airport until I would finally fall out of the short-term pick-up gate. The trip home was predictably silent.

On occasion, as I was crying into my beer, Ben would diplomatically mutter, 'Perhaps it would be better for you if you went home.' God bless him.

Most of the time, Ben and I were sympatico. We were both obsessed with poker machines and spent our nights at the Dee

Why RSL, a three-storey casino-style establishment. The barman, Omar, was most fond of us, due partly to our exorbitant tips but also because he thought we were amusing. And I must say, when Ben and I got going, we were an outstanding comedy team. We could be hugely and inappropriately funny. Omar enjoyed getting us pissed as the more we drank, the crazier we became. His Canadian Club and sodas with a wedge of fresh lime would kill a brown dog. Ben and I would bump into each other, break into a soft shoe shuffle, and in unison, sing, 'I've been Omar-ed, oh yes siree bob, I've been Omar-ed!'

We made a lot of friends, pokies friends that is, with the conversations limited to things like, 'Oh wow, look at that. You got five in a row! Yeah.' We'd encourage each other, boosting egos, clinking glasses and practising liquid lyrics, with an underlying knowing we would lose it all again but being too inebriated to care. I reckon we put three cars through those machines. What evil things they are.

Then there were the countless times I would drink to oblivion on my own, with Ben looking on somewhat baffled. Because I couldn't remember anything the next day, and with a feeling of despair in the pit of my stomach, I would hide until Ben had left for work. Those days were spent shuddering, cooking up a storm and hoping for forgiveness. When he returned home, I'd gush, 'Hello, darling. How was your day? Look, I've made you your favourite spinach and ricotta pie. Would you like a beer with that?'

I'd be silently praying, *Please say yes to a beer. Then I can have a legal wine.* I had already snuck a couple, just to stop the tremors, you understand.

I decided that, just in case Ben's covert wine supply ever ran out, on pay day I would stock up. I found cowboy boots were ideal for hiding bottles.

Ben stashed his gold coins; they were his insurance for a rainy day. Many times, suffering not only a hangover but also skint yet aching for a drink, I would search for those coins, scrambling through his belongings, draws and pockets. When I found them,

I would get excited, filling my overall pockets and jingling to the club, delusionally envisaging a jackpot and replacing his coins. It never happened. I would pray Ben wouldn't notice but I would inevitably hear, 'Hey, where the hell are my coins? Not again. Jeeezus.'

In Sydney, I had my fourth joint replacement, my left shoulder. On being discharged from hospital, while mainlining Oxycontin, Celebrex and Tylenol and with my arm in a sling, I insisted we go to lunch, as I needed a drink. Bennie was incredulous, saying, 'You can't drink on all those drugs, and the doctor said drinking retards the healing process so just cool your jets babe.'

I begged and begged until he relented. My hand was shaking so much I could hardly hold the glass, so I sculled the wine, which instantly came back up in a projectile manner all over Ben and our lunch. His face said it all. These moments hit so hard. The powerlessness I felt, the agitation before the drink and the acknowledgement of the baffling and cunning nature of this disease.

As an aside, what I didn't know then and do now, is that the drinking is but a symptom that aids in treating the mental illness. The drinking enables us to cope with our addiction.

The plonk killed any sense of a conscience, and I was still a kleptomaniac; I couldn't stop. On one occasion, at our local Woollies, I had forty dollars' worth of stolen cosmetics in the mix, when I heard, 'I'll let you go this time, but next time I'm calling the police.'

That's it, I swore to myself. *No more*. Well not quite no more. I also stole tofu from the Asian deli, stupidly as it was only four dollars. I put it down to the thrill of the chase. It was a Sunday and the shop was packed. When the tofu was discovered in my bag, the owner started crying, 'Why? Why, when we are so bery, bery busy? I call porice if me not so busy. This one bad, bad lady. Get out and never come back.'

Why did I do this? This was my hometown.

I was becoming recognisable for all the wrong reasons. Again, I just couldn't stop. Everything was an addiction. Every time I think I've stopped, I would do it again. Recently, I was caught at the self-serve checkout at my local Coles by a store detective who looked through my on-screen receipt and asked me why there were seven 'brown onions' listed. I wanted to say, 'Because brown onions are the cheapest thing in the store, dar.'

> **Diary excerpt Sept 12, 2012:** *I have gone three days without a drink and I can't stop crying. I have started journalling again. I feel like I am losing my mind, noticing my constant mood swings. I feel fragile, hollow and restless on or off the booze. Today is Greer's birthday so I should have a drink for her, even though she's in Bali, she would want me to celebrate her day of birth. Wouldn't she?*

~

I found a volunteer job at the local Dee Why Lifeline Op Shop. My colleagues had been there forever. Their houses, children and dogs were dressed compliments of the shop. These were old, stuck-in-their-ways, 'insular peninsular' women who had their heads so far up their own arses they couldn't see daylight and were as much fun as leukaemia. They would give me all the shit jobs. I had to sort clothing in the downstairs dungeon for hours where it was dark and smelly. I was virtually a garbage sorter.

It was from there that I picked up a ten-metre roll of fabulous red Indian silk. As my sister and her girlfriend were coming to stay, I thought I would use it to jazz up our drab unit. I covered every piece of furniture with silk and hung fringed light shades. I filled the place with candles and incense, had Krishna music playing and I made beef rendang, dahl and pappadams. When they sat on the silk-covered couch, they slid off.

Bennie took one look and said, 'This place looks like an Indian joss house.'

I had nauseating hangovers at the op shop. The manager commented that I was irritable and agitated and said it wasn't good for customers. I was only irritable before lunch, because at lunchtime I had a few cheeky bevvies with the always-available Tom. Besides, who was she to judge? One day she had a prolapse, with her insides falling onto the floor of the shop. 'How was that good for business?' I enquired.

And then there was Gwen, who had the biggest boobs in the whole wide world. They were complemented by her massive body, which was squeezed into two-sizes-too-small, skin-tight stretch jeans which she wore with acrylic T-shirts printed with puff paint cartoon animal heads. She would dab at her one functioning eye with a tissue retrieved from her left bra cup, which would then go back into the left bra cup along with price tags, notes, coins and business cards. Her left boob looked like a lumpy Mt Everest.

One day at work, I had a full-on anxiety attack – a major meltdown no doubt brought on by my suicidal drinking. Instead of recommending me to their other Lifeline services such as mental health counselling, they fired me. Such compassion! 'Don't let the door hit you in the arse on your way out!' Who gets fired from a volunteer job? Me, that's who.

Bennie's sister and brother in law had been members of the Hare Krishna movement (The International Society for Krishna Consciousness), for forty-five years and so, forever searching for the meaning of life, I decided to give this a red hot go. We attended several Diwali festivals where we chanted along with a bunch of spiritual beings. With a full band, drums, sitars, tambourines, flutes, I would find myself swept up in the infectious energy, transporting me to a realm of unbridled joy and freedom. The chanting grew louder and more insistent, drawing me in with an irresistible force until, as if propelled by an unseen energy, my hands clapping, feet and body moving faster and faster, I was transported to a different dimension. Gazing up at the heavens, the words of the chant 'Hare Krishna, Hare Krishna' seemed to echo deep within my soul. I would notice Bennie in the same euphoric state, arms in the air, worshipping Krishna. The sea of white robed devotees around me appeared as a unified entity, as I would lose myself in the collective ecstacy of the moment. The beat of the drum grew faster until it seemed to reverberate in perfect synchronicity with my pounding heart. And all the while my mind caused havoc as I had a deep longing to be part of this vibrant community and yet, a nagging sense of disconnection lingered, making me aware that my lifestyle marked by substance abuse, cigarette smoking and meat eating seemed worlds apart from the principles of this spiritual tradition. The feeling of imposter syndrome that arose was almost palpable, threatening to undermine the fleeting sense of connection I had felt. I couldn't help but wonder if, again, I was merely a pretender, an outsider looking in on a world that was fundamentally at odds with my own. The joy I felt in these moments was next level. Why couldn't I choose this life instead of the destructive one I led.

After being sacked from the Op Shop, I found a nanny job, driving rich people's SUVs and picking up their snobby children from kinder and private school. One particular eight-year-old child instructed, 'you don't need to come to the classroom. Just wait outside.'

Her five-year-old brother would throw tantrums, with me having to carry him to kinder. When we arrived, he would wave his hand, saying 'Put my drink bottle and bag in my locker then leave.'

I had to ring their mum, as I didn't know how to start her ridiculously massive keyless Jeep.

I did their washing, ironing and cleaning. One army major complimented me on my meticulous folding of his jocks. Before I left, I would spray the house with jasmine, leaving a tall vase of fresh flowers. The windows shone, the shirts hung steamed and buttoned, the clothes pressed, in four piles on their beds. Whatever the task, it was completed with an almost reverent precision. I believed that if the floors gleamed brightly enough my insides would match. I was a paradox, a perfectionist, needing total control and yet at the same time I was imperfect and loose, with a longing churning inside me, as I inevitably fossicked through the house looking for liquor.

It seemed I couldn't do anything without the dreaded drink. I somehow justified this behaviour, ignoring the simple truth that this wasn't my liquor to take and these people deserved more respect.

I also cooked for these families, the affluent working women handing over their credit cards for me to buy whatever I wanted in the way of food, which I would turn into yummy meals, filling their fridges for the week. I became close to one of these women, whose name was Marsha. She had a personal trainer for a husband who treated her appallingly. I would scrub their bathroom and toilet spotlessly and every time, as soon as I finished, he would take a dump, leaving poo all over the bowl. He told me not to go into his office, so of course I would, where I proceeded to re-arrange his drawers and hide his stuff. One day I arrived and Marsha asked me for a hug, whereupon she burst into tears, telling me she was pregnant with a down syndrome child who she wanted desperately to give birth to but jerk hubby told her she had to abort. They moved house during this time and she gave me a George Foreman grill, a fridge, a blender, a juicer and a microwave. I still think about that gorgeous woman.

One of these jobs was with an Irish family who had a four-year-old child named Emmett. He was a darling. We went for long park walks, coffee/baby chinos with marshmallows and then sleep. He slept for a long time so, after meticulously cleaning the house, I decided that I deserved a drink or two, attacking their liquor cabinet. Being Irish, theirs was a smorgasbord, and by the end of the day, I would be sideways. The woman rang me after a couple of weeks of this and explained that she didn't require my services anymore, as her mother was moving over from Ireland. *A bit far-fetched* I thought.

~

Every Christmas, Ben and I packed up our car and headed down the Hume Highway to spend Yuletide with our families. By the end of our time in Sydney, we had driven this road twenty-one times. We loved it. We would pack food, CDs, Trivial Pursuit cards and an Esky, traditionally stopping in the middle of nowhere at a tomato farm where Bennie would buy boxes of his most beloved tomatoes, including oxtail, Tommy Toe and Black Russian varieties. You name it; this wonderful old man had them all. The last trip we made we discovered an abandoned house and no tomatoes. Bennie was devastated.

The closer we got to family, the more anxious I became and the more I drank. My family were all good drinkers, with the difference being they knew when to stop. On Christmas Day, whilst playing a karaoke game, my niece howling into the microphone and sounding like a dying cat, I morphed into a viper, grabbing the microphone and screaming at her to stop. She was in tears, yelling, 'I hate you! I hate you!'

At these times, my alter ego kicked in and so did the stinking thinking, and I became somebody no one recognised, least of all myself. Those demons lurking like parasites under the skin released themselves in all their glory.

The next day, while I was on it again, the subject came up. My niece was crying, hoping for an apology, and I was loaded, telling her to 'Grow fucking up, and stop taking everything so personally.'

Big mistake. My eldest niece was mortified, and asked if we could talk before Ben and I left for Sydney. I agreed. It was the least I could do given I had ruined everyone's Christmas. At the allotted time of the meeting, I was at the local, hammered. I rang her to say I wasn't going to make it. The next morning, I snuck out of the house before they woke up. Riddled with guilt, I drank all the way to Sydney bitching and whining to Bennie about my family.

Alcohol is causing a looseness in me whereby my moral compass goes missing for hours. My soul is suffering, paying a huge price for this self-destructive behaviour. I have a fundamental inability to be honest. I have surrendered my sense of self to the addiction. I am seeking physical solutions to spiritual problems. I am the architect of my own misery.

~

That time, I was ostracised by my whole family. My sister told me she didn't want me in her or her children's lives if I continued to drink. My mother called me a shrew. *Where was the support? Didn't they know how soul destroying this disease was? Why couldn't they offer to help me instead of reprimanding me?* I needed empathy not verbal abuse. I was in so much emotional pain, and I didn't know how to make it stop. All I wanted from my only sister was her approval and my behaviour achieved the exact opposite. The shame was overwhelming.

How I hated my family. It was their entire fault. I felt misunderstood by them. They were a bunch of prima donnas – self-righteous, know-it-all fucks. *Couldn't they see, I was the victim here?*

Reflecting on this now, I am in disbelief. I can't imagine ever thinking that way. My family are the most precious people in my life, and I love them dearly.

At this point, I was receiving numerous threats and ultimatums from friends and loved ones. Things I couldn't unhear. This simply exacerbated my drinking, transforming me from feelings of hopeless dread to an entirely numb dread.

> **Diary excerpt present time:** *Alcohol has become my obnoxious consistent companion; thoughts of suicide ever present. Three bottles of wine simply normalise me. There are times when I can't succumb to the urge for whatever reason, must be a good reason, the urge then gets replaced with an absent sort of bleakness.*

~

I began cooking at the Manly Salvos soup kitchen. After work one day, still reeling from the divorce from my family, I was on my own drinking after work in a Manly bar, sobbing into my beer, when two men walked in and sat down next to me. One was in white robes and the other wore a suit. They asked me why I was crying, and so I told them my story. Their eyes never left mine, and they listened intently, nodding and taking in every word. After what seemed like an eternity, the one in robes took my hand in his, saying, 'you don't need to drink. Look at you. You have everything going for you. You are denying yourself the opportunity to be who you were born to be. You have a beautiful soul, and the drink is destroying it.'

I made a promise to them both that I would stop drinking, not believing for a moment that I would.

They gave me their cards. It turns out the one in robes was a Buddhist Monk living in a monastery in the Blue Mountains, and the other one was a psychologist and motivational speaker.

The monk asked me to visit him at the monastery, advising, 'Only if you're sober.' The psychologist offered me a free consultation.

I was convinced God had sent them. Always expect miracles.

I felt enlightened. I ran home, blurting out the story to Ben. He agreed that this was a God job. He was hopeful. He, too, had had enough.

The next day I joined the Dee Why fellowship of Alcoholics Anonymous (AA). I was accountant for my home group and attended sunrise meetings. I did one hundred and twenty meetings in ninety days.

During this sober time, Greer had moved to Sydney and was living with her stepbrother in Newtown. She suggested we do the ten-day noble silence Vipassana meditation course. 'The most powerful form of self-discovery available.'

Ben drove us the hour and a half to the Blue Mountains, where it was so cold there was frost on the grass.

A very loud bell rang at 4 a.m. whereupon we entered a huge hall, full of cross-legged, poncho-draped peeps, listening to tapes of the Buddhist Monk, S.N. Goenka. The chanting sound is hard to describe but is similar to a relentless, low, guttural moan.

Greer and I made sure we sat on different sides of the room, as far away from each other as possible so that there was absolutely no eye contact or we would have lost our shit. They had to find a chair for me as my replaced knees wouldn't allow me to sit cross-legged on the floor for nine hours – even nine minutes would have killed me.

Apart from three food breaks, we sat and listened to this disturbing noise until nine p.m., while trying not to choke on the incense smoke. Again, we made sure we sat on different dinner tables as we weren't allowed to talk to others or have eye contact while eating the tasteless indescribable vegan mush.

On the second day, Greer ran into my room close to tears, saying, 'Mum, we've got to get the fuck out of here.'

I concurred, but it was not an easy feat. We were summoned to the head guru who was sitting cross-legged on a stage, while we sat looking up at her, trying to think of a valid excuse for leaving. Unprepared, suddenly I blurted out, 'We've both got unexpected heavy periods, and we didn't bring any tampons, so we must go.'

Greer looked horrified, 'Mum, you're post-menopausal!'

After an hour, she let us go. We rang Ben and asked him to pick us up. He told us to get the train. Having called a cab to take us to the station, we escaped as quickly as possible. We jumped in the taxi, giggling. The cab driver, who looked like a bushranger, was incredulous. 'Well, I seen crew come outta there cryin', I seen crew come outta there psycho, but I never seen crew come outta there that quick.'

We decided that the only form of discovery manifesting from that experience was that we can't go forty-eight hours without talking and we're crap at meditation.

Unfortunately, my time at A.A. was short lived as I didn't have a sponsor, I wasn't committed and I hadn't surrendered to Step One. In surrender we receive. I didn't have the willingness to stop, and after eight months, I drank again. It happened so quickly.

Ben was away. I opened the fridge and found a lonely can of bourbon and cola. I heard it saying, *Please drink me. Please throw away eight months of well needed sobriety, of freedom from a self-induced prison'*. And because I was a people pleaser (in this case, a 'can pleaser'), I ripped the top of it and shotgunned it down my throat. This was strange, really, as I hate bourbon.

Needing more alcohol, I rang my mate Tom, 'hey Tommy, the drought is over, come and party man, and bring wine'. His reply, 'no fuckin way am I having anything to do with your relapse, I'm turning my phone off.' He knew me well.

The following day, I flew to Melbourne where Ben and I were attending a fiftieth birthday party. Still pretending I was sober, I spent the night sculling wine in the dunnies, plastering on layers of lipstick and mascara, delusionally thinking no one knew.

The day after that, my daughter and I flew to Darwin to visit my stepdaughters, one of whom had recently had a baby. I hadn't told my daughter that I had relapsed. How could I? It was so hot in Darwin, all I could think about was frosty Fosters. I looked longingly at their beers; I knew I was a goner. It was back in my bloodstream, and I couldn't stop now. I sneakily cased my stepdaughter's place for booze when I found a stash of spirits hidden at the top of a tallboy. Before I knew it, when everyone was asleep, I found myself on a stepladder, involuntarily sculling neat vodka and gin from the bottle. By the time the week was up, I managed to finish it all, replacing the liquor with water. All I wanted to do was nurture that new baby, my step-grandson, but my maternal instincts were overtaken by my will to drink.

I was so baffled. I had again abandoned myself for the booze. They say every relapse is worse than the last and a truer word was never spoken. When you relapse, you are drinking on knowledge which negates any enjoyment whatsoever. I didn't know how to stop. I had tried sobriety and that didn't suit me. What choice did I have? Reality was still out of the question.

I had created a prison for myself. I felt like my nerve endings were outside of my body. The roots of my hair ached. I thrashed in my sleep, waking up soaking wet, blankets on the floor. I was mainlining ibuprofen. I had headaches you could photograph. My brain felt like it was sloshing around in my head, unattached.

I couldn't recognise myself. I had reached the end, the absolute devaluation of self.

Back to School

This is a new year. A new beginning. And things will change. They must.

Taylor Swift

Ironically, I enrolled in a Certificate IV in Alcohol and Other Drugs and Certificate III in Counselling at TAFE. I figured being back in the classroom would surely stop me drinking. Alas, I still found a way. We had 45 minutes for lunch. I would make excuses as to why I couldn't join the others in the canteen for a pie and chips and off I would go to the pub to throw back a few bevvies, after which I would interrupt the teacher with rhetorical questions, loving the sound of my own boring voice. I had a crush on the teacher who was very cute. I would dress up for him, wearing lots of bling, headscarves and glitter eye shadow. I'm sure he thought I was really annoying, although he gave me distinctions for all my assignments.

As part of the course, we were required to undertake work experience for six weeks. I was assigned to Phoenix-Kedesh Rehabilitation Centre in Manly. My job was taking the daily urine tests and checking the rooms for contraband. Under a mattress, I found bottles of vanilla essence, which contains alcohol. Go figure. *I wish I'd known that earlier.*

Fitted with a duress alarm, I drove the residents to doctor's appointments, the video shop and the supermarket, accompanied them on walks and helped them cook and prepare their meals. I sat in on counselling sessions and workshops. I felt like I should be one of the residents, not an outside observer. At the end of the placement, and being surrounded by serious social workers, I decided I didn't want to pursue a career in counselling. I found the whole scene to be somewhat depressing.

I found work as a cook at several cafés in Collaroy and Dee Why – along with every dickhead in the business. At one of these jobs, the chef would sneak up close to me and scream in my ear, 'BEHIND! BEHIND! BEHIND!'

I would get such a fright that I would drop the plates.

I worked for a woman who had a criminal thug for a boyfriend; he was just out of the pen. She gave me the keys to do whatever I wanted as she had too many bruises on her to show her face. I was opening at 5.30 a.m. in freezing cold temperatures and pouring rain. I did a whole new menu and was in charge of the staff, who were young stoners and who sat out the back smoking joints. I was in charge of ordering, cleaning and cooking breakfasts and lunches. I was paid seventeen dollars per hour. I persevered until I came in one day and found that the stoners had put my magnificent Napolitana sauce, which had taken me all day to make, in the blender, as they had run out of soup!

This woman and her criminal bloke lived opposite Ben and me. There was a constant police presence, the smashing of windows and one day she was lying on the grass covered in blood. It was such a shame as she was a nice girl. Very sadly, her five-year-old daughter had been backed over by a Range Rover at the school and killed. 'She didn't even apologise,' she would wail.

Following this job, I worked for a German man. He was about seven foot tall and would lean over my shoulder, breathing down my neck and watching everything I did, commenting, 'zat slice of cheese is crooked on zee bread.' 'You need to cover zee crusts with zee mustard.' 'Don't use so much of zee pickle.' 'You put that container in zee wrong place; it needs to go to zee left of zat one.'

He rang me at home once, saying 'Suzie, you have left food in zee grate of zee zink!'

Fortunately, this was a licensed bar, and I convinced him I needed white wine in my carbonara, my coffee cup never leaving my side.

Feeling like I must have needed more torture, I found a position at Guiseppe's Pizza and Pasta in Narrabeen. Guiseppe, the owner, was a good-looking older Italian man, a bit Robert De Niro-esque.

These people were affiliated with the mafia and owned half of Narrabeen. Guiseppe's wife was a nasty, bitter and twisted old cow. She hated me because I flirted with her hubby. Whenever she passed by, she would intentionally bump me. One such time, she rammed my hip into the door jamb which really hurt. I swore at her in Italian, saying, *'vaffanculo, stronza!'* (fuck off, bitch), while throwing my apron in her face and storming out, grabbing a bottle of Riecine Chianti Classico Riserva on my way. I yelled at Guiseppe, 'your wife gives Italians a bad name. Oh, and by the way, I have my pay in my hand, so we're even. Ciao bello.'

We weren't really even as that bottle was worth more than his house. However, it would have cost them a lot more had I taken them to court for grievous bodily harm.

~

I'd had enough of these idiots and hospitality in general and decided to do some more volunteer work. Through Manly Council, I found a position at the women's shelter which provided support for women in crisis. I held cooking classes, took the women shopping and accompanied them to court. We had some violent husbands turning up at the house, screaming and yelling from the street, and there was a constant flow of police. These women were traumatised. One had been living in a bus shelter for six months. I was thrilled to be able to practice my newly acquired counselling skills. Here, I also offloaded my op shop clothes, and the women were so appreciative.

Around the same time, I met an English entrepreneur at Fitness First in Dee Why, whose name was Amanda. She was a high-level network marketer for USANA skincare and supplements, an American company. I had a passion for both products so attended a party plan at her apartment, where I drank too much and signed my life away. And so began a financially rewarding and yet torturous time of my life.

Amanda was a powerhouse. She was a tall attractive blonde woman who sang the end of every sentence. Imagine a cross between Miss Hathaway from the Beverly Hillbillies and Julie

Andrews and that was Amanda. I knew I was a good salesperson – I could sell ice to Eskimos. I was once the top Victorian salesperson for Nutrimetics.

Amanda began training me as her first downline. She bought me a keypad and mouse and would hang over my shoulder at the computer, singing instructions at me, becoming louder and louder and increasingly aggressive.

At my first party, I signed up five ladies, taking $1,500 worth of orders. I was on my way to the top. My only problem was Amanda. I had never met a more annoying person in my life. She caused me such anxiety. She had her claws into me and wasn't letting me out of her sight as I was making her rich. She sang on her knees, hands in prayer, 'You're my little rock staaar.'

I was New South Wales USANA top salesperson for the month. This little rock star was a-rockin' baby, but I had to get out otherwise I would have to kill 'Amanda-hug-and-kiss'.

~

With my earnings from USANA, Ben and I flew to Bali. My days were spent at the beach, drinking ice cold $1 Bintangs delivered to me by Wayan. I said yes to all the beach vendors, and had my feet and back massaged, my body tattooed, my hair braided and my nails painted. I bought sarongs, T-shirts, sandals, watches, bracelets and rings. The more Bintang I drank, the more I spent. At the end of the first day, Ben took one look at me and said, 'Oh my Lord. I reckon you have single handedly saved the Indonesian economy.'

I would stay on that beach until there was no more sun and no more beer.

My very pregnant daughter came over for a week, and the three of us travelled to Nusa Lembongan, an island off the southeast coast of Bali. It was exquisite. We snorkelled in deep warm crystal-clear water. On this leg of our journey, I had made myself quite sick from arrack, a Balinese liquor, and would sneak away to puke. I hid it from the others as I didn't want to have to stop drinking.

I had recently read Schapelle Corby's book *My Story: Schapelle Corby* and Kathryn Bonella's *Snowing in Bali*, both of which spoke extensively of Kerobokan prison. Having once been a crim's moll, and with a sordid fascination for anything involving crime – along with a strong sense of empathy and compassion for criminals (no doubt because I'd been one myself) – I decided I was going to get myself into the prison.

Having completed a Certificate IV in Alcohol and Other Drugs and a counselling course, I felt I could offer assistance to any Australians in the prison who had no other support in Bali. So, as advised, I bought cigarettes, magazines, soaps, fresh fruit and veggies and off I went. It was an hour's cab trip away. I got there with half an hour to spare so decided to have a 'Bali coppee' nearby. I was chatting to the locals there about my venture, and they were trying to tell me something but I thought nothing of it. I got to the prison only to find it was closed. There was just one day each week that Kerobokan Prison was closed to visitors – Sunday. And it was Sunday.

When I arrived home disheartened, Greer and Ben thought that would be it for me but not to be deterred, I went back the next day. I marched myself up to reception with my big heavy bag of goodies and spoke in Indonesian to the sleazy guards.

I've read all about you, you corrupt knobs, I thought. Instead, I lied and said I was a counsellor from Australia and was here to help any Aussies without support. One guard looked at me quizzically and said, '*Saya tidak mengerti* (I don't understand).'

I was desperately scanning my Indo/English dictionary, when he asked, 'You want to see Bali Nine?' then laughing, '*Menyesal* (Regret/my mistake), Bali Seven!'

You heartless prick. Despite this, I nodded. The guard called over a regular visitor who spoke English and, without question, escorted me into Kerobokan prison. It was surreal. I was searched and patted down, as they went through my bags. A guard stamped my wrist and gave me a ticket. Again, with a snigger, and a wink, the guard advised, 'If you lose this one, you never get out.'

l was led into the communal visiting room I had read so much about. I sat down with the visitors on a dirt floor in the foreigner section. Next to us was a small fence, with the local visitors and prisoners sitting on the other side. The room was huge and stifling, and we were squeezed in like sardines. The smell of body odour hung heavy in the air. I sat next to an Australian girl with a beautiful baby. She was visiting her husband, and father of her child, who was serving ten years for drug trafficking. She instantly handed the baby to me, and I was grateful, as it was a distraction from the filthy glares I was getting from the Australian women, who were demanding to know why I was there. Fair enough, I mused.

I began to question my own motives. *Why was I here?* I felt uncomfortable, like an imposter, an intruder. I needed to get out of there. I was kidding myself thinking I could help anyone in this room.

I saw a couple of the Bali Seven, and strangely, they looked happy. After twenty minutes of being interrogated by the Australian visitors, whilst trying to explain that I was here to help, I decided to leave. I gave away the goodies to whoever put their hands out and ran out of there at lightning speed. Sometimes I just don't understand why I do the things I do. *What was I thinking?*

Our hotel didn't have a pool, but next door was one of the most luxurious hotels in Bali, the Puri Saron which had an infinity pool with a bar inside it. Here, I was asked for a room number in order to charge my drinks. I invented one, and proceeded to enjoy the complimentary cocktails, lounging on the pool beds and eating chicken satay with fluffy rice. Eventually I was caught out, given a hefty bill, and asked to leave.

As I was being escorted from the premises, struggling to grab all my stuff while licking out the inside of my banana daiquiri cocktail glass, I haughtily exclaimed in my poshest voice, 'Well, I'll have you know, I've been thrown out of better joints than this'. I definitely hadn't.

As previously mentioned, I got stuck into the vodka – big mistake. It is a mystery bag and is laced with arrack. Good arrack contains over sixty per cent alcohol. It is lethal, causing stomach and bowel horrors.

My eyes lit up when I found a karaoke band on Kuta Beach. Suffering arrack-phobia, I decided to give it a go. The stage was so high, I had to ask a band member to help me up. I chose Meghan Trainor's song *All About That Bass*. I only knew the chorus: *'yeah, my mama she told me don't worry about your size, she says, boys like a little more booty to hold at night.'* I was rolling my hips and shaking my booty like Meghan, and the crowd was going mad. The guitarist was also mad as he kept thrusting the song sheet in front of me, saying 'sing the verse, sing the verse.' I ignored this angry man, continuing to please my adoring fans: *'because you know I'm all about that bass, 'bout that bass, no treble'.* I felt like a true star.

When I finished, because of my head rush I forgot how high the stage was, and fell off. I twisted my ankle but, due to the inebriation, didn't feel a thing. That was until the next morning, when it swelled up like a balloon. I saw some of the audience the next day. They congratulated me on my performance.

We spent some time in Gili Trewangan, one of the three Gili Islands, which are near the coast of northwest Lombok Island. We saw sea turtles swimming off Turtle Point and rode push bikes around the exquisitely beautiful island. We spent many hours at the reggae bar on the beach, dancing to Bob Marley with strangers from all over the globe, dressed only in a sarong. I swear I was born in the wrong country.

With a six pack of Bintang in tow, I joined a cooking class where a couple of cute young boys taught us how to cook satay, curry, spring rolls and bami goreng. They put on Aussie music for me, including Men At Work and INXS. I shared the beers and sang *Down Under* into a spatula, the foreigners grabbing wooden spoons and joining in.

I swear one day I will live in Indonesia. Ben concurs with this. He has spent thirty years surfing in The Mentawai Islands, and he speaks their language fluently. It's like home to him. Everything about the place suits us. Their simple life, their culture and their sense of deep joy, their religious ceremonies, the weather the traditional food, such as nangka mekuah (Balinese Jackfruit), and the piece de resistance, the Islamic call to prayer, known as the adhan or azaan, which is broadcast from the mosques five times a day to signal the times for obligatory prayers. I find that sound so spiritually powerful.

~

When we returned to Sydney, I volunteered at the local Childcare Centre.

Eventually, I was offered a full-time casual job. I could choose my days so if the sun was out, I didn't work. I was assigned to a four-year-old boy called Harry, who was autistic. Now that was a challenge! Harry would body slam me, throw frightening tantrums, toss his food all over me and then hug me. He had horrific accidents and there would be poo everywhere. I would throw him in the shower, and he'd be howling and whacking me. I wrote a daily journal on Harry's progress and his milestone achievements; he had an interesting mind. Together, he and I were kicking goals.

I became fascinated with autism and researched the syndrome extensively. The most memorable bit of research was through the work of Temple Grandin, who connected with cows' psyche and redesigned cattle yards to calm the animals before slaughter, hence producing better quality meat. This helped me better understand little Harry. I felt like he had been waiting for me, and I had been waiting for him. We were helping each other navigate this strange world. I feel we all have a bit of Harry in us.

That job ended a bit like the rest of them. And here's why. Manly Council threw the Christmas party of all Christmas parties. Partners weren't invited. I didn't know many people and I was nervous, so I decided to take an ecstasy tablet beforehand. My outfit screamed mutton dressed as lamb. I drank bubbles, socialising, chatting at a million miles per hour. Suddenly the pill kicked in and rocketed me to another dimension. I danced furiously to eighties and disco tunes – I couldn't stop moving. The mayor of Manly was a lovely community minded chap called – to his detriment as it turned out – Mr Wong. I began chasing him around the room, calling out, 'Mr Wong, Mr Wong. I got the wong card, Mr Wong.'

He was walking faster and faster, avoiding me, when I grabbed his hand, dragging him onto the dance floor. In my way-too-high heels, I was towering over this little man. Looking awkward, a smile cemented on his dear little face, he began the 'old man shuffle' while I was boot-scooting to *Achy Breaky Heart*, jumping on Mr Wong's toes, declaring 'Look at me, Mr Wong. I can dance.'

I was having trouble talking as my tongue was glued to the roof of my mouth, so I found myself a pool cue and joined the band. Channelling Rod Stewart, I threw the pool cue in the air, neglecting to catch it as it smashed into the amplifier. Everything came to a halt including the band, whose microphones started screaming with static. I froze. The silence was deafening, and everyone was looking at me, stunned. I was high as a kite as two burly security guards grabbed either side of me, escorting me from the premises, as I yelled, 'Sowwy, Mr Wong. I'm bery, bery sowwy.' *What was I thinking?*

And so, ends another chapter in the life of a would-be rock star and one-time childcare worker.

~

Considering I was a natural with children, I decided to go back to TAFE to study Certificate III in Early Childhood Education and Care. I found a job at Collaroy Early Learning Centre. I worked in the kitchen and in the rooms. I enjoyed these children, and they me. I would play their favourite tunes on the big screen, grooving and singing to Taylor Swift and Katy Perry. Again, it was suggested to me that my teaching was unorthodox, but hey, what fun we had. I told the children to call me Miss Suzie Darling as a joke, and because they thought this was my actual name, they did. This name stuck, and even the teachers and parents called me Miss Suzie Darling. I overheard one of the pre-school children quietly say to a younger child, 'If you want anything from her, you have to say "Please Miss Suzie Darling".'

I had three quarters of an hour for lunch, and the pub was three minutes away. I timed it perfectly, arriving at the pub at 12.04, hiding myself in a corner as occasionally one or other of the kindy fathers drank there. At 12.40, I would guzzle my third and last wine then hightail it back to work, arriving at 12.45, sucking peppermints on the way. Always red faced, and gushy on my return, I would be over-enthusiastic, crawling around like an animal and making strange noises. The kids loved pissed Miss Suzie Darling.

I wondered if the director and teachers knew what I was up to? Nothing was said. I guess they liked me, as drinking while in charge of children is against the law, and a sackable offence. Again, my need to drink overtook my need for employment. The consequences, for example not being able to ask for a reference and losing respect from those whose respect I craved, were so far from my mind. None of it registered when I drank. I connected with these children; I was their equal. My addiction had prevented the natural occurrence of my emotions. I, too, was a child.

One of the first things you hear in AA – one of the first things that makes core, gut-level sense – is that in some deep and important personal respects you stop growing when you start drinking alcoholically. The drink stunts you, prevents you from walking through the kinds of fearful life experiences that bring you from point A to point B on the maturity scale.

Caroline Knapp – Drinking -A Love Story. Release date 19/10/2012

Joy of joys, l got to resign from this job. Ben and I were going back to Melbourne. My break-up night was a hoot. We all drank way too much and took a bunch of funny photos. In one shot, I decided to hang one boob out, resting it on the shoulder of the girl in front of me. In the photo, the other girls are looking at my boob and shrieking. One girl decided to put it on social media.

On Monday, when I arrived at work, the place was in an uproar. The centre manager was horrified, as were the mums and dads. 'What was she thinking?' was heard throughout the kindy.

'She's a teacher, for God's sake.'

My aim was to go out with a bang, and that I did. Miss Suzie Darling and her boob have left the building.

Return to Melbourne

The most common way people give up their power is by thinking they don't have any.

Alice Walker

After seven years, in 2017 our time in Sydney was over. I was melancholy leaving my 'beach office' – The Strand – and the semi-tropical climate. I would miss the Manly Ferry, the Manly Wharf Hotel and the harbour with its sun-splashed glassy waters.

However, I was excited about our return and the pending birth of my first grandson. I was, however, dreading being back in the family fold.

Ben and I found a small house in a triplex in St Kilda, which backed onto the Sandringham train line, the passing trains causing the walls to tremble and the windows to rattle. There was a Balinese garden with bamboo plants and a large buddha. The place also came with a complimentary fridge.

We had a wonderful neighbour. She and I spent a lot of time drinking together in the garden that first hot summer. When I ran out of alcohol, she would nip next door to grab another bottle. When she ran out, I would drive to the Inkerman Hotel, justifying it to myself, as the pub was only a hop, skip and a jump away.

Ben was going back to Sydney to work in the early days, so I was on my own a lot. None of my old friends were around anymore, having mostly moved to the east coast to live. I hadn't lived in Melbourne for a long time. I left the city when I was thirty-five years old, and I was back at sixty-three. I didn't expect it would be the same – I wasn't delusional, actually I was, – but I was lonely for my old mates and my former Melbourne lifestyle of pubs, dinner parties and late-night clubbing. It was all so different this time around.

The booze was taking its toll on me, physically, spiritually and mentally. *How am I going to deal with a new grandchild in this condition?* I knew I had to stop again; the clock was ticking. I was finding it hard to look in the mirror. I had red blood vessels exploding out of my moon-shaped face, morning tremors and a throbbing liver.

I was enjoying living on my own. Without my vegetarian partner at home, I cooked crispy tail chops every night, filling the house with smoke. I watched whatever I chose on the TV, which didn't include cricket, football or Judge Judy. I was also on the phone a lot, crying to my Sydney mates.

A great deal of my time was taken up yelling down the phone at my arsehole surgeon landlord who didn't give a proverbial fuck about us. Surrounded by smoke this one evening, there was suddenly a sound-barrier-breaking, ear-piercing alarm. I rang the landlord, holding the phone out for his benefit. Apparently, the house alarm and the smoke alarm were connected, 'you need to punch in a code to de-activate both,' he was yelling down the phone, trying to be heard over the screeching alarm.

'What the fuck?' I bellowed, 'why are you telling me now and not when we moved in?'

I became panicked, the alarm piercing through the core of my soul. I grabbed a broomstick and whacked the living daylights out of the little black box. Sparks flew and it fell to the floor, smashing into a million pieces. Elation. I ate my burnt chops in peace and smoke. My ears were ringing for days.

I recently read a diary excerpt from this time in my life.

> **Diary excerpt June 20 2017:** *I feel helpless; I'm heading down a deep black hole which I have discovered has a basement. I need to claw my way out. Instead, I'm digging deeper and deeper. I feel fragile, irritable, discontented, restless, on or off the booze.*

> *I am sick and tired of being sick and tired. Why am I always comparing myself to others? Nothing I ever do is good enough. I'm so hard on myself. Why can't I listen to my own intuition instead of living by others' opinions? Comparison is the thief of joy. I am seeing myself through the disapproving, hypercritical eyes of others. My shadow is haunting me. It is blocking the light.*

I had an affinity with St Kilda as I was born there. Ben and I acquainted ourselves with the local pubs and the pokie rooms, and it wasn't long before the bottle shop attendant, Frank, started greeting me by saying, 'Hi, Suzie. The usual?'

I used all the bins in the street for my empties, sneaking out in the middle of the night, carefully placing them so they didn't clink. I continued doing the same old shit I had always done, doing it more and hating it more.

I had never agreed more with the legend Wayne Dyer when he said, 'You can never get enough of what you don't want.'

Mum, who was thrilled having us home, made sure I had a car upon my return. I was set; I had a great boyfriend, a new house with a Bali Garden and complimentary fridge, a grandson on the way, and summer on the horizon. So why was I so fucking miserable.

~

Ben eventually got work in Melbourne, and he has been subcontracting for the same Irish guy ever since. I decided I had to work again. My daughter and I organised my CV, and for someone who didn't think much of herself, my resume wasn't too shabby.

I had achieved quite a lot in my life: secretarial skills, shorthand, typing, word processing, computer skills, volunteering certificates at the Salvos and Lifeline, a Certificate III in Childcare, Certificate IV in Alcohol and Other Drugs, Certificate III in Counselling, certificates in Food Handling and Safety, Menu Planning, Occupational Health and Safety and Nutrition, a Certificate

III in Commercial Cookery and a Certificate in Rehabilitation Assistance. Not bad for a drunk!

So, considering I was a multi-skilled, multi-talented wonder woman, it made perfect sense that I would now be cooking for fifteen mentally ill live -in residents in a big old house in St Kilda. I certainly understood these folk and their psychological disorders. None of us had filters, everyone spoke their truth and we all got on amazingly well. I worked for Prahran Mission, (Uniting Victoria and Tasmania), for five years and I loved it.

I became close with one of my colleagues who is a carer and a rock star. He's the lead singer of a Led Zeppelin tribute band called Shed Zeppelin, and yes, he is the dead spit of Robert Plant. He had me at 'Stairway to Heaven'. Over the years, we have rocked it out to many of his gigs at different pubs in St Kilda. He is also known as the King of St Kilda and is a man of great notoriety in that town. He is a Taurean like me and we shared birthday celebrations, dressing to the nines at superbly organised Eurovision wing dings. He has and will always be a great friend to Ben and I.

Again, I lied to the manager about needing wine in my cooking, 'for mentally ill people?' he questioned. I explained that it didn't matter if I was cooking for the King of England or people with mental health issues; I cooked with wine, because food tastes better that way.

So out came the coffee cup again, only château cardboard was on the budget but hey, I've drunk worse.

~

The time came on 16 February 2017 when my grandson was to enter the world. I had requested to attend the birth. My son-in-law, Stuart has a weak stomach and can't stand the sight of blood, so I stood at the receiving end and he held Greer's hand.

I thought that little bugger would never come. We were there for hours. His head would appear, I would clap and yell, 'Come to me, Maxi. Come to grandma,' while making wild pulling movements, my hands in prayer, begging him to show himself. The crown would disappear, and my heart would sink. After a while Stuart had to stop looking at me as he couldn't deal with my distorted facial expressions.

Eventually he arrived, Maximilian James Murray. We breathed again. I was so proud of my tough, resilient daughter. What a trooper. She was beyond exhausted as she held Maximilian for the first time and said, 'I hope you're not expecting any siblings.'

Max became a huge part of our lives from the get-go. He was an easy baby, and I loved having him. He gave me a new lease of life. I would walk the pram to the local cafés for lunch, and he would have a bottle of milk and I, a bottle of wine.

Greer and Stuart, bought a house in Woodend where I spent two days a week babysitting while they trained it to work in the city. I felt calm and focused with Max in Woodend. I dressed him in his Seed-branded clothing, attending rhyme time at the Woodend library then the pub for lunch. When Ben visited, we sampled the twenty-eight beers on tap at the local brewery, often drunk in charge of a pram. My winter afternoons were spent ironing, knitting baby clothes and cooking for the workers, with the Coonara roaring and Max sleeping.

This should have been such a serene time in my life, but I questioned everything.

Was this really my life? Perhaps I'll stop drinking now I have a grandchild – stop to smell the roses, breathe in the fresh mountain air, enjoy the frost-covered lawn in the morning. Woodend is indeed a magical place.

The fear and anxiety that goes with addiction was not allowing me to relish this extraordinary life of mine. I wanted to focus on this beautiful child through sober eyes.

Alcohol had become my medicine. I was in a self-induced prison; I was as sick as a research monkey. My drinking had become an isolated, lonely event. Drinking socially was no longer an option. I didn't want to be the bitter and twisted person I had become.

I detested the fact that I was powerless over alcohol. From the minute I opened my eyes, it was all I thought about. When I wasn't drinking, I was thinking about drinking. When I was drinking, I was thinking about how I didn't want to be drinking. When I had a drink in my hand, it was all that mattered, everything else around me paled into insignificance. By this stage, Max and Ben were the only ones who saw me drink. Max didn't seem to notice and Ben tried to ignore it. Ben knew better than to comment as he valued his life too much. He would tolerate my drinking until I reached for the third bottle when he would politely excuse himself for bed.

I saw the Light

We cannot become what we want by remaining what we are.

Max DePree

On 23 June, 2017, I was on my own, babysitting fourteen-month-old Max. I had finished two bottles of red wine. I won't say that I was drunk because no matter how much I drank I didn't get drunk. Numb, more like it. At this stage I had become de-sensitised to alcohol, however I was in a state, 'stinkin thinkin' rampant. I was screaming at the telly like a banshee. I turned and looked at that adorable child and thought to myself: *What would I do if he hurt himself and I had to get him to hospital?* I had a vision of the drunken old granny and the baby, off to hospital in a cab, and then and there I had an epiphany.

I don't want to be a drunken old granny. I am better than this, stronger than this, tougher than this. I want to live. I want to be at Max's twenty-first birthday. I don't want to go insane, more insane.

I found myself on my hands and knees, tears streaming, as I prayed to God to take away the pain. I swear I heard a very small voice say 'I'm here for you and I can help you' Goose bumps prickled my skin. A luminous white light surrounded me and there was deathly silence. I looked towards the heavens, hands in prayer. 'Thank you, God.'

I can't say whether any of this actually happened, but I got a clear message that night from Him upstairs, and I knew that was it. I felt a euphoric sense of calm. *So, this is the 'spiritual awakening' they all talk about?*

To this day I can't believe what occurred that night.

The next morning, I attended an Alcoholics Anonymous meeting in St Kilda. A woman shared; her name was Suzie. She told her drinking story which was my drinking story. She directed her share at me, looking straight into my eyes. I cried throughout the meeting. I have been to hundreds of meetings in the area since and I've never seen her again. I have no doubt she was sent from the heavens.

Before we go any further, I might make mention here of the undeniable fact that I have been seeking help for my disease since 1990. I don't understand why we must wait until we hit rock bottom before we stop. Why can't we stop when we first become powerless? It's a conundrum. Again, the God aspect is difficult to comprehend. I had spent a lifetime looking for messages from God in graffiti on public toilet walls, in fortune cookies, while gazing at the moon, in the bottom of a wine glass and in toilet bowls while 'riding the porcelain bus'. I never took God seriously, until now. Sure, I had asked him for favours, such as 'Please God, please don't let me be pregnant,' or, while driving with one eye closed, 'Please God, stop me from killing anyone. So here I was, back at AA, seeking answers, and a new life. I was so grateful for this fellowship.

Alcoholics Anonymous is a simple program for complicated people, and we are such complicated people. Generally, we are perfectionists with inferiority complexes, egotists with low self-worth, sensitive, yet arrogant. We take everything personally. We are catastrophisers, and we thrive on drama. We are egomaniacs with crippling low self-esteem and an enormous sense of entitlement. We have a deep dissatisfaction of life. We can't stand ourselves and yet we create our own 'manifesto of amazingness'. We don't like the person we are, and yet we never stop talking about ourselves. Alcoholics are pleasure seekers, reality dodgers, avoidants, lost souls. Our denial is protection from pain, guilt, shame and anything too real. No one has the power to fuck ourselves up like we do. We would never treat anyone else the disgusting way we treat ourselves. Alcoholics Anonymous teaches us how to handle sobriety.

AA has many meanings for God. G.O.D: group of drunks, good orderly direction, grace over drama and great outdoors, depending on where your head is at. Truth be known, I have always felt that God is within.

We need to accept that it is a 'God of our own understanding', an entity more powerful than ourselves, someone or something you hand your shit over to. Why try to analyse it? Do you question the light going on when you flick the switch? If we don't have faith, what do we have? Faith gives us hope. Faith is the opposite of fear, and fear separates us from love. We need to stay connected and close to a Higher Power. The Al-anon catch phrase is: Don't fight it, don't fix it, and don't figure it out. Trust in the universe instead.

Alcoholics Anonymous is awash with acronyms such as A.N.G.E.R.: always negatively gathering emotional responses; S.O.B.E.R.: son of a bitch, everything's real; A.A.: altered attitude/allergic to advice; and H.O.P.E.: hold on, pain ends. It is also referred to as psychosomatic medicine, benevolent interpersonal relations, group psychotherapy and collective consciousness. It's a plan for a lifetime of daily living, a map for life.

The Twelve Steps, developed by AA – are an archetypal spiritual program, a set of guiding principles and practices, and the source of intense self-examination.

In early sobriety we are told to avoid the H.A.L.T.S.: hungry, angry, lonely, tired, stressed.

I have my own version – S.T.A.R.T.S.: (p)sycho, teary, angry, ratty, tortured, shattered.

That just about summed me up!

Quitting for me is the ultimate version of living responsibly. Nobody is coming! Nobody is going to protect me. Nobody is going to look at my life and say 'that life's not serving you'. That's my job. The definition of the word responsible – able to respond. If something doesn't suit me, or service me, I need to get rid of it. My job as a sober person is to protect my peace of mind at all costs.

Glennon Doyle

I had never been so uncertain about anything. I needed to be content in the unknown and to have faith. 'Let Go Let God'. I wanted certainty but it was out of my reach. I figure certainty is the enemy of tolerance. If there is only certainty and no doubt, there would be no mystery and therefore no need for faith. Life is a mystery, celebrating that mystery might be as close as we get to the truth.

Even though this wasn't my first gig, I felt like it was. I had no memory of my eight sober months in Sydney. Here I go again, and again. I disliked the rooms initially. 'I'm still not sure I'm an alcoholic,' I would repeat over and over, resulting in a word from my sponsor, 'well, something got you here and the same thing keeps bringing you back.' It's blatantly obvious to me this time around that living away from the fellowship of Alcoholics Anonymous is living in a danger zone.

What I should have been asking myself is not, 'am I really an alcoholic?' but 'is this life good enough for me?'

This time around I was determined to stay sober. I knew I was defeated, and as the saying goes, 'the defeated don't get to dictate the terms of their surrender'. I found a sponsor and did the Twelve Steps. I did ninety meetings in ninety days. I found a home group, helped put the chairs out and swung on a tea towel whenever the chance arose. Compliant and obedient, I wanted what those people had, and I was determined to get it. I had another chance at a happy life, and I was going to make the most of it.

It was drummed into me over and over that we must put sobriety first and foremost. We must do the work daily. Half measures don't prevail. The only way out is through.

I believe the Twelve Steps should be compulsory for every human being, as they demonstrate how to live a conscious, guilt free, fulfilling and authentic life.

I have completed the Twelve Steps three times now.

The most difficult step is Step Four: Made a searching and fearless moral inventory of ourselves. This step did my head in and is the cause of many relapses. It is brutal but life changing. My Step Four consisted of twenty-five pages – twenty-five pages of 'emotional sherpa', a lifetime of baggage.

My sponsor listened patiently. There were a lot of tears, remorse and pain but it was enlightening and cathartic. 'Anything else you haven't told me?' she would ask. I'd look at the ceiling, then at the floor, wiping my hands, and say, 'Ah no. That's about it for me. All done.'

'Out with it,' she would scorn.

At twenty years sober, they know. And if we are not completely honest with someone who understands us, our shadow self will start running the show from our mind's most morbid place. Addiction doesn't rest it simply waits.

My sponsor encouraged me, pointing out that Step Four is what I'm capable of, not who I am, and to forgive myself. 'Don't let your past destroy your future,' she said. 'We are not bad. We are sick.'

Step Eight was a doozy: Made a list of all persons we had harmed, and became willing to make amends to them all. Uh-oh! This was followed by the most challenging, Step Nine: Made direct amends to such people wherever possible, except when to do so would injure them or others.

When I made amends to my sister, she was most understanding and asked, 'so what now?'

I replied, 'Now you have to forgive me.' I followed this with, 'aren't you lucky we don't do you? You certainly dodged a bullet there!'

Clearly, I had a long way to go.

After completing my amends to all and sundry, I felt so proud of myself. I thought they'd say things like, 'Oh, not only are you not the selfish, self-absorbed bitch I thought you were, but you're actually an angel. I'm going to tell everyone about you and even write an article in the local paper about the miracle that is you.' One can only dream.

The fact of the matter is, we don't skip into the rooms of AA; we drag ourselves in, reluctant, depressed and fearful. However, I eventually came to love the meetings. I felt at home, as if I belonged. It was comforting. Their hunger was my hunger. Their frustration was my frustration. Here was a room full of former miserable wrecks who were pro-actively doing something about saving themselves, and who realised that divulgence of their pain was helping others. I met some great people, and I was surprised at how happy these folk were. I became close to one particular lady named Irene. She was such a hoot. She was a chronic relapser but was always so positive. During one meeting, in which her ex-lover was also in attendance, she sent me a photo of his penis. I ran to the toilets, choking on my Earl Grey Tea.

I sat at the back and, as instructed, took the cotton wool out of my ears and put it in my mouth. I shared and cried to rooms full of total strangers. I realised how much I had been holding in, how many secrets I was nurturing. Note: 'We are only as sick as the secrets we keep'. I was even surprising myself as the words spewed forth. Being able to release all of this was a form of psychological relief. Nowhere else could we be this honest, without judgement, without shame. No one else, including our families, would understand. 'Normies' don't get us. We are one in the rooms, like-minded people who get each other. This disease is the greatest leveller; in the rooms, we are all equal. Addiction doesn't discriminate. There are peeps from all walks of life here including lawyers, Australian Rules football players, actors, musicians of renown and even movie stars.

The overall feeling in the rooms is that of equanimity and benevolence. Here, we are reminded that it is our ego (Edging God Out) creating unrealistic expectations of people, causing feelings of superiority and separating us from others and ourselves. The truth is, we are interdependent beings. We need each other to survive. After a time, my need to share became monumental. I would be disappointed if I wasn't asked. I loved being centre stage, everyone listening to me, watching me. It was still all about me.

These people didn't drink anymore, but they still smoked like there was no tomorrow. The outdoor fagging and chatting pre-meeting was strangely comforting, even though since quitting myself, ciggie smoke up my nostrils now gave me an instant headache. And let it be known, I had no problem quitting, as soon as the booze went so did the ciggies. You can't have one without the other.

When you quit booze, your desire for baked goods rises sharply, thanks to the deprivation of sugar that your body would normally extract from alcohol. Meetings tend to be fuelled by vanilla slices and lolly snakes. For an annual sobriety birthday, there was a cake, a medal marking the number of sober years and hugs galore as we sang our own rendition of Happy Birthday to You: *Happy birthday to you, happy birthday to you, keep coming back ... SOOOBEEER!*

I was in a daze most of the time, a dreamlike state. *Is this really my life?* And yet there was something so euphoric about the process. I preferred the women's meetings. Some ladies knitted, including me, and some brought children and babies in prams.

And still, I kept asking myself questions. *Do I belong here? Do I qualify?* The truth is alcohol use disorder is self-diagnosed. There is no blood test or biopsy. It is a gut feeling, a deep, inner knowing. This is a progressive disease. The progression is slow but constant. It creeps up on you when you're not looking. We need more and more alcohol as the years go by until it stops working altogether.

Addiction is complex and variable. Addiction is a symptom of the pain of separation and loneliness we suffer. We are often separated and lonely before we even pick up a drink.

Generally, disconnection is intolerable for human beings. We substitute a lack of love and connection with the drink. The problem with substitutes for love and connection is there's never enough. The opposite of addiction isn't sobriety, it's connection.

I find the 'disease' concept comforting. We are not terrible people; we have a 'disease'. We are unwell people struggling with life on life's terms.

My doctor put me on Naltrexone, an opiate blocker designed to stop cravings. Fact: overuse of alcohol raises oestrogen levels, causing confusion, poor memory, depression and anxiety.

Removing it suddenly can cause monumental imbalance to our internal settings. This wonderful GP was vital in my initial sobriety. She made a poignant point when she said, 'If alcohol was discovered today, it would never be legalised, being a dangerous toxic substance.'

She also prescribed me with a mild anti-depressant to 'take the edge off' and to help me sleep. It worked, so much so that I have taken one a night ever since. I question my need for a daily pill (as they say in AA, 'pills are for dills') but if it ain't broke…!

Sober, I no longer had a buffer against the world. I had to come to accept that my life, as I knew it, was dead. The armour was off. The mask was gone. My security blanket was no longer. Here, I was, vulnerable, raw, exposed, emotionally crippled, a spiritually bankrupt half a person, no longer with an identity. What will I be? Who will I be?

The more sober I became, the more proud I became of the sophisticated, pro-active, grown-ass woman I had become. However, I was never happy being labelled and stigmatised as an alcoholic, as I find it diminishes the full spectrum of my humanity, overtaking the fact that I am an extraordinary, amazing person. Alcoholism is such a specific pathology. People put you in a box, saying 'Oh, she's an alcoholic,' which they think gives them *carte blanche* to wipe out any responsibility for their own behaviour.

Re-evaluating the past, I can see the drinking caused the dismissing of my boundaries which were unstable to begin with. It became a demon, a demon that followed me around sucking every ounce of confidence out of me. Alcohol hardened my heart.

~

There were some horrendous times in early sobriety, including two-day-long sobbing fits, violent mood swings and paranoia. A poor internet connection could lead to catastrophic frustration. Adding to my torment was the fact that, even though I was on Naltrexone, I was going through unassisted detox and a cerebral reboot. My nerve endings felt exposed. I was irritable, restless and so fucking angry. I look upon anger as unmet needs. Anger tells you what you need. Anger causes our bodies to over-heat, triggering nerve activation. My mind played havoc with me, imagining catastrophes, disasters and accidents involving my loved ones. I call it 'dress rehearsing tragedy'.

If Ben was five minutes late home, I thought he had been decapitated in a car accident. If those three little dots didn't manifest into a text message in the next second, they too were dead. I had gruesome thoughts. When I saw a woman holding a baby, I imagined grabbing that baby and throwing it over a fence or tossing it in front of a car. These thoughts sickened me and yet they were ever present. I wondered where they came from and why? *Did they manifest from a need for attention, for people to please notice me, please see and feel my suffering? Or from a desire to cause a reaction and pain in the mother whose baby I had thrown over a fence, to destroy her perfect life and her perfect baby? Why should these people be so happy when I was so miserable?*

I recently read another woman's 'drunkalogue' and she, too, expressed the same imaginings, which I found comforting.

My early sobriety dreams were disturbing and intense – mostly involving drinking, justifying it, hiding it, being held down and sat on, force fed alcohol, warped faces on strangers, maniacal laughter, waking up with young boys I didn't know, drowning in a deep, dark, frightening ocean, smashing cars. A strong, looming sense of guilt and remorse hovered over everything – me, always the sycophant, always pretending. I awoke sweating; sometimes crying, relieved it was a dream and that I was still sober. Still to this day, according to my dreams, my other life, I have never stopped drinking.

Whenever my dreams involved my partner, it was always Greg, not Bennie. This is still the case. I wonder what that signifies.

I Want to Feel Again

All I want is emotional sobriety. Is that too much to ask?

I missed drinking. Without it, I didn't feel complete. I was desperate to drop a toe in that river again, or fall in. I missed the drama. I wanted to feel hungover; I wanted to feel shame. I wanted to feel something, anything. I reminisced about the days when a couple of bevvies would fill me full of hope, energising me, kick starting me. Now that was so out of reach.

Early sobriety, known as the 'pink cloud', is tricky. The days dragged on. I wish I could have skipped that part. I hated the slow and aching present. Sometimes I would do three meetings in one day – one before work, one at lunchtime and one in the evening. The meetings became my spiritual thermostat.

At times, I became so depressed, not knowing how I would live without booze. The future seemed ominous, and I pondered upcoming events and my ability to stay sane and sober throughout. Christmas, New Year, Easter, birthdays, weddings, funerals, long weekends, bar mitzvahs *(I should be safe there)*, anniversaries, live music, any day that ends in a 'y'. God help me, kill me now, I had to stop thinking. It had to be one day at a time. I had to stop going against the grain, stop bashing my head against the wall.

Where will I go? What will I do? I'll have to get rid of all my friends, not that I had any friends. I had managed to insult or punch all of them. Instead of isolating in active addiction, I'll be isolating in sobriety.

In the haze of recovery, my alcoholic mind finds itself wrestling with a profound sense of disconnection from the world and those in it. I was constantly questioning, desperate to understand this plebian society. Like the married couple walking hand in hand at Bunnings, discussing which lamp would suit their newly built house in their newly build suburb, the one with no trees. Does it really matter what fucking lamp they choose? Will the right lamp make them happy or will the wrong one ruin his day at the office or play on her mind at school drop off, or when she's wandering through the supermarket desperately trying to decide what to cook for dinner, again! What do they have to look forward to? The annual Bali holiday where they will do what the million other families do, while resort dining with their braided hair? Does that make them happy? Or the old married couple dining at the RSL with their one glass of wine and their roast of the day. What makes them happy? What do they have to talk about? What will they do after lunch? Sit in the same chairs? Watch the same news programme, tut-tutting about the disgusting state of the planet?

I yearn to understand, but more importantly I yearn to know my place within this tapestry. I yearn for a life which is not just about surviving but about truly living without a need to numb myself.

The thought of a sober life, a colourless, flat and dull life, was overwhelming. *How will I deal with people and the relentless small talk?* No more drinking away the boredom, the awkwardness of social situations. Alcohol had an uncanny way of transforming complete bores into fascinating people.

Sober – what a frightening word. There are a number of definitions for the word in the dictionary, including serious, sensible, solemn, severe. Being sober, I began questioning every little thing, the 'analysis paralysis' causing so much anxiety. *Why are we here? What does it mean? What is the point?* I'm with Bono; I still haven't found what I'm looking for.

I recall my ex-husband handing me over to Greg, saying 'I hope you can make her happy. I certainly couldn't.'

Maybe I will never find happiness. Maybe I'm not meant to. Maybe I don't deserve happiness. Maybe I've de-sensitised myself to it.

Even though we are no longer in active addiction, the reality is alcoholism never goes away. We need to accept this and move on. Abstinence can be its own fierce motivator – after all, who in their right mind would risk waking the beast by feeding it alcohol again?

I have to say, I love the simple dignity of waking up without a hangover – the dignity of being who I am, enjoying who I am. I no longer have to act. There's no more pretending and no more exhausting myself trying to please everyone around me.

So many good things come with sobriety. Like concerts, where I can remember everything, where I'm not spending the night queueing at the bar or the toilets and missing the show, (or on occasion peeing my pants). I have crystal clear memories of A Day on the Green concerts - Robbie Williams, The Waifs, Cindy Lauper, Fat Boy Slim, Midnight Oil, Sting, Foo Fighters, Rod Stewart, the Chicks, all thanks to sobriety and my beautiful mate, who runs the show and who allots us front row seats to all the gigs. *Respect.*

The cravings have almost gone, but I still have a problem dealing with the 'defects' of character that caused me to drink in the first place. As stated in Step 6, we must be entirely ready to have God remove all defects of character. This step builds upon the self-awareness gained in previous steps where we identified and admitted our character defects. Step 6 is about cultivating a willingness to let go of these negative patterns and behaviours.

I'm not sure if God has taken away my shortcomings just yet. I don't know if he has that much power or if he was even listening. For example, my judgement of others is scary, but how do you abandon something you've been conditioned with your whole life?

I pray for tolerance. I told Bennie off tonight because he used a wooden spoon to cut a piece of spinach pie out of the baking dish, ruining the square shape of the pie. I was so angry. Next to me in the gym changing room was a millennial putting on her face powder. She was using a brush with a dab, dab, dab and bang, bang, bang on the bench, over and over. After internally chanting *pause, pause, pause, breathe, breathe, breathe*, I heard myself say, 'Can you shut the fuck up? That banging is giving me a fucking headache.'

I have an ongoing shimmering resentment of people and their ways, spending a great deal of my time sanitising the character flaws of others. *Why can't they be the way I want them to be? Why can't they think the way I think?* These resentments fester, lingering and torturing me. I have let them live rent free in my brain for way too long. It's time to go.

~

In early sobriety we received a wedding invitation. I began to sweat as I looked at the gold calligraphy on the envelope. It was like opening a bomb. I thought about throwing it in the bin before Bennie saw it, but they were good mates and we had to attend. The wedding was at a winery. *Perfect! What are they thinking? How can they do this to me? How can they have a wedding at a winery when I no longer drink wine?*

We were sat at a big round table, where charming waiters offered us a choice of the local wines. I couldn't believe I was placing my hand over the top of my glass. Previously I had moved away from people who did that as they were not people I wanted anything to do with. I had marvelled at this common gesture and now here was I doing the same.

Sipping my Evian, I found myself counting their drinks. *Doesn't she know she's had enough? She's making a fool of herself, her lipstick is smudged and she's flirting with a guy young enough to be her son. Talk about mutton dressed as lamb, could you put anymore red lipstick on, it's all over your teeth for God's sake'. Disgusting.* I smiled and nodded a lot. I wanted to say 'Hello, my name is Suzie, I am an alcoholic, and this is fucking torture' *'God grant me the serenity … God grant me the serenity …'* But these people are having so much fun. I should be happy for them, but I hate them. I hate them so much.

When I was one hundred and twenty-eight days sober, I agreed to performing in a play held at the Arts Centre Melbourne. The play, *All the Sex I've Ever Had*, was written and produced by Darren O'Donnell, a remarkable Canadian man who delves into 'social acupuncture' with people from all walks of life, races and ages. There were six of us on the stage, and at sixty-three, I was the youngest. We each had a script outlining our lives and the pivotal points within. In turn, chronologically, we told our stories. It wasn't all about sex but that was the focus. A microphone was passed around the audience as they relayed similar experiences. There was laughter, tears, dancing, confetti throwing and raw, honest confessions. The energy was palpable. It was a huge success, so we added extra shows. This was a tough gig as everyone on stage had a glass of wine in front of them and there was drinking before and after the show. My sponsor came; she was so impressed. Darren called me 'the milker' as I had a way of capturing the audience with, perhaps, too much detail!

So many women identified with my story and my early sobriety. In the foyer at closing, there was a queue of women wanting to share their drinking stories with me. It became glaringly obvious that the subject of female alcoholism is still so taboo. I was buzzing being back on the stage and am so grateful for that experience. I was interviewed by the Australian Broadcasting Corporation which aired on the entertainment channel. I had the bug again; the stage was where I wanted to be. I began looking for repertory theatres to sign up to. My sponsor, however, warned me, saying 'Don't make any big decisions or changes in your first year of sobriety.' She was such a buzz kill.

~

It was 25 December, 2017. I thought I'd be okay but I was far from okay. I was having an internal meltdown. I noticed things that shouldn't be noticed. I felt disconnected. A drink would have instantly connected me. *Why can't I find joy at Christmas time?* It should be a happy day, full of love. I envy those who find joy after one glass of champagne, becoming chatty and telling stupid jokes from the stupid bon bons. I hated those stupid jokes. I hated those stupid bon bons. I couldn't find anything to say, and there was a looming silence from within. I am no longer the party girl, and I'm grieving the loss of her. The relatives face timed from New Zealand and 'Merry Christmas' is wished back and forth. I avoided the camera. *What would I say? Merry Christmas. Oh, don't you all look happy. Do you have turkey or prawns?* Fuck that. I couldn't give a rat's arse if they had turkey or prawns. *Will this ever get any better? Will I ever have life in me again?* I felt numb. I was as flat as a tack, plateauing, and my eyes were transfixed on nothing. I wonder if everyone is talking about me; I imagine it. 'Gosh she's not nearly as fun as she used to be, is she?' 'She doesn't look happy, maybe she should drink again, at least alcohol made her interesting.' 'Why doesn't she stay at home, the boring bitch?'

And it doesn't help when my mother says, 'You're so uptight.'

'Would you rather I drink again, Mum?' I snarl. 'That didn't seem to please you either. What would please you, mother dearest? Bitch.'

She is ninety-six now and I despise the way I am around her. I revert to a twelve-year-old child – insecure, desperate for her approval and love. I hate that I still resent her; it eats away at me. I pray for the patience to answer her rhetorical questions which go twenty-four seven. I want to love her, to be kind and tolerant, but she pushes my buttons like no other. She also holds a mirror to me. I despise that part.

I wandered from the Yuletide table, feeling desperately forlorn, and found myself in my mum's camp. I open the fridge and there are two uncorked bottles of wine inside. I pick one up and I put it to my mouth. *No one will know, just one sip. I'll feel better after one sip; it will normalise me. I won't need any more, just one sip, but I need this.* My body broke out in a sweat. Shakily, I put it back. *What was I thinking?*

I took two-year-old Max to the beach to collect shells. Bliss. He is so intuitive, and I sensed he was feeling my sadness. He held my hand as we walked, chatting enthusiastically as best he could. What would I do without this child? He is my saviour. I love him so much, I feel as if I love him too much at times.

This is the toughest thing I have or will ever have to do in my life. The obsession is ongoing. How do I explain that booze calls to me from the fridge and the cupboards? Booze sings its siren song to me, luring me, enticing me, teasing me.

I want to be one of those organically happy people who make others feel good. I have chronic social anxiety. I no longer know how to make people laugh, and I struggle daily to be an acceptable human being.

And then there's the inevitable question from friends and family: 'How are you going?'

How are you going? How the fuck do you think I'm going?! However, my standard answer is, 'Fine, I'm just fine. I'm just fucking fine, thanks for asking.' FINE: fucked up, insecure, neurotic, emotional. Tick, tick, tick, tick.

Before I go on, let's get one thing straight. I have no regrets. My drinking life and its titanic turbulence served me well until it annihilated me – laughing till my stomach ached, urinating at inappropriate times and in inappropriate places, sleeping with randoms, sexually transmitted diseases, bitch fights, bloke fights, unexplained bruises, stomach evacuations, endless bouts of diarrhoea, brain-bursting hangovers, police cells, DUIs, cocaine-induced nose bleeds, tremors, broken blood vessels, migraines, paranoia, anxiety, suicide ideation, isolation, family war and a general obliteration of my nervous system. I wouldn't change it for the world. Note: my tongue is firmly planted in my cheek. I will never go back to that self-induced prison. What a lonely life that was.

When you stop drinking, you lose a huge part of yourself. There may no longer be any of the above and it may seem as if there will be no more fun but the sober fun is authentic fun, as opposed to the drunken fun, which was superficial fun, and came with a dread of how it would end.

Tough times never last, but tough people do.

Robert H. Schuller

There are many mixed emotions, opinions and reactions when someone gives up drinking. There is also the fascination, the envy and the guilt of those who are still drinking, and the questions, including 'Why did you stop drinking?'

'Because I made bad choices when I drank, put my life and the lives of others in danger. I was sick in body and mind and spiritually bankrupt. I had a fatty liver, and I was going insane.'

Their faces say it all. 'Shit, I have all that. Maybe I, too, need to stop,' or 'Yeah, well, I don't trust people who don't drink,' or 'I'm not there yet.'

And of course, there are the sober shamers, the ones who are threatened by my sobriety. 'Why can't you just have one?' asked one of my friends who is in Overeaters.

'Why can't you just have one piece of chocolate, fatso?' was my grown-up reply.

Some feel attacked by my sobriety. At times I feel guilty for stopping. Drinking is our social connection; sobriety is isolating. From total connection with my girlfriends, sober, I can barely meet their eyes. There is no longer a commonality of interest. Back when I was drinking, I remember whenever one of my friends announced, 'I'll have soda thanks. I'm not drinking.' I wanted to ask her to leave the table. Drinking was a shared activity. One person's abstinence was a violation of protocol.

Once you give away the drink, you soon learn who your real friends are. The ones who love you unconditionally don't go anywhere. And most of them are relieved, thrilled in fact. Mum was so happy she bought me a car!

Unless you have alcohol abuse disorder, you can't possibly imagine what an enormous effort it is to stop. Alcohol is so deeply stitched into our social fabric. It's ubiquitous.

And then of course there's the bullshit inner conflict. *Maybe I can learn to control drink. Maybe I could just have a couple.* I tried control drinking once. I controlled what everyone else drank, as when they left the table, I would scull their drink. They'd return and ask, 'Where did my drink go?' I would shrug, gazing at the ceiling, 'No idea.'

We Are the Fortunate Ones...

... as we are given the gift of losing hope in alcohol to find hope in recovery

Now I honestly believe we are the fortunate ones, as we have been given the 'gift of desperation' – abstinence is our only option. It is a common conception that if we keep drinking, we will end up in jail, a mental asylum or dead. If nothing changes, nothing changes. Humans are hard-wired for change; it's in our DNA. If we don't change, we die.

> **Diary excerpt June 23, 2018:** *I am six month sober. Today I saw a clairvoyant. She told me I will write four books, and that I will be a 'star'. I told her I had always been a 'star', to which she replied: 'Stop. If you get those two stars confused it will be deadly. You need to forget about that old you or she will get in the way of the new you and your current success.' I knew what she meant.*

Through this process, I have come to the realisation that from a young age we need to know our worth. If we don't, someone will assign it to us, and then we will have to change to suit. This brings me to the part where I am reading Glennon Doyle's book *Untamed*. Here's an excerpt:

> *My mother watched the spark in my eyes fade during my twelfth year on Earth. Now, sixty or so years later she was witnessing the return of that spark. In the past few years, my entire posture had changed. I looked regal to her, majestic. And a little scary. After that day I began to ask myself,* 'where did my spark go, at twelve, how had I lost myself'.

I was at a young age when I got on the 'Hedonic Treadmill', always trying to change my life situation but never feeling any different. I've done my research and learned this. Twelve for me is when we learn how to be good girls, and real boys. Twelve is when children begin to hide who they are in order to become what the world expects them to be. Right around twelve is when we begin to internalize our formal taming. Twelve is when the world sat me down, told me to be quiet, and pointed towards my cages: These are the feelings you are allowed to express, this is how a woman should act, this is the body you must strive for, these are the things you will believe, these are the people you can love, those are the people you should fear, this is the kind of life you are supposed to want. Make yourself fit. You'll be uncomfortable at first, but don't worry, eventually you'll forget you're caged. Soon this will just feel like: Life. I wanted to be a good girl, so I tried to control myself. I chose a personality, a body, a faith and a sexuality so tiny I had to hold my breath to fit myself inside. Then I promptly became sick, sick mentally, looking for comfort, searching for ways to dull the pain and confusion, looking for a solution, an escape.

~

Through my drinking years, I sought help from many doctors. Initially not wanting to stop, hoping for a magic pill which would enable me to keep drinking.

I would lie:

> Doc: 'So, how much do you drink?'
> Me: awkward silence.
> Doc: 'Well, how much? The equivalent of one or two bottles of beer a day?'
> Me: attempting to lighten the situation: 'I spill more than that!'

However, as time went on, I would seek out the health professionals, almost begging them to tell me to stop, alas, one mentioned that my liver count was elevated, der, another mentioned that down the track a fair way I may develop oesophageal haemorrhaging and die. '*Down the track*'?' You would think forty-five years of drinking was 'down the fucking track' wouldn't you?

They would skirt around the problem, ignoring the obvious signs, and then write me out a script for anti-anxiety medication. Doctors are enablers.

While writing this, I am reminded of how booze was the dominating factor in our lives. It was, and still is, acceptable, and in a way, compulsory. In society, we say things like 'If you don't drink, don't come,' and 'Go hard or go home.' We think drinking is dangerous, edgy, and cool. The marketing sucks us in. Drink champagne to celebrate; drink champagne if there's nothing to celebrate. Alcohol is glamorised. It's plastered on billboards and advertised on television. It's the glue that keeps social situations together, the petrol in our tanks, the endless quotes. 'I used to run but the ice cubes kept falling out of my glass.' 'A day without wine isn't over yet.'

This is extraordinary, considering it is estimated that alcohol kills three million people throughout the world every year. Around one in every twenty deaths worldwide is the result of an alcohol-related disease, injury, accident, murder or suicide.

Alcohol is the base cause of sixty diseases. More people die from alcohol related diseases than AIDS, violence and tuberculosis. It is a group one carcinogen, and is a huge factor in breast, pancreatic, brain, liver and stomach cancers.

World Health Organization statistics – September 2022

Recovery means breaking free from the habit of chasing quick fixes – understanding how what once felt good became destructive. It's about looking inward, asking why we're ruled by impulses. Why the constant unease? Why do we keep walking back into hurt and pain? Why the self soothing shame? Why the self-medicating anxiety?

It is thought to be in our DNA or that we are born with a predisposition to alcoholism, however the jury is still out on that one. It is a fact that I may have inherited poor impulse control or low frustration tolerance, some features that make me more vulnerable to anxiety and therefore craving numbness, but still not convinced I was born with the disease. Latest research suggests that there is no single gene for alcoholism.

According to epigenetics, our behaviours and environment can manifest changes that affect the way our genes work, in turn activating or deactivating certain genes.

Continued substance use can cause neuro-adaptive changes in the brain that are the basis for craving, bingeing, tolerance and withdrawal.

Who knows when and if a heavy drinker crosses the line into alcoholism? And how much of that is significant and how much of it is inherited? Where and when is that magical line between use, abuse and addiction? When do we switch from liking to needing alcohol? We do know that alcoholics continue to use long after the pleasure and thrill are a distant memory. We become sensitised to alcohol and the choice to drink is taken from us. As far as I'm concerned, we have the 'isms' of alcoholism in our DNA. From an early age we feel misaligned; our inside doesn't match our outside.

Addiction specialists have found that people in active addiction experience abnormalities in the reptilian brain, the part of the brain that controls instinctual and impulsive actions. Addiction and the severity of it is reliant on so many factors or stressors; genetics, lifestyle, gender, social disconnection, sensation seeking, social rank or hierarchical status. These factors are unconscious and powerful and mostly out of the addict's control. The addict craves the dopamine and the ensuing pleasure, however chronic alcohol use leads to reduced dopamine production and fewer dopamine receptors, which can result in a 'reward deficit' and potentially contribute to alcohol dependence. Alcohol is cunning, powerful and baffling and therefore leaves the addict feeling 'hopeless and a failure'. Neurological and learned behaviours are depictions of addictive conduct. Societal fragmentation and fracturing of meaning lead to experiences of disconnection from each other. This is called 'poverty of the spirit'. Addiction is a cry for help, spiritually and mentally.

~

When I think of the booze I have hidden, drunk behind backs and stolen, the years of deceit, the people affected by my addiction and those I let down and disappointed due to hangovers or inebriation, it brings tears to my eyes. I feel ashamed thinking how my ignorance and silence hurt others.

I would sever solid friendships if they couldn't keep up with my obsessive drinking, 'Sorry, I can't be friends with you anymore. You don't drink enough.'

I have lived with an empty heart for so long. I now know that sobriety, is a panacea for a full heart. I feel I have missed most of my life. All I want now is to feel it all. I have been resurrected. *Here I am. This is me, starting over. I have come home to me. I am reborn.* Recovery is freedom.

> **Diary excerpt June 23 2018:** *After twelve months, the fog has lifted. My head feels clear, transparent, alert. I feel organically happy, with a sense of peace, a serenity I haven't felt in years. I love me, the strong me, the one who has released me from jail, remarkable me, amazing me. I am so proud of me.*

Relentlessly, I remind myself and my sponsees, the need to keep a sense of humour about ourselves. 'Never take yourself too seriously,' my father's words repeating in my ear. 'Always look for the funny side, because there's always a funny side.'

We didn't stop drinking to be miserable.

Having said that, there are still the odd days when I wonder how I'm ever going to get through, fearful that if I stop doing the work I'll drink again. I still have feelings of anxiety when around people drinking, not because I want to drink but because I have trouble dealing with my feelings. *Why did she say that again, she just said that? Why is she pouring herself another drink? She's already pissed. Doesn't she know how boring she is? Guess I should feed the kids and wash the dishes. None of these drunks are going to do it. Maybe I'll just peel off unnoticed and jump on a meeting. I wonder how long they are staying. I'm so bored. How much fucking small talk can I muster? Why didn't they bring their own beer? Why are they drinking that person's wine? Fucking freeloaders.* And aren't I the ultimate hypocrite. People are forever holding mirrors to me. I was such a freeloader. I spent a lifetime botting, constantly broke, having pissed all my money up a wall. I used and manipulated people; I stole from my best mates' wallets and liquor cabinets. I resented those people because they allowed it. They humoured me, observing my self-centred behaviour without comment. I had no respect for them or myself.

My restlessness turned outward – into obsession, planning, scheming – anything to avoid being alone with myself. That craving for control was really an escape from the turmoil within. It wasn't about power; it was about survival. I was trying to contain emotions I couldn't understand. My energy spilled onto others, as if my worth depended on their approval. This is the seed of co-dependency: the moment our own inner world becomes too painful to inhabit, so we start living through others instead. We fix, we manage, we manipulate, we charm – all to keep fear from swallowing us whole.

I once relished drunken conversations. I excelled at them with my bullshit, outdoing all the others and their lies, exaggerations, amplifications, baloney, fabrications, falsehoods, fantasies, misrepresentations, embellishments and repetitions. I trumped all. I was a one-upper, a catastrophiser and a terrible gossip with a caustic tongue, often causing torrents of vituperation to spew forth from my mouth. I would demand attention by putting other people down, using sarcasm as a weapon, telling others' secrets, showing off, dominating every situation, delusionally thinking I was being so hilariously amusing and witty. I still have nightmares about those times, I still see their faces reflecting horror, disgust, shock, sadness. Injured faces, wounded faces, people leaving the table or the room due to my words. How did I not see I was committing social suicide?

A friend commented recently, saying, 'You set the larrikin bar so high, you could barely keep up.' It is clear now that my behaviour was destroying my authentic internal power.

I was a paradox, I had always had a deep intuition, a gut feeling when it came to people's characters and motives and yet the alcohol dulled my instincts. Instead of using those insights to benefit all around me, I chose to shut them down.

In conversation with my daughter, 'Can you ask your dad if I can attend his sixtieth birthday party?'

Her reply was, 'He said no because you will take over.'

Now, I pray to God to help me be an altruistic, self-effacing person, like so many in the rooms of AA. I pray to be self-forgetting; I pray for willingness. I pray all day every day. Scientifically, prayer is extremely effective.

Nowadays I see things so differently. It is hard to imagine that the drinking me and the sober me are the same person. Once upon a time, I would only do favours for people if I got something in return. When I gifted someone I would expect thanks, and acknowledgment. Now I give to be generous, I do service to help others with no expectations. And it feels so good. That is my reward.

It seems as if the self-absorption never goes away. It was all about me when I was drinking, and it's all about me when I'm not drinking. Either way, it's still all about me!

To quote me: 'That's enough about me. What do you think about me?'

I'm forever having to concentrate on not interrupting others when they are talking about themselves, as I can't wait to get back onto me. I'm mentally rushing their words.

Now that I am unshackled from my addiction, I understand why addicts take their own lives. They can't live with the booze, and they can't live without it. When I think of the times I considered killing myself, I physically shudder. I thought ending my life was the only way to stop the pain. It's funny how emotionally flimsy we are, even when we think we are so tough.

The ceasing of the drink is just the beginning. It's no longer a 'drinking disease', it is now a 'thinking disease'. We need to change the way we think. There are so many unsubstantiated thoughts – the stories we tell ourselves that have nothing to do with reality. They are merely thoughts, and we are not our thoughts. We need a daily meditation practice and a daily gratification list. We need to find our truth as opposed to the illusion our addiction holds us in; we need to find our authentic selves.

I listened to a share recently, and he said, 'I thought when I came to AA I would have to get rid of me, but what I learnt here is that it's okay to be me.'

Toning Body Mind and Spirit

To strengthen the body's muscles, exercise; the mind's muscles, read; the heart's muscles, laugh; and the soul's muscles, love.

Matshona Dhliwayo

A strong incentive for kicking the booze was my intense vanity. I have always been boringly self-conscious and obsessed with body image. There isn't a reflective surface I don't fall in love with. Now, without the ageing effects of booze and ciggies, I had a real chance at looking hot again. I'm still delusional!

I joined Fitness First for Pilates, pump and CX classes. My old body ached. I became acutely aware of how invisible I felt. I was surrounded by Elle Macpherson and Arnold Schwarzenegger lookalikes. Nobody spoke to me, maybe because they didn't see me. After all, my 5'1" was so much closer to the ground than the rest of them. Gone were the days when heads turned as I entered a room. Gone were the wolf whistles. I marvel remembering doors opening for us young, attractive girls. Now doors were closing everywhere. I felt unseen and unheard. But none of that mattered. I was sober.

I became a member at the St Kilda Sea Baths as they overlooked the bay, and there was a pool for aqua aerobics. I also found myself a personal trainer, I called her Madam Lash. I met her at 6 a.m. five days a week to be tortured. During my first session, dressed like Jane Fonda including towelling head band and leg warmers, a tad out of touch, I went flying off the back of the cross trainer, landing on my arse. I persevered, as this gym was where the St Kilda football team trained. I salivated as I watched them running in and out from pool to ocean in their budgie smugglers. Such incentive.

I decided to find some much-yearned-for cosmic relief to further my journey of self-discovery. I chose yoga. In the past, I have been of the opinion that yoga is only for superficial hippy wankers with too much time on their hands. However, something – or someone – sent me into a studio in Inkerman Street, where I was greeted by an angel – a spiritual warrior with a luminous, transcendent beatitude about her. She greeted me like you would a long-lost friend. 'There are no coincidences in this life.' Her sessions are essential to my recovery. Kundalini yoga – the yoga of self-awareness, together with her Nidra yoga, visualisations and meditations are a source of joy and when I'm in that space; I feel at peace. I still have a problem finding 'that space' though. I have a problem living in the present moment. As explained in Buddhism, 'If we don't live in the present we are forever grasping onto past experiences and reacting according to them.' I have come to the conclusion that the reason I wrestle with living in the present is because I'm scared of finding serenity. I have been so accustomed to turmoil, chaos and living in a pressure cooker. *What pray tell, would I do with peace of mind? I fight the yogic state as I'm scared of the truth.*

I have found a rewarding way to serve and that is, along with other AA members, through running meetings at the Dame Phyllis Frost Centre, a maximum-security women's prison, every Friday morning. These women are incarcerated for drug and alcohol-related crimes. We have lived somewhat parallel lives, the difference being, I didn't get caught. I have such compassion and empathy for these women. When it comes to the program, they can't get enough. They virtually run their own meetings, with us sharing our experience, strength and hope. Our shares are brutally honest, and we have a lot of fun. We inspire them; we offer them hope. We are the evidence that there is joy after substances and prison. I am currently doing the Twelve Steps with a group of them, and it is such rewarding work.

In 2020, we were in the middle of a global corona virus pandemic, which was an unprecedented time. We were in lockdown for nearly three months. Greer, Stuart, my grandsons, Bennie and I were all living together in an old Jewish house which had two sinks, one for dairy and one for meat, and a mezuzah outside the front door. Considering my Jewish heritage, I felt this is where I belonged. The synagogue was in the next street, and we were the only gentiles in the area. Here was my chance to get to the nitty gritty of this fascinating religion, or lifestyle as it's referred to, talking and hanging out with the plethora of Jewish people in my midst. However, it was not to be, as they acted as if we didn't exist, when we passed them on the street, they would look down.

I was still working throughout the lock-down, as I was an essential worker. I had to carry a work permit at all times. Bennie still had a job because he's a tradie. Greer lost her high-profile job and had Max, four, and Charlie, two, at home as they were taken out of day care for safety reasons.

Melbourne was in stage 4, whereby most businesses were closed, except bottle shops, supermarkets and chemists. The drinking rate went up by eighty per cent, as did domestic violence, robberies and crime in general.

There is a silver lining to a pandemic. The planet thrived. Widespread social-distancing measures produced some jarring effects across land, air and sea. The world became quieter. There was hardly any traffic on the roads; dogs were happy as they were getting walked more. I saw a comic of a dog hiding on top of a wardrobe, with a speak bubble which read, 'If one more bastard takes me for a walk …'

Social media went mad with people isolating, working from home, filming themselves venting, dancing and singing. With fewer trains, buses and people pounding the pavement, the usual hum of public life vanished, and so did its dependable rhythms. It was literally reflecting a slowdown of our lives. We had to socially distance from supermarket cashiers who had plastic screens over their faces. I'm not sure why they call it 'social distancing'; there's nothing social about it. People didn't seem to chat in the street as much or even say good morning, as pandemics create paranoia. It was all so weird and yet I have a feeling that this is God's plan and a way of culling the population. He was telling us to slow down, re-evaluate our relationships, stop destroying our planet, smell the roses and practice empathy towards all mankind.

Since people were only allowed to leave the house for shopping, medical issues, exercising and essential work, there was a sharp decrease in the vibrations produced by human activity. People were getting to know their neighbours, cooking for each other and generally showing a compassionate side of themselves they didn't even know they had. Parents were spending more time with their children.

Stage 3 saw borders between states closed. So many people were not seeing their loved ones, but they were appreciating them more, and maybe for the first time.

In September 2020, our restricted life in a locked-down city became too much for us. Greer called a meeting, saying, 'Hands up who wants to move back to the coast.'

Big show of hands.

'Good,' she grinned, 'because I have rented us a big house in Ocean Grove.'

And it was a big house, with two living areas, three bathrooms and seven bedrooms. I had a perfect 'office' in the yard, a sheltered hot box. My 'tan-orexia' was alive and thriving. On the property, there was a built-in playground for the kids, an outdoor barbecue area, lawns covered in numerous fruit trees, a large veggie garden, four chickens and two dogs. We stayed there for four wonderful years.

I spent a lot of time with the grandchildren, took up boot scooting, which involved a concentrated hour of real country and western music. Yee-haaaa! I did aqua aerobics, yoga, reformer Pilates, qi gong, and a course in Buddhism.

Bottom line, I am still an alcoholic with a spiritual malady, but I am learning to live with it.

~

I decided I had too much time on my hands as, for the first time in my life, I was unemployed. One of my friends in the fellowship suggested that, like her, I study a Bachelor of Arts at Universities Online. *What a great idea*, I thought. This would allow me to use my brain, which was a novelty at this point. I decided to major in Sociology. After two weeks of unsuccessfully navigating the university website, struggling with readings – none of which made an ounce of sense to me, nor seemed relevant to the subject at hand – emailing my lecturer, constructively criticising the course structure, questioning the necessity of the number of readings and highlighting the pressure she was putting us all under, and explaining that I was a very mature-aged student and that she needed to back off a tad, and after requiring an extension on the first assessment and having no idea how to do that, I quit.

I joined the Ocean Grove Baptist Church. And here's why. A month after we moved here, I noticed an incident in the next court over from ours. I strolled down, thinking it was a drug bust or the like. There was a crowd of rubberneckers, and the court was roped off. There were two ambulances and two police cars plus a Nine News helicopter overhead. The locals were filling me in on the history of this court, known as the 'happy court', as all the families are friends, the parents take it in turn driving the children to school and kinder and there was a permanent chalk hopscotch drawing on the road.

On the nature strip, there was a blonde-haired woman, head in hands, racked with sobs. *She must be the wife of the man who has been busted. I can relate.* I didn't really think that at all but it was better than thinking what deep down in my gut was the unthinkable. After a while, and none the wiser as to what happened, I walked home and hesitantly put the news on the TV. The announcer was reporting, 'A one-year-old child has been killed by a car in Naples Court.' Apparently, the mum didn't see her and with her other two children in the car, ran over her.

For weeks I had nightmares about the sobbing mother and the baby. I took flowers to the house, thinking I would be adding to a pile of tributes, but there was nothing. The court had shut down and the family in question had moved out. A local eventually explained to me that there would be no tributes at the home as they had moved to their parents' house at the Baptist church, of which the family were the custodians. Now it all made sense.

I had to get to the church. I desperately needed to be prayed for. For someone who had only been to church for Sunday school, funerals and weddings, this was big. This church was at the end of our street and I had heard the heart-warming Hillsong Church-style anthems coming from the building, and it sounded awesome.

I sat in the packed church, listening to the pastor talking about the incident and offering prayer to those in need. I was racked with sobs, head in hands, when the woman next to me asked why I was crying? When I told her, she hugged me then fetched the pastor and his wife. They lay their hands on me and prayed. 'Dear God, please remove Suzie's pain and grief, as a mother and a grandmother. Release her trauma.'

They reassured me that the family's faith has saved them and that their baby is safe and in God's arms. It was like having a second spiritual awakening. I was sold. If believing in God, Baby Jesus, the Holy Spirit or whatever you wanted to call him/her could get them through something like this, then I wanted what they had. I already knew there was no other way but now I was convinced. Without belief in a God, higher power or whatever you wanted to call it, I could never remain sober.

I skipped out of that church feeling like the load of a lifetime had been lifted. The overwhelming sadness had gone. I went to the funeral of little Hava. Her name, ironically, meaning 'life'.

I believed that little girl was sending me a message, and I am so grateful to her for leading me to this place of worship where I feel so calm and peaceful. I went to church every Sunday for months. Yes, that's right, I became a fully-fledged happy clapper, God-botherer.

Along with the rest of the congregation, a full band in attendance, I raised my arms to the heavens belting out the upbeat gospel hymns such as *What a Beautiful Name* and *Relentless*. I was in a state of total euphoria. I wanted to embrace every part of it. I felt I had been missing out on something so powerful and fundamentally spiritual.

Having just re-read this, I can't help but question my fickle nature. I signed up for the Alpha course, where the church folk questioned my interest in Buddhism, stating there is only one God and religions like Buddhism teach us to fear God. What a load of bollocks. Buddhism is a philosophy, it's not about God and it follows the same principles as Christianity. For example: don't kill anything with a nervous system, and acknowledge the first Noble Truth – the truth of suffering.

But being the sober and enlightened soul that I now am and not wanting or needing to justify their ridiculous opinions – none of which were vaguely true or made any sense whatsoever – I thanked them for their time, walked out and never went back. Fucking fanatical, God-bothering, bible thumping, happy clappers!

Which brings me to the saying – 'religion is for those who are scared of going to hell, spirituality is for those who have already been there' Amen.

Speaking of 'don't kill anything with a nervous system', my dog recently attacked a rather large rat, which lay bleeding on the lawn. Priding myself on my Buddhist beliefs, I decided to save said rat, mend its bleeding head and send it on its way. With my six-year-old grandson looking on, I went to pick the rat up when it viciously sunk his two deadly sharp teeth into either side of a large bunion on my finger. I have never felt pain like it! Thinking it was going to attack him next, my grandson took off screaming, "help, Suzie's got a rat biting her hand, help, help …' as I shook my hand trying to remove the rat which clung on for dear life.

With blood pouring out of my hand and the rat's head, Bennie came and yanked it off me, smashed the living shit out of it with a spade and threw it over the fence. He looked disbelievingly at my bleeding finger, saying, 'I'm not sure if Buddhists are allowed tetanus shots but this Buddhist needs one asap.'

Off I go, with my grandsons, to the only doctor I could find at short notice on a Saturday. He was a gorgeous short round African man who had a big smile and not much English. When he asked what happened, I explained using part words and part charades with my grandsons joining in. Suddenly the doctor began to laugh so hard that he started us all off. We were crying hysterical tears. He was wiping his eyes with a tissue as he gave me the injection. On our way out, I could hear him mumbling, 'Ha-ha, a Buddhist, ha-ha, trying to save a rat, ha-ha.'

My grandsons told their schoolmates, who still regularly ask me to tell them the rat story.

The Simple Life

To be richer, happier and freer, all you need to do is want less.

Francine Jay

My life now is simple, uncomplicated and boring, and I love it. One of the highlights of my day is when I get to do the school pick up for my grandchildren. I wait outside their classrooms, anticipating their beautiful little faces lighting up when they see their grandma, running to jump into my arms. They mainly ignore me. Apparently, I have a reputation at the school as being the 'cool hippy grandmother', so not to disappoint, I make sure I dress accordingly, including bright orange lippy which I wipe off as soon as I get back in the car. I'm still pretending.

My life may sound dull, but it suits me just fine. Often, I witness my daughter and her friends partying at our house, ranting and raving, singing raucously, shrieking with laughter, the table strewn with pizza boxes, wine bottles and ashtrays, ciggie smoke billowing, some of them sliding into the pool fully clothed and others singing from the table top. I am not envious. I simply say to myself, *been there, done that. Whatever you're doing, I've done a million times over and better, bitches.*

Maybe I am a little envious.

Not long after we moved, I began volunteering at the church op shop. Due to past experience, I put my hand up to be chief window dresser. Before my arrival, the windows were drab. After I finished with them, they featured lots of animal print, colourful jewellery, hats, scarves and scantily clad models. I was constantly reprimanded, 'Suzie, your windows are un-church like. Tone them down a bit and cover those models.' I ignored them. Seems I am still a chronic controller of people, places and things.

I am also a nanny to a few local families, including looking after four young girls. I find it refreshing hanging out with small females after all the testosterone in our house. I love putting lip-gloss on them, plaiting their hair and answering their girly questions. They are so affectionate compared to my boys. Up until now, I had never realised how fundamentally different little girls are from little boys.

On Friday afternoons, several AA members and I travel to rehabilitation centres around Geelong, spreading the AA message, reading 'the big book' and discussing the Twelve Steps with the residents. I am hesitant entering these places, feeling like the harbinger of doom. 'You can never drink again!' They are such vulnerable humans, so attentive and like sponges. It is liberating, seeing the positive effect we have on these people and how much they enjoy our visits. It gives them hope. It also gives me hope. I learn something new every time. This, too, makes me feel so grateful for my life.

One girl told me she had recently been released from prison after six months for breaking and entering. She had an ice addiction before rehab. Her mother, who is five years sober after a lifetime of heroin and ice addiction, confiscated her six-year-old son and refuses to give him back. Her father is in prison for murder. She was cheery about her future, optimistic and determined to get clean for her son's sake. We don't know how lucky we are. At the same time, my head goes to that place. *I'm not as bad as these people or so many in the rooms. Maybe I'm not an addict?* I wonder if those thoughts will ever cease. ...

I also volunteer at the Baptist church soup kitchen in Geelong every fortnight, feeding the homeless. I start at 7 am, cooking bacon and egg sandwiches. This service runs 365 days of the year. I am constantly reminded of the fine line between them and me. If I hadn't gotten sober, I too could be receiving the food rather than cooking it.

In past years, I have had many sponsees through AA. This is rewarding and satisfying work and helps keep me sober. Unfortunately, they have all relapsed! This is heartbreaking and frustrating, but I need to remember that I have planted the seed. Statistically, one in ten will stay sober.

Once a week for twelve months I have been doing service on the AA helpline and would like to think I have helped a lot of lost souls. The feedback has been excellent and the success rate encouraging.

I have also gone back to 'receiving light' through Sukyo Mahikari. 'Sukyo' meaning universal principles and 'Mahikari' meaning True Light. Originating in Japan, the stated aim of the organization is to help people improve the quality of their lives and attain happiness by practicing universal principles, as well as a method of spiritual purification of the soul called the 'art of True Light'. My bro has been part of this movement for thirty-five years and he has always made sure I receive light on a regular basis wherever I am. Again, this is profound and hard to explain but when it's happening, I feel a spiritual energy vibration, and in the long term, a cleansing of the soul. I just love it.

I recently took part in a stage play called 'Imagine', based on the book by Alison Lester. My character, the nanna, was played out on an imaginary mobile phone screen built into the stage as I conversed with my stage grand-daughter who was on the other screen. It was shown at the Geelong Performing Arts Centre and was taken all around Australia. It was a great success. I still hear, 'hi nanna' around the town. And I'm still waiting for Hollywood to call me. Nothing yet.

~

I was also blessed to be offered a spot at a female meditation and yoga reset retreat on North Stradbroke Island run by a magnificent spiritually enlightened woman. We rose at five am for sunrise walks, journalling and yin yoga. We also partook in art class where we created a mandala from garden and beach findings, had massages, went whale watching, participated in women's embodiment practices and workshops covering emotional wellbeing, meditation tools and techniques for living wholly, enjoyed delicious vegan meals, full moon kirtan sound healing and sunset walks.

On the final day, we participated in a 6 am full moon release ceremony. On the beach, the moon was sinking on one side of the sky and the sun was rising on the other. We were instructed to find an object, such as a rock or a stick, and verbally offload everything that no longer serves us into it, then write the same on a piece of paper. We then sat around an open fire, screaming out our unwanted curses, throwing our pieces of paper into the fire and our objects into the ocean. It was enlightening as I imagined the anxiety and fear leaving my body. I was floating. I began running around in circles, singing and clapping my hands, and then I threw myself into the ocean fully clothed! Our guru looked at the others, and grinning said, 'Seems my job here is done.'

We were then presented with a crystal, into which we were to manifest our desires, e.g. love, acceptance, willingness, forgiveness, tolerance, patience, open-mindedness, peace of mind and most of all serenity',

I bless that crystal every morning of my life.

~

Until now I never wanted to burden anyone by asking them to help me in my plight. I didn't know that was a thing. Now I ask for help and help is always available. Buddhism makes sense to me, more so than anything I have ever taken on: be still and know; suffering is caused by attachment. (Buddhists call addiction 'attachment on steroids'); try to practice loving kindness and meta meditation ie: 'may all sentient beings live without suffering'.

There is no ego, no 'I' and no 'me'. There is only equanimity, the Four Noble Truths and the Eight-Fold Path. Why are we constantly seeking happiness and avoiding sorrow? Ironically, we might experience sorrow more often than joy, with the reason being we learn and grow from the sorrow. Rejoice in suffering; it produces endurance.

I frequent Drohl Kar, the Buddhist Temple, participating in meditation sessions with monks. I have found the answer: Meditation is medicine. I have joined a Buddhist recovery group called Recovery Dharma. I find it a lot softer and less judgemental than AA. I am also doing Tuesday night meditation with a Buddhist monk, who is a learned, realised being and so very funny. Currently, we are talking about karma. What I have learnt is that when it comes to our past sins, if we feel remorse, if we apologise and redeem ourselves, it is no longer classed as bad karma. Hallelujah! Salvation.

~

And just when I thought I couldn't possibly be any more enlightened, my mate insisted I do an Ayahuasca Ceremony with him, saying 'Brownie, you are ready for this. This is the next part of your journey; it's a natural progression.'

We flew to the Gold Coast, where we were picked up by the shaman who took us to a great house in the hinterland with a pool and world-class views. The first ceremony began at 8 p.m. on Friday and was attended by six males and me, sitting in a circle, dressed in white. Provided were floor chairs, buckets, pillows and rugs. We were read prayers, and then smudged with sage, which was wafted over us with an eagle feather to clear our energy of any negative ions.

We were then administered the first of three cups of the foul-tasting tea which is a psychoactive and entheogenic drink brewed from the leaves of the *Psychotria viridis* shrub and the stalks of the *Banisteriopsis caapi* vine from the Amazon.

The name Ayahuasca combines 'aye', meaning death, and 'yhuasca', meaning vine. I assume this refers to 'death of the ego'. The music begins and continues throughout, consisting of guitars, drums, maracas, didgeridoos and divine singing. We are instructed to concentrate on the words in the song books as this keeps us focused, although I'm not sure how as it's all in Portuguese.

It wasn't too long before I was vomiting into the bucket and then, as instructed, followed a fairy-light lit path to a hole in the ground into which I threw the spew, asking it, 'What are you?' The spew answered me with one word, 'Fear.' Dah.

The hallucinations began, taking over my psyche, with thousands of tiny jokers and pranksters in cartoon form slamming into my eyes, laughing at me and ridiculing me. I felt my bowel about to burst so I banged against walls trying to get to the dunny, which seemed unreachable. *What the fuck! I can't do this. I'm tripping. I'm not allowed to trip. I'm a recovering alcoholic. I don't do drugs. This could be a trigger.*

My eyes refused to open so I lay down. This was a bad move. A fly wire screen formed between me and the others, and what appeared to be spirits in flashing light form bounced off a statue of Jesus, going back and forward, back and forward, while my body twitched and itched uncontrollably. The shag pile carpet morphed into millions of worms with purple mushroom heads, coming towards me and trying to eat me. 'Help,' I cried. 'The worms are eating me.'

'Let them eat you,' announced the shaman.

Time for the second cup. *Oh no. When is this going to get better? Aren't I to be enlightened? Where are the messages, showing me my truth, healing me? It's medicine after all. This isn't healing; this is torture, when will my ego die?*

At 3.30 am, after three cups of this gunk, we were dismissed. While the men sat and debriefed, I took a Valium and lay down. I felt like I'd been dragged through a wringer and back. All I could think about the next day was going back into that torture chamber, so to distract myself; I sun-baked and swam in the pool, listening to Rod Stewart. My mate slept all day. There is no conversing with others; we are all on our own journey. At 9 p.m., we sat for the next session. With the promise of an easier ride by the participants, one of whom was up to his seventeenth ceremony, I felt more confident.

Alas, it was a repeat of the night before. At 12.30 a.m., after my second cup, I removed myself from the circle, bounced off walls to my room and took two Valium. My head was reeling with thousands of cartoon characters, smashing my frontal cortex. In the mirror, my face morphed into a ninety-year-old's. The shaman came in and advised, 'Suzie you can't take Valium with Ayahuasca. You'll have to come back to the room, and I'll make you a bed there. I have to keep an eye on you. I have a duty of care.'

I was angry, so very angry. I glared at him, and spat, 'Fuck off, you. This is a cult. You are a drug dealer, and all these freaks are addicted to psychoactive drugs. I'm a recovering alcoholic and I can't take drugs. Now leave me alone.'

At nine the next morning, the shaman's assistant came back, asking me to return for the closing ceremony, which I did. The others were all still there, glowing in their crumpled white clothing, and I was in my nightie. We did a tribal dance to the beating drum, my braless boobs bouncing up and down. We then shared, and I admitted I had been resisting the effects of the medicine, as I feared the truth. I promised that next time I would let the worms eat me.

The others understood, thanking me for my feminine energy and for being so brave. The shaman told my mate he was worried about me as he thinks I have 'complex trauma'. Me? Later, I was told the medicine was way too strong for me considering it was my first time.

I did some research and discovered that the 'jokers' were telling me to lighten up and the 'mushrooms' are a traditional symbol of good luck and new beginnings. Maybe there is something in this.

I organised my next ceremony, close to home, with a milder dosage and people I know. I need to get to the bottom of this and won't stop until I do. Having completed the second ceremony, I can report that I now know why we put ourselves through this torture. The first night went something like the last one, with horrendous hallucinations, dark purple vomit and diarrhoea, after which I announced to all and sundry that I would not be staying for the second night. However, I was talked into it and, after the first cup and a similar experience, I was calling it a night when the shaman asked me to sit for a bit longer. And then it happened. I heard a voice saying repeatedly, 'It's you. It's you.'

I asked the heavens, 'What's me?'

That's when I heard, 'you are all you need, everything you have been looking for is in you. It's all there. God is within you. Nurture this; keep it close to your heart. Don't give it away. You are everything and everything is you. Stop searching.'

The voice was so clear, so succinct, that I was gazing around the room looking for its source. 'Is that you?' I asked the closed eyed shaman.

He smiled, shaking his head, saying 'No, that is Grandmother Ayahuasca.'

At last, I had the answer I had been looking for, or at least what I had always known deep down was irrevocably confirmed.

I got up to leave the room, thanking the shaman for asking me to stay. He smiled a knowing smile. He knew that was coming. Twelve years of living in the Amazon jungle practicing Shamanism will do that I'm guessing.

I lay down, noticing the ceiling was covered in big black clouds, which gradually cleared to reveal a bright light in the centre. I stood on the bed to take a better look and there, as clear as day, was a brightly lit outline of a foetus. I knew what that meant: new beginnings, new life.

And now I am hooked. I plan to do another one soon in the country with my mate. I am nervous and excited. Grandmother Ayahuasca is healing medicine. She comes from love and only love. She has so much to tell us and she is calling me.'

I recently undertook a Unity Field Healing course with a beautiful soul I met at the retreat. This is similar to Reiki, and is an evolutionary form of energy medicine which transfers energy and clears blockages. It works through the quantum field of energy of your personal DNA using a quantum field light template. I know, again, how profound, however it has made such a difference to my psyche as it has cleared away energy blockages, of which I had many. I feel lighter, less bogged down and closer to my truth.

Bennie and I just celebrated our eighteenth anniversary, and I love him now more than ever. He brings me breakfast in bed daily; he cooks for me at night, and reliably entertains me. He has supported me every step of the way and has tolerated my moods, and my spiralling out of control episodes in early sobriety. He has allowed me to grow within the partnership, to be me and only me. This is the first relationship in my life where I have felt supported and safe. He is my rock and my best friend. God sent him to me, that I know.

Recently I was made aware of the 'Buddy System', relating to relationships and that's what Ben and I have. 'A safety support method where two individuals operate as a unit, monitoring and assisting each other.' When I tell him 'I love him', I mean I love him and not 'I love how you make me feel' as in past relationships. We are not each other's possessions. This is unconditional love. Love like I've never felt before.

He had a radical prostatectomy in January whereby they left behind cancer cells, which manifested in his lymph nodes. He endured seven weeks of daily radiation therapy which had some nasty side effects and he is to be on hormone therapy for four years. Even though this caused hot flushes and hair growing in strange places, he took it in his stride. I pray for his recovery. I sent God into the hospital with him daily to oversee the treatment. And through it all, that guy maintained a sense of humour, asking me daily for new jokes to write on the blackboard in the hospital. He finds positivity in all aspects of life. He wakes up singing as he watches cartoons with the grandkids while making their breakfast. They too adore him. So much laughter emanates from that room. Those three boys speak in tongues, and they have their own language. They are like The Three Stooges.

As an aside, according to the medical profession, tomatoes contain lycopene, potassium and antioxidants and from all accounts if you eat enough of them, you will never get prostate cancer. Bennie hasn't gone a day in his life without eating tomatoes. There goes that theory!

He now has regular check ups, which monitor his PSA levels. So far so good. I'm pretty sure his positive attitude reflects his condition.

I recently went to a Rod Stewart concert. I wasn't expecting much as he is now seventy-eight, but I was gobsmacked. I was three rows from the front, and I could almost touch him. He's still got it. Oh yes, he is still 'Rockin' Rod', and he still has a wonderful sense of humour. I turned to my friend Poppy, and said, 'I'm sure he's looking at me. I think he remembers me from 1983 when he opened his hotel door to me in his leopard print jocks.' Sorry Bennie, but Rod is, and will always be, the love of my life

I'm not sure why but the more sober I get, the worse my obsessive-compulsive disorder becomes. If I straighten another thing, I'll scream. Everything has to be lined up or at right angles. The boys' shoes must be in pairs in rows. I have an anxiety attack when they reach for them shouting, 'Hey, boys, you don't need shoes. Let your feet breathe, ay?' and 'I SAID DON'T TOUCH THOSE FUCKING SHOES!'

I can't leave the house unless my bed is made, with the pillows in order. No longer do I have a 'floordrobe'. Now, my clothes are colour coordinated in my cupboard. I am hesitant to wear them in case I ruin the order. I got halfway to Geelong yesterday then had to drive back home to turn the iron off – the one I knew I hadn't left on. I text Stuart, Greer and Ben to say, 'Can you please check I blew out the candle in my room?' or 'Can you please check I turned the gas off?' This, in itself, is a mental illness.

I have had blinkers on for so long, I now feel open to everything and anything. I feel like, until now, I had been living under a rock. Now, I am a sponge, soaking it all in. Now, I walk slower and breathe mindfully, and my sense of smell, touch and hearing seem magnified. I now stop to smell the roses, I howl at the moon, repeating my Sankalpa three times: 'I am a successful author'. And if you're reading this, maybe I am?

I wish on the stars, I am now aware of cloud patterns, I walk in the rain and marvel at the stunning sunrises and sunsets, taking photos and posting them on Instagram. My friend's comment, 'You know you are not the only one who sees sunsets!'

I am noticeably more aware of nature and the importance of it. Bennie and I walk the dogs most days on our magnificent beach and even in winter, I swim in the ocean. I no longer analyse everything and everyone. I now know that ninety-nine per cent of outcomes are out of my control. And while we're on the subject of control, I no longer need to control everyone and everything. As Glennon Doyle points out, needing to control is about fragility of our own worth. The fear of losing control is actually the fear of death. And I have always feared death, but not anymore. I believe the Buddhist concept of death nowadays, which is that it is not viewed as an ending, but rather as a transition within a continuous cycle of life, death, and rebirth, known as 'samsara'. Navigating the concept of death is about surrender.

I am a member of the AA Melbourne Rise and Shine group and attend their zoom meetings at 7.30 am five days a week, and Hampton Sunrise zoom meetings at 7 am on week-ends, as well as attending Geelong and Ocean Grove live meetings when I can. I am so grateful to Alcoholics Anonymous and I can honestly state that the fellowship saved my life.

I feel incredibly blessed and I am so grateful for Bennie, my beautiful daughter, son-in-law, grandkids and family. I haven't been easy to live with – that is a grand understatement – and yet they have all stood by me with an unmatched sense of loyalty, encouraging me every step of the way. I love them so much. I have learned to practice acceptance, and doesn't that make life simpler? Now, when I feel unheard and unseen, I don't react; I just cop it sweet. I need to be right-sized at all times, after all, I am a mere blip on the planet.

I now try to live with an attitude of gratitude, and I would like to think after all these years of searching and potential healing, I live without regret – knowing that regret is the biggest pain of all. At least the guilt is slowly becoming a thing of the past.

On that subject, during my ninth step, whilst redeeming myself to Greer and apologising for putting my addiction before her wellbeing and safety, I was not expecting her reaction. Seemingly unaffected, she said 'That's okay, Mum. I only remember the good times like when you would take me down the street to get a frozen yoghurt and we would laugh a lot, and our seven years of calisthenics, you sewing sequins on my outfits and doing our make-up.' Dodged a bullet there methinks.

There was no mention of the times when she would cry, 'I never see you anymore, Mum. I need to see you more,' when she was eight years old. Or at twelve years of age, when she would yell at me 'I hate you, I never want to be like you. It's always about you. I hate you. I hate you'. Or the numerous times, in a sad voice, when she would say, 'You only tell me you love me when you're drunk.' I heard that more times than I would like to remember. And there was no mention of her friend's mum having to take her to school because we were sleeping off hangovers. God only knows if she had breakfast or a lunch box. Need I go on?

As she matured and showed signs of following in my footsteps, in all the wrong ways, my standard answer to her 'I never want to be like you', was 'then stop trying'. Her early teens were tough years. I didn't know what she needed from me; I don't think she did either. Even if I had worked it out, I doubt I would have been able to give it to her, I wasn't capable. I felt a deep-rooted hatred from her, and I didn't blame her, but rather than make the effort, I distanced myself from her and drank more. She would lash out at me at times and it would debilitate me. I remember her crying, stating, 'our lives depend on you and Greg's moods, I don't know whether I'm to be happy or sad until I look at your face'. Our states of mind were her thermostat.

In order for our children to be OK they need to see that we're OK. I have a feeling that in her late twenties, this psychological abuse impacted Greer's ability to form healthy relationships as it had taken a toll on her self-esteem and trust in others. Until she met Stuart, her soul mate, she struggled to navigate romantic relationships, often finding herself drawn to partners who mirrored the toxic dynamics she experienced in her childhood. That guilt, my friends, will never leave me.

Your child uses the psychological stiletto in your back in exactly the place they know will hurt you most. How? Because they've been watching you their whole life.

David White

I am endeavouring to make amends through my two grandsons who have never seen me drink and hopefully, will never see me drink. I am trying my darnedest to give my all to them, to be an enthusiastic, funny granny. I harp on about the importance of manners, reminding them constantly 'manners are free so use them.' And of course, I teach them about respect and the importance of respecting others. I tell them, 'Hey, boys, girls are to be put on pedestals, worshipped and obeyed, don't ever forget it,' whereby I am met with blank faces. From when they could first talk, every morning, I would ask them, 'What do we expect?'

And they would answer, 'Expect miracles!'

Always expect miracles. Never settle for anything less than magic.

We have a lot to do with our grandsons, minding them on Sundays, watching their many sports, at which they excel. We now have separate houses and we live two streets away so there are many pre-school morning drop ins 'we're hungry, we're thirsty ...' as they Frisbee their plates back at us in the kitchen, 'more please ...' They are amusing, intelligent, delightful, intuitive boys and they fill my heart.

The boys are far more efficient when there's a bribe involved. We're talking car wash, dog walk, and I'm working on 'foot rubs'. I had to give the youngest five dollars just to brush his matted hair!

Here I must mention my daughter and son-in-law's outstanding parenting skills. When it comes to their sons they are focused and devoted. When I witness them interacting with their kids I feel envious and that of a failure.

But at the same time I take credit for this because if I hadn't been such a lousy mother, Greer wouldn't be such a brilliant one. And that's enough about me!

My ninety-six-year-old mum has moved from Melbourne and now lives in a granny flat in the front yard of Greer and Stuart's house. This has been an unsettling time for us all, especially mum as she suffered 'relocation depression', yes, there is such a thing, however now she seems quite calm. We finally got her car licence taken from her after she drove through a stop sign, causing a nasty accident. Now she buzzes up and down to Coles, the library, the Elderly Citz and the Community Centre on a covered in motorised scooter, which looks like something from the Jetsons. She is becoming the talk of the town.

Greer and Stuart have a successful business in Pt. Lonsdale. A very popular café, I work there sometimes but they haven't asked me back as on two occasions they found my rings in the salad. Both from a hospitality background, Greer, for twenty-five years having managed some of the best establishments in Melbourne and Stuart, who is also *au fait* with the business, producing amazing culinary delights and when they are busy, which is most of the time, they are dynamic, pumping out coffees and meals like machines. They have a loyal following as they are friendly and welcoming to all, and Greer, front of house, always with a smile, has a fabulous contagious laugh that echoes throughout the café. They are to be congratulated.

It blows my mind, considering our collective backgrounds, that here we are, the almost nuclear family, with the white picket fence, literally, four cars, two dogs, two children and a Granny flat in the yard of our seaside suburban street. I would never have envisioned this life of gentle routine, revolving around work, school and sports, as we barrack for our relatively normal grandsons at basketball and football, even cutting the oranges for half-time. Amidst the normal chaos of everyday responsibilities, we have found solace in the simplicity of our existence, savouring each moment as it comes. It is a life that isn't flashy or extraordinary, but it is ours and we cherish every bit of it. Whoever would have thought such diverse folk such as ourselves, could now be living ordinary yet satisfying lives. I applaud us.

To be honest I never thought I would still be here to tell this tale. Life is full of surprises and magic.

In June my family took me to the Philippines for a holiday. We had an amazing time in that beautiful country with its joyous people. There is something about the folk in third world countries that resonates with my desire for a simple spiritual life, where they measure well-being through relationships, rituals and reverence rather than through possessions, where the transcendent is woven into everyday gestures – sharing bread, lighting incense, greeting a stranger with peace.

In a couple of days, I am off to a yoga retreat in Keramas, Bali, with my local yoga group. I never take these opportunities for granted, as I know they are only available to me because I am sober.

~

In May 2025, I turned seventy-one and for my birthday my family gifted me a tattoo that reads, 'Sweeter after difficulty' (and in Latin, *Dulcius ex asperis*) which encapsulates the idea that overcoming challenges and hardships makes the subsequent success or reward even more satisfying.

Amen to that.

On June 23, 2025 I was eight years clean and sober. One day at a time. My family and friends are so proud of me but not as proud as I am of myself. I no longer worry about the future. 'It is what it is', 'take it easy', 'keep it simple', and 'let go, let God', being my mantras. But my most powerful mantra, and the question I ask my fellow AA members at the end of my shares, is 'What would love do?' This, my friends, is the answer to the human condition. Any situation, positive or negative, any dilemma or altercation, any problem can be solved by asking yourself, 'What would love do?'

And I may also add here that paramount to my ongoing sobriety is the ceasing of expectations of others.

The solution for me is staying close to my God, my Higher Power. I know she is looking after me, guaranteeing peace of mind and serenity.

Upon reflection, I never thought what I did had an effect on people around me because I didn't think they cared. How wrong I was. I was also of the opinion that I didn't deserve to be happy. I didn't trust happiness. Being happy, I figured, would bring on suffering. I have learned that contentment is never out of reach. It is available to us all. We can be as happy as we set out to be. Joy comes from the strength of our relationships.

Our connection with others is only as solid and deep as our connection with ourselves.

Brené Brown

I now realise that I didn't have to spend my life trying to be someone I wasn't when all I had to be was me. I believe we are in the exact place we are meant to be right now. I believe God only gives us what we can handle. I believe fear is my indication that I'm doing what I need to do. I believe everything does happen for a reason and all will be revealed when the time is right.

This memoir is for all of you out there who struggle with addiction. Know that you are never alone. Know that you are enough. Know that because you were born, the miracle has already happened. Honour your truth and uniqueness. Listen to what your soul is telling you. Be brave, be authentic and smash the shit out of life.

From my heart to your heart. With all my love and gratitude.

Suzie (Brownie)

www.ingramcontent.com/pod-product-compliance
Lightning Source LLC
Chambersburg PA
CBHW061206070526
44583CB00025B/3127